FUNDP
NAMUR

Model-based Management of Information System Security Risk

Nicolas Mayer

April 2009

Doctoral thesis for the degree of Doctor of Science
Computer Science Department, University of Namur

PRESSES
UNIVERSITAIRES
DE NAMUR

Model-Based Management of Information System Security Risk

NICOLAS MAYER

Doctoral Thesis in Computer Science
Namur, Belgium, 2009

© Presses universitaires de Namur, 2009
Rempart de la Vierge, 13
5000 Namur (Belgique)
Tel : +32 (0)81 72 48 84
Fax : +32 (0) 81 72 49 12
E-mail : pun@fundp.ac.be
Site web : http://www.pun.be

Dépôt légal : D/2008/1881/28
ISBN : 978-2-87037-640-9
Imprimé en Belgique

Les coûts d'édition et de production de cette thèse ont été assurés par le Fonds National de la Recherche Luxembourg.

 Fonds National de la Recherche Luxembourg

Committee

Prof. Jean-Marie Jacquet, University of Namur (President)
Prof. Eric Dubois, Centre de Recherche Public Henri Tudor (Supervisor)
Prof. Patrick Heymans, University of Namur (Supervisor)
Prof. Jean Ramaekers, University of Namur (Internal Reviewer)
Prof. Jean-Noël Colin, University of Namur (Internal Reviewer)
Prof. Haralambos Mouratidis, University of East London (External Reviewer)
Prof. Guttorm Sindre, The Norwegian Institute of Technology (External Reviewer)
Mr. David Hagen, Commission de Surveillance du Secteur Financier – Luxembourg (External Reviewer)

The PhD defense was held on the 21st of April in the University of Namur.

Abstract

During the last twenty years, the impact of security concerns on the development and exploitation of information systems never ceased to grow. Security risk management methods are methodological tools, helping organisations to take rational decisions, regarding the security of their IS. Feedbacks on the use of such approaches show that they considerably reduce losses originating from security problems. Today, these methods are generally built around a well structured process. However, the product coming from the different risk management steps is still largely informal, and often not analytical enough. This lack of formality hinders the automation of the management of risk-related information. Another drawback of current methods is that they are generally designed for being used a posteriori, that is, to assess the way existing systems handle risks, and are with difficulty usable a priori, during information system development. Finally, with method using its own terminology, it is difficult to combine several methods, in the aim of taking advantage of each of them. For tackling the preceding problems, this thesis proposes a model-based approach for risk management, applicable from the early phases of information system development. This approach relies on a study of the domain's own concepts.

This scientific approach is composed of three successive steps. The *first step* aims at defining a reference conceptual model for security risk management. The research method followed proposes to base the model on an extensive study of the literature. The different risk management and/or security standards, a set of methods representative of the current state of the practice, and the scientific works related to the domain, are analysed. The result is a semantic alignment table of the security risk management concepts, highlighting the key concepts taking place in such an approach. Based on this set of concepts, the security risk management domain model is built. This model is challenged by domain experts in standardisation, risk management practitioners and scientists.

The *second step* of this research work enriches the domain model with the different metrics used in a risk management method. The proposed approach combines two methods to define this set of metrics. The first one is the Goal-Question-Metric (GQM) method applied on the domain model. This method allows to focus on reaching the best return on security investment. The second one enriches the metrics identified with the first approach, through a study of the literature based on standards and methods addressed during the first step. An experimentation on a real case of these metrics is performed, in the frame of supporting a SME towards the ISO/IEC 27001 certification.

Finally, in a *third step*, a set of conceptual modelling languages dedicated to information security is noticed in the literature. These languages are mainly coming from the requirements engineering domain. They allow to tackle security during the early phases of information system development. The conceptual support proposed by each of them is evaluated, and thus the gap to bridge for being able to completely model the different steps of risk management too. This work ends in an extension proposal of the Secure Tropos language, and a process to follow for using this extension in the frame of risk management, illustrated by an example.

Résumé

Durant les vingt dernières années, l'intérêt pour la sécurité lors du développement et l'exploitation des systèmes d'information n'a cessé de croître. Les méthodes de gestion des risques de sécurité sont des outils méthodologiques, qui aident les organisations à prendre des décisions rationnelles sur la sécurité de leur système d'information. Les retours d'expérience sur l'utilisation de telles approches montrent une réduction considérable des pertes liées aux problèmes de sécurité. Aujourd'hui, ces méthodes sont généralement construites autour d'un processus bien structuré. Cependant, le produit issu des différentes étapes de la gestion des risques est encore très largement informel et souvent pas assez analytique. Ce manque de formalisme est un frein à l'automatisation de la gestion des informations relatives aux risques. Un autre inconvénient des méthodes actuelles est qu'elles sont généralement destinées à évaluer a posteriori comment les systèmes d'information déjà existants gèrent les risques, et sont difficilement applicables a priori, pendant la conception de tels systèmes. Enfin, chaque méthode utilisant souvent une terminologie qui lui est propre, il est difficile de combiner plusieurs méthodes afin de profiter des points forts de chacune. Afin de répondre aux problèmes mentionnés ci-dessus, notre contribution propose une approche basée sur la modélisation de la gestion des risques, utilisable dans les phases amont de conception de systèmes d'information. Cette approche est fondée sur une étude des concepts propres au domaine.

Notre démarche scientifique se compose de trois étapes successives. La *première étape* vise à définir un modèle conceptuel de référence relatif à la gestion des risques de sécurité. La méthode de recherche adoptée propose de fonder le modèle sur une étude approfondie de la littérature. Les différents standards de gestion des risques et/ou de sécurité, un ensemble de méthodes représentatives de l'état actuel de la pratique, ainsi que les travaux scientifiques se rapportant au domaine, ont été analysés. Le résultat est une grille d'alignement sémantique des concepts de la gestion des risques de sécurité, mettant en évidence les concepts-clés intervenant dans une telle démarche. Sur base de cet ensemble de concepts est ensuite construit le modèle du domaine de la gestion des risques. Ce modèle a été confronté aux experts du domaine, provenant du monde de la standardisation, des méthodes de gestion des risques et du monde scientifique.

La *deuxième étape* de notre recherche enrichit ce modèle du domaine avec les différentes métriques utilisées lors de l'application d'une méthode de gestion des risques. La démarche proposée combine deux approches pour la détermination des métriques. La première est la méthode Goal-Question-Metric (GQM) appliquée sur notre modèle de référence. Elle permet de se focaliser sur l'atteinte du meilleur retour sur investissement de la sécurité. La seconde enrichit les métriques identifiées par la première approche, grâce à une étude de la littérature basée sur les standards et méthodes étudiés lors de la première étape. Une expérimentation sur un cas réel de ces métriques a été réalisée, dans le cadre de l'accompagnement d'une PME vers la certification ISO/IEC 27001.

Enfin, dans une *troisième étape*, nous relevons dans la littérature un ensemble de langages de modélisation conceptuelle de la sécurité de l'information. Ces langages sont issus essentiellement du domaine de l'ingénierie des exigences. Ils permettent donc d'aborder la sécurité lors des phases initiales de la conception de systèmes d'information. Nous avons évalué le support conceptuel proposé par chacun d'eux et donc le manque à combler afin d'être à même de modéliser intégralement les différentes étapes de la gestion des risques. Le résultat de ce travail permet de formuler une proposition d'extension du langage Secure Tropos et une démarche d'utilisation de cette évolution dans le cadre de la gestion des risques, illustrée par un exemple.

Acknowledgments

First of all, I would like to thank my first supervisor Eric Dubois without whom this PhD would not have been possible. He introduced me to the topic of security risk management and supported me during the whole PhD. His availability and his kindness were prominent and a great source of motivation. I thank him for the trust he gave me from the beginning of the PhD until now: trust was the key factor of this collaboration (...and hopefully not the highest risk). I would like to thank warmly my second supervisor Patrick Heymans from the University of Namur. His implication and interest in my PhD were really important and had a huge impact on the results obtained. His availability, his open-mindedness and his warmth were always a great help for me.

Although they were the greatest instigators helping me to achieve my PhD, my advisors were not the only ones playing a key role in this research work. I am first indebted to Raimundas Matulevičius for the collaboration we had together. His knowledge in so many research domains was an added value for me and his availability was greatly appreciated. Then, I would like to thank Jean-Philippe Humbert, who gave me so much feedback about my work. He helped me improve not only my research skills but also my professional behaviour. Our collaborations were always interesting and very efficient despite the fact we most of the time worked in Tudor's bar. I also thank Vincent Rosener for the 'never ending' afternoons spent working on conceptual modelling. His competence in modelling and analysis are no secret for anybody who knows him, and his advices on my work helped the results to get better.

Another key institution of the PhD I would like to thank is the LIASIT, not only for providing me a grant, that is obviously one of the cornerstones of a PhD, but also for the feedback and advices of the professors. I think mainly of Thomas Engel, Christoph Meinel, Björn Ottersten and David Basin. I would like also to thank particularly Magali Martin for her availability and her always excellent mood.

Thanks to all of my colleagues from the CRP Henri Tudor. Thanks to my CRP 'coaches' Béatrix and Norbert, and to André and Djamel leading the main projects on which I worked. Sébastien Pineau for providing me a great help concerning the evaluation chapter and for his enjoyable conversations. Sébastien Poggi for the work done on the security topic during the day and the harder work done in pubs during the evenings. Hervé, Marc and Jordan, the best tennis players of the CRP. Naturally, I also thank all of my other enjoyable colleagues of the CRP. They are too many to mention.

Thanks also to other people interested in my work and who provided feedback. Thanks to Matthieu Grall and the members of the 'Club EBIOS', the members of ANSIL (particularly Cédric Mauny) and the Codasystem team.

Special thanks to all my family, my parents and my brother for their support and love. My greatest gratitude goes naturally to Audrey.

Nicolas Mayer
Luxembourg, April 2009

Contents

List of Figures

List of Tables

Acronyms

ADOM   Application-based Domain Modeling

BSI   Bundesamt für Sicherheit in der Informationstechnik

CC   Common Criteria

CCTA   Central Computer and Telecommunications Agency

CORAS   Risk Assessment of Security Critical Systems

COTS   Commercial off-the-shelf

CRAMM   CCTA Risk Analysis and Management Method

CTCPEC   Canadian Trusted Computer Product Evaluation Criteria

DARE   Domain Analysis and Reuse Environment

DCSSI   Direction Centrale de la Sécurité des Systèmes d'Information

DITSCAP   DoD Information Technology Security Certification and Accreditation Process

DoS   Denial of Service

EBIOS   Expression des Besoins et Identification des Objectifs de Sécurité

ENISA   European Network and Information Security Agency

FMECA   Failure Mode and Effect Criticality Analysis

FODA   Feature-Oriented Domain Analysis

FTA   Fault Tree Analysis

GQM   Goal-Question-Metric

GMITS   Guidelines for the Management of IT Security

GSN   Goal Structuring Notation

HAZOP   HAZard OPerability study

ICT   Information and Communication Technology

IDS	Intrusion Detection System
IEC	International Electrotechnical Commission
IS	Information System
ISMS	Information Security Management System
ISO	International Organization for Standardization
ISSRM	Information System Security Risk Management
IT	Information Technology
ITSEC	Information Technology Security Evaluation Criteria
MARION	Méthodologie d'Analyse de Risques Informatiques Orientée par Niveaux
MEHARI	MEthode Harmonisée d'Analyse du Risque Informatique
MELISA	Méthode d'Evaluation de la Vulnérabilité Résiduelle des Systèmes d'Armement
MICTS	Management of Information and Communications Technology Security
MTTR	Mean Time To Repair
NIST	National Institute of Standards and Technology
OCTAVE	Operationally Critical Threat, Asset, and Vulnerability Evaluation
PDCA	Plan-Do-Check-Act
RE	Requirements Engineering
RM	Risk Management
ROSI	Return On Security Investment
RUP	Rationale Unified Process
SE	Software Engineering
SEAM	Security Enhanced Actor Model
SEGM	Security Enhanced Goal Model
SQUARE	Security Quality Requirements Engineering
SP	Special Publication
TCSEC	Trusted Computer System Evaluation Criteria
TR	Technical Report

Chapter 1

Introduction

Information systems (IS) are everywhere. They have a large impact on the everyday life of organisations and individuals. In the light of ambient, pervasive and ubiquitous computing, this impact is increasing significantly. At the heart of these IS, security aspects play a vital role and are thus becoming a central issue in IS effective usage. IS are required to be more secure in order to resist to a potential large number of attacks. The importance of security technologies and of their enabling technical platforms has been widely recognised and is therefore receiving a continuous attention (see e.g., new encryption algorithms, public key infrastructures, etc.).

However, organisations are also more and more considering the management dimension attached to security. As an example, we can observe that many organisations (like e.g., banks) have first introduced public key infrastructures, considered as the most secure technical platform for coping with authentication, confidentiality, integrity and non-repudiation security issues. But after a while, many of these organisations have abandoned such solutions for lighter platforms, because of the generated costs. Sources of these costs are mainly related to associated management activities, interoperability issues, and also indirect costs, due to the difficulty of usage by their clients. To summarise, many security solutions and infrastructures exist and can be deployed, but the key question is to know if their associated direct and indirect costs are well adapted.

The ROSI (Return On Security Investment) issues, related to the cost of security technologies with respect to their benefits, are thus becoming a vital question in many organisations. As a consequence, we can observe that the traditional role of IS security officers is evolving more and more from a pure technical profile to a new profile, where a mix of business and technical competences is required. Those are needed for being able to evaluate the fit that must be established between the secure Information Technology (IT) infrastructure and the assets to be protected at the business level of an organisation. Central to this business/IT alignment problem [HV99] is the Risk Management (RM) process. This need for the set-up of security RM processes within organisations is further reinforced at the Institutional and/or sector-based levels, with large initiatives like the Sarbanes-Oxley Act [SoRiC02] governing the integrity of financial and accounting data or, in the banking industry, the Basel II agreement [Bas02], which requires banks to comply to instructions for defining the level of their capital requirements, in relation with the maturity of their RM activities.

1.1 Motivation and research objectives

IS Security RM (ISSRM) is paramount because it helps companies to adopt cost-effective security measures. Indeed, security threats are so numerous that it is impossible to act on all of them because (1) every technological security solution has a cost, and (2) companies have limited resources. Hence, companies want to make sure that they adopt only solutions for which the ROSI is positive. This is done by comparing the cost of a solution with the risk of not using it, e.g., the cost of a business disruption due to a successful security attack. In this sense, ISSRM plays an important role in the alignment of a company's business with its IT strategy.

1.1.1 Problem statement

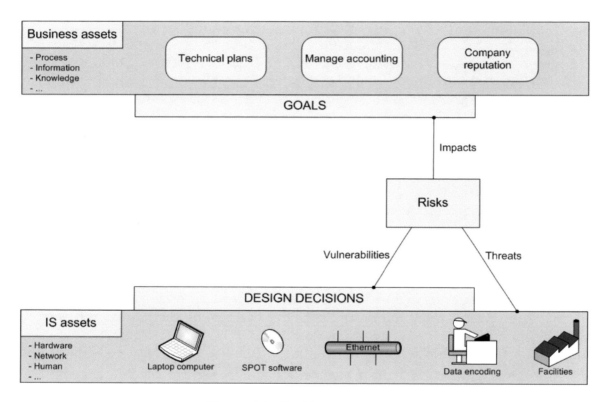

Figure 1.1: Problem statement

A key to a good alignment between business domain and security of the IS, is to keep the focus on the *assets* of the *business*. Assets are defined as anything that has a value for the organisation and that is central to the achievement of business *goals* [ISO05b]. Figure 1.1 shows different kinds of business assets extracted from the coming running example about an architecture engineering consulting firm in the building domain (Section 1.6). For instance, business assets are information like "Technical plans" or processes like "Manage accounting". Several other classes of business assets can be identified (knowledge, reputation, relationships between employees, etc.). All those elements are part of the business of the company and have their own value in the business model.

In parallel, we are calling *IS assets* those IT resources or other components that are part of the IS, linked to the business assets. IS assets are often considered as the 'mirror' of the business assets, because many business goals are achieved with the assistance of the IS. Coming back to the running example, IS assets are basically the computers, the software, the network components, etc., used within the organisation. People and facilities are also considered as IS assets, because they are part of the IS and so they are essential to a good information security. As an obvious example, despite of confidential data being encrypted, if an employee knowing the decryption key is not aware of security, the information security is in danger (this point is further explained in Section 1.4). IS assets are therefore the IS components needed to be secured, in order to ensure the achievement of the business goals. The set of IS assets is part of the IS architecture and they are selected through *design decisions.*

Assets need to be secure, because they are exposed to security *risks.* Security risk is most often defined by three components :

$$\text{Risk = Threat * Vulnerability * Impact}$$

In other words, risk is characterised by the opportunity of a *threat* targeting IS assets, to exploit one or more *vulnerabilities* originating from the design decisions, and leading to an *impact* on business goals. Figure 1.1 depicts these components and their relationships.

1.1.2 Research domains and objectives

In the preceding context, the objective is naturally to *mitigate* the risks by introducing countermeasures that satisfy adequate *security requirements* (Figure 1.2). In this context, a lot of work has already been done in the *security RM* domain and particularly on risk analysis and risk assessment, which are the activity of analysing threats, vulnerabilities and impacts on each component of the IS, and comparing them to the security needs driven by business goals. Many industrial methods based on risk assessment [AD01b, DCS04b, CLU07b, SGF02] already exist. However these methods are generally applied bottom-up, once the architectural design has been defined (represented by the links between security RM and the IS side of Figure 1.2). This allows only an "a posteriori" approach to IS security, resulting in a gap between security requirements and business security needs. An "a priori" approach to security engineering, based on RM performed during RE, could improve IS security much more significantly. Therefore, this work is more focused on the *RE* domain, linking business assets with security RM, instead of being only focused on *architectural engineering.*

Another remark about security RM concerns the product of its performed activities. Existing methods and standards are generally focussed on structuring the different steps and activities to perform as a good security RM. Their added value rely also on the knowledge bases of risks [DCS04b, ISO08, CLU07b] and/or security requirements [ISO05c, DCS04b] they provide. They are the input of the activities performed. The methodological aspects are thus generally rigorous, because they are standing on a well-defined process and structure to follow. However, products (i.e. documents produced as output of the different steps of the process) are generally informal, most often in natural language, possibly complemented with tables for structuring the information. This lack of formality prevents the automation (reasoning, evolution, monitoring

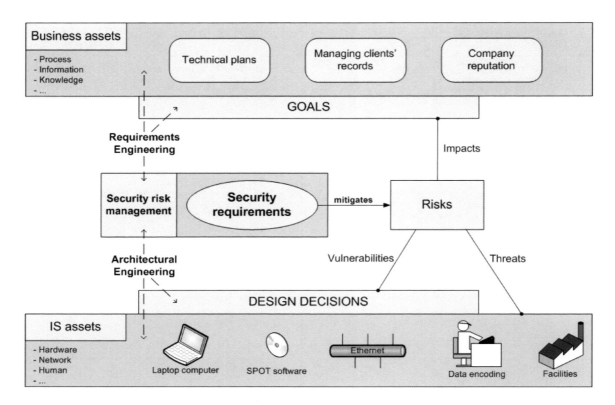

Figure 1.2: Problem statement and security risk management

and traceability) of RM-related information. For a long time, IS engineers (including requirements engineers) have been using 'models' as a way to achieve a better formality and quality mostly to benefit from abstraction in order to tackle complexity. This thesis proposes to introduce a modelling component, that provides a better support for the formalisation of the knowledge created and exchanged during RM activities.

The results of this research work shall help to reach four different research objectives:

- to deliver **secure IS** (generally in terms of confidentiality, integrity, availability, very often mentioned through the CIA acronym [ISO05b]);

- to create a link between business security needs and system security measures, provided by **risk-based approaches**, to obtain the best ROSI;

- to perform **a priori** security (i.e. before IS design), as opposed to a posteriori;

- to produce deliverables under the form of **models** as proof of security management.

1.2   Requirements Engineering

RE takes place during the early phases of the development of an IS. For this work, the following definition for RE is adopted: "Requirements engineering is the branch of software engineering concerned with the real-world goals for, functions of, and constraints on software systems. It is also concerned with the relationship of these factors to precise specifications of software behavior, and to their evolution over time and across software families" [NE00]. Although this is subject to debate, researchers often differentiate between early and late RE [Yu97]. Early requirements analysis put the emphasis on understanding the *whys* of the system-to-be rather than the *what* it should do. *What* the system should do is addressed during late requirements analysis. As further explained in Section 1.3.1, security should be addressed all along the IS development, from early RE. In this context, we define a *requirement*, like in [Jac97], as "a condition over the phenomena of the environment that we wish to make true by installing the machine".

1.2.1 Security requirements as non-functional requirements

It is generally accepted that *functional requirements* define 'what' the system should do [Gli07, RR99, IEE90, Som95]. Functional requirements are opposed to *non-functional requirements*. As explained by Glinz [Gli07], no clear consensus has been found on what is precisely a *non-functional requirement*, and many different definitions have already been proposed [Ant97, RR99, Wie03, etc.]. A definition of non-functional requirement is "a property, or quality, that the product must have [...]" [RR99]. Security requirements are generally considered as non-functional requirements in the literature, like usability, performance, etc. However, regarding security requirements, they can be sometimes functional requirements. For example, as depicted in [Gli07], "The database shall grant access to the customer data only to those users that have been authorized by their user name and password" is a security requirement that is functional. Nevertheless, most of the time, security is considered as a non-functional requirement [ISO00, IEE98, Ant97, RR99, Wie03]. In the context of this thesis, and mainly because most of the security-oriented modelling languages we study consider security requirements as non-functional requirements [CNYM00, MG07a, vL04, SO05], we adopt this convention.

1.2.2 The important role of RE in the ISSRM context

The role of RE with regards to ISSRM can be highlighted as illustrated in Figure 1.3.

ISSRM can be characterised as a specific case of the general business/IT alignment challenge [HV99]. IS (mostly based on IT infrastructure, but also including human-based tasks) is supporting the realisation of the business strategy and of its associated value proposition. This value proposition is made from knowledge and services created and managed through processes, mobilising competences of the organisation [OP04, GPW06]. Because of the required alignment, risks associated with the IS have a direct impact on the business value, and thus, this mis-alignment requires to be mitigated. Various controls and countermeasures can be set up for managing the required mitigation. Still the difficulty is in the selection of the most appropriate one. This is where RE and more particularly Goal-Oriented Requirements Engineering (GORE) approaches helps [BGG+04, Yu96, vLL00, Jac01]. GORE has been proved to be useful in the management of requirements, that can vary in their granularity and be used at different decision-making levels. More precisely, as depicted on the right part of Fig.

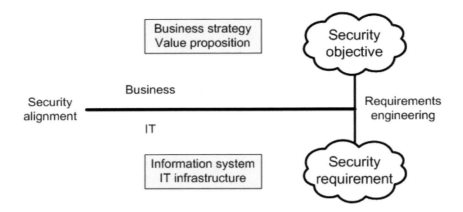

Figure 1.3: Business/IT alignment at the level of security

1.3, GORE can be used:

1. At the business level, to understand the security objectives associated with the business strategy, and the value proposition components of the organisation;

2. At the IS level, to express the requirements associated with the controls to be put in place in response to attacks to the IS components, arisen from the IS' environment. Requirements will express expected properties of these controls in terms of their impact on the malicious behavior of the attackers from the environment.

3. At the business/IT alignment level, the progressive refinement of business security objectives, in terms of IS security requirements, is supported by the goal hierarchy, where the different alternatives regarding the fulfillment of security goals by security requirements are systematically investigated.

1.3   Background and research work assumptions

As seen previously, this research work relies on three main assumptions:

- Dealing with security during the early phases of IS development is better than later in the development process or once the system is already designed;

- Using a RM approach provides beneficial results to define the security requirements of an IS;

- To have a model-based approach supporting the ISSRM process improves the product coming from the various ISSRM steps.

The objective of this section is to explain the assumptions and the orientation of the research work.

1.3.1   Security and early phases of requirements engineering

Security is currently too often considered after design of the IS or even once the IS is already running. It has been extensively argued that security should be considered during the whole IS development process and it is generally accepted considering security during RE phases of IS engineering helps to decrease the total cost of detection and removal of security defects [DS00]. Various approaches were proposed to cope with security in different development phases [vL04, SO05, MG04, LBD02, Jö2]. Some of them address design phases or architectural engineering [LBD02, Jö2]. An assumption we adopt in this work is that it is more efficient to take care of security as early as possible. During early RE, and more generally when reasoning on business goals [Let01], examining security allows IS developers to discard design alternatives that do not offer a sufficient security level. Furthermore, to correct some security defects once the IS is already designed could decrease other IS qualities such as maintainability and efficiency, also recommended to be discussed during the early phases of RE [CNYM00]. To cope with security during early phases of RE helps to reach the best trade-off between all of the non-functional requirements needed by the IS. The scope of the thesis is thus focused on early phases of RE.

1.3.2 Security requirements and risk management

The application of any ISSRM approach has usually three main outcomes [SGF02]:

- The improvement of IS security;

- The justification of budget and investment for IS security management decisions;

- The assessment of the level of confidence that customers or partners can have in the IS.

Therefore, the first advantage of ISSRM is that it helps to deal with the three main stakeholders concerned by IS security: IS developers, organisation's managers and organisation's clients. It provides for each of them results at their concerns' level, i.e., technical level, financial level and IS trust level. ISSRM has some other advantages compared to traditional security engineering. First, ISSRM methods aim to reach the best ROSI for the studied IS. The ROSI is (informally) defined as the final cost savings in avoiding security incidents compared to the global cost of security measures taken [CLU04b]. By proposing a comparison between security needs and potential security risks, ISSRM is a powerful tool for arguing around ROSI. Second, to prioritise security requirements (or even requirements in general) in terms of importance or implementation order is usually seen as a challenge in RE [HD08]. Requirements prioritisation is a tough research problem and several research works have already been done in this field. Many requirements prioritisation methods have been defined [KR97, BGL05, Dav03]. However risk-based approaches have already shown to be efficient in prioritising requirements for various domains [Wie99]. Using an ISSRM method for defining suited security requirements brings by nature the prioritisation of the requirements.

1.3.3 Security risks and model-based approaches

In the building domain, the classical approach adopted for a long time is to produce maps of the building before starting the construction. In software engineering, the same approach based on modelling has also been adopted, mainly driven by the generalisation of the use of the UML standard [Obj]. Regarding IS security risks, the introduction of a model-based approach is motivated by several factors, related first to the efficiency of the ISSRM process, and second to the relevance of the product resulting of the performed process:

- It is an efficient support to communication and interaction between stakeholders involved in a risk assessment [VML+07]. This is expected to improve the quality of the results coming from interviews and analysis, and also speed up the risk assessment process.

- Models have the ability to describe precisely concepts (in a non-ambiguous manner) and especially at the right level of granularity. It is clearly more difficult to have the same by using natural language. It helps also to have a clear traceability link between the different concepts, compared to relationships expressed with the help of tables [DCS04b].

- Formalisation of ISSRM through a model-based approach allows some automatic reasoning (e.g., consistency and completeness checking, alternative selection, etc.) [vL01]. Despite such abilities are not directly expected as outcomes of the thesis, the work done brings the background to go towards such functionalities.

- Some standards requiring compliance with their requirements involve ISSRM activities [ISO05b]. Documentation of these activities are a key point of such standards. Models are thus a good mean to improve the documentation of ISSRM activities.

- ISSRM is always seen as an iterative process, needing to be continuously monitored and reviewed [AS/04, ISO08]. A model-based approach improves the maintenability of ISSRM steps and helps to speed up the updates of ISSRM results, needed after performing a new iteration of the underlying process.

- As seen in the preceding sections, to integrate RE and RM provides several benefits. A model-based approach seems to be a cornerstone of this integration. Many RE methods, and mainly goal-oriented approaches that are moreover well-suited to early RE steps [vL01], are standing on modelling. To introduce modelling activities in ISSRM is a way to reconcile RE and ISSRM, and ease in general the reuse of ISSRM results in other projects.

1.4   Scope of the work

This research work is standing in the Information System Security Risk Management domain. In this section, we define step by step the different concepts and the boundaries of the work, summarised in Figure 1.4.

1.4.1   Information System

A lot of work has been done in the frame of IS terminology (and already on 'system' terminology in general [Moi77, VB93]) and many definitions were already proposed

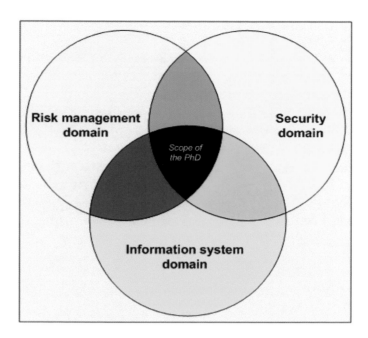

Figure 1.4: Scope related to the Information System Security Risk Management domain

[Moi77, FHL+98, RFB88][1]. However no agreement has been found in defining what is an IS [Car00]. The definition of IS used should generally be related to the domain it is applied. The one provided by Wikipedia [Wik08a] is a good example regarding the scope of this work: "*A system, whether automated or manual, that comprises people, machines, and/or methods organised to collect, process, transmit, and disseminate data that represent user information*". It is thus clear that the domain of this thesis encompass not only security of software system or IT architecture, but takes care of people and facilities playing a role in an IS and so in its security. For example, people following a procedure and encoding data or air conditioning for server room is as important as software or network security. As an illustration, let's consider the assumption that the client's database of *@rchimed* and its associated network are highly secure, using the best practices currently known in terms of encryption, authentication, data redundancy, etc. If the employees are not aware of security, some attacks using social engineering on an employee can be successful [MS03], leading to disclosure of their personal login information to the attacker and making all of the technical security measures useless. Thus, regarding the state of the art, it will be focused on literature targeting the whole IS security and not literature focused only on security of IT components. Moreover, different terms are used for meaning the security of an IS in general, and they are usually used (wrongly) as synonymous: "Information Technology Security", "Information and Communications Technology Security", "Information Security", etc. Considering the scope of this thesis is clearly focused on a whole IS, this work uses the term "Information System Security" (IS security), that seems to be the most relevant to the research context.

---

[1]This list is clearly far from being exhaustive, considering the number of publications trying to define the concept of 'Information System'

1.4.2   Risk Management

The most generally agreed upon definition of risk is the one found in ISO/IEC Guide 73 [ISO02b]. There risk is defined as a *"combination of the probability of an event and its consequence"* [ISO02b]. Following this definition, RM is defined as *"coordinated activities to direct and control an organisation with regard to risk"* [ISO02b]. Depending on the context, RM can address various kinds of issues [The01], [ISO04a]. For example, risks can be related to the organisation's management (e.g., illness of a key person in regards to the business), finance (e.g., related to investment), environment (e.g., pollution), or security. In this thesis, we focus only on security RM in the context of an IS (following the definition proposed in Section 1.4.1). Other kinds of risk such as financial or project risk, even related to an IS, are out of the scope[2].

1.4.3   Security

In the literature, security is generally understood in two different manners. The first kind of approaches [Fir03] use the term 'security' for what concerns malicious (or deliberate) harm on the IS, and they use the term 'safety' for what concerns accidental harm. Firesmith [Fir07b] uses the broader notion of defensibility to cover both security (in the above sense) and safety. The notion of security that we adopt in this work, and that defines the scope, is broader. Actually, it is a synonym of defensibility according to Firesmith. The different standards, methods and frameworks studied are standing in both domains, and thus dealing with malicious and accidental harm, as depicted in Figure 1.5. We decided to keep the term 'security' because it is the most commonly used term in the ISSRM literature [ISO05b, ISO04b, DCS04b, CLU07b, AD01b, VML+07, etc.] for this domain.

The second typical difference recognised between security and safety is related to the objective to reach. Security aims at protecting the confidentiality, integrity and availability of information and/or processes in an organisation [ISO04b, Com06a]:

- Confidentiality is the property that information is not made available or disclosed to unauthorised individuals, entities, or processes;

- Integrity is the property of safeguarding the accuracy and completeness of assets. Accuracy could be threatened by (unauthorised or undesirable) update or tampering. Completeness could be threatened by altering or deletion;

- Availability is the property of being accessible and usable upon demand by an authorised entity.

Some other criteria like authenticity, non-repudiation or accountability might be added when the context requires, but they are usually deemed secondary [ISO04b]. Safety relates to risk that may affect human life or environmental health [UK 96, LCJ05]. This notion is commonly used in aeronautics and other transport systems [Lev95]. This domain is not in the scope of this thesis as we focus only on information security.

---

[2]The reader should not overinterpret this statement as saying that those various kinds of risk are unrelated. On the contrary, they are often related, e.g., an increase in security risks is usually accompanied by increased project and financial risks for a company. The sole purpose here is to state that for a question of feasibility only security risk is a direct object of study for us.

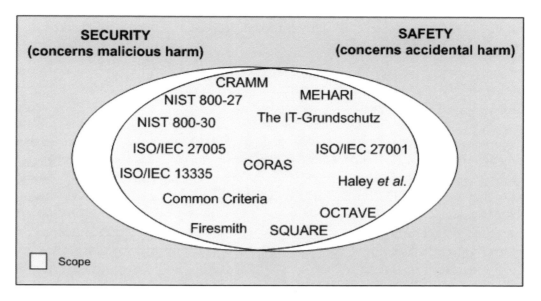

Figure 1.5: Security and safety differentiated by the cause

All of the standards, methods and frameworks studied aim at maintaining confidentiality, integrity and availability of information. However, information security can sometimes be related to human life or environmental health. This intersection is especially growing as IT components are embedded in all kinds of products, and more and more of organisation's infrastructures are managed through IS. For example, some medical information can need integrity, otherwise patient life can be in danger. This case remains in the scope, as depicted in Figure 1.6, denoted by the coloring of the intersection between the two sets.

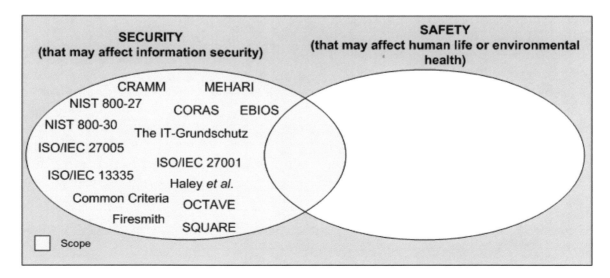

Figure 1.6: Security and safety differentiated by the objective

Summing up, the objective of ISSRM is thus to protect essential constituents of an **IS**, from all harm to IS **security** (confidentiality, integrity, availability) which could arise accidentally or deliberately, by using a **RM** approach.

1.5   Claimed contributions and research questions

1.5.1   Proposal

Our contribution aims at proposing **a model-based approach to support ISSRM**, mainly for early phases of RE, but also applicable in general. This thesis focuses on the *modelling language* part of such an approach, and does not address the methodological part or the tool support. More specifically, the first research question addressed in this thesis is: *what are the concepts that should be present in a modelling language supporting ISSRM?* Once the ISSRM concepts are elicited, this work is completed with the associated metrics. The second research question is therefore: *what are the metrics relevant to perform ISSRM and to reason about ROSI?* Finally, to propose efficiently a modelling support to ISSRM, we need to investigate existing languages and compare their modelling capabilities to the conceptual needs. Then, we can propose ways to improve them, in the aim to provide the best support to ISSRM. The last research question of this thesis is thus: *what is the ISSRM support provided by security-oriented modelling languages and how it can be improved?*

1.5.2   What the PhD is not...

After defining the contribution and the research questions tackled by this research work, we would like to clarify what is out of the scope of this PhD thesis.

Tools or techniques for identifying new kinds of risks

In the risk management process, the risk analysis task aims at identifying and estimating risks and their components. A lot of tools have already been proposed for precise identification and specification of new kinds of risks, threats or vulnerabilities . We can cite for example *attack trees* [Sch04] or *software fault trees* [HWS⁺02] using trees to precisely define attacks. This research work does not address this issue. This thesis is more in line with the risk management approaches that provide tools and techniques for supporting the whole ISSRM process. For the risk analysis task, those build on existing risk/threat/vulnerability knowledge bases [DCS04b, CLU07b, ISO08]. The user will use them to choose the most relevant components to his context. However, risk elicitation approaches [Sch04, HWS⁺02] are complementary to these risk management approaches and can be used to refine and improve the knowledge bases.

Tools or techniques for formulating security requirements

Much research work in RE is focused on the elicitation of requirements [NE00]. Precise, complete, non ambiguous, etc. are qualities often requested for requirements and RE techniques are developed to reach them. As in the preceding section, this research work assumes the existence of security requirements knowledge bases [ISO05c, DCS04b]. The artefacts we produce are not meant to improve the formulation of security requirements, but rather help the user to choose the best matches in the existing knowledge bases. Generally, the examples of security requirements presented in this thesis are not defined by the author but extracted from standards or methods [ISO05c, DCS04b, DCS04a].

Tools or techniques for defining security requirements for a security product

As described in Section 1.4, the scope is limited to risk-based analyses that focus on the whole IS. Conversely, other approaches address the definition of security requirements for *products* [Com06a], like security products (firewall, authentication system), operating systems or network components. These methods or standards are considered out of the scope.

1.6 Running example

In order to illustrate the different sections of this thesis with examples, we introduce a running example. A running example is an example used all along the thesis to explain the different concepts and proposals. The running example is extracted from a case study [DCS04a] of the EBIOS method [DCS04b]. This case study has been developed for illustrating the EBIOS method on an example. The document [DCS04a] describes first a company called *@rchimed*. Then, a security analysis is performed, based on the EBIOS method.

In the context of this thesis, to use such an existing example with risks already identified, is effective considering the PhD objectives. In this thesis, the emphasis is placed on how to manage risks already identified and improve their management, but not on the identification of new kinds of risks in a given context, as described in Section 1.5.2. By using such an example, the research questions addressed in this thesis will not be dependent on the risk identification, because the risks are already defined.

In this section, we first introduce the running example by describing the *@rchimed* company (Section 1.6.1). Then a brief overview of its IT infrastructure is provided (Section 1.6.2).

1.6.1 Description of the *@rchimed* company

The *@rchimed* society is a (fictitious) architecture engineering consulting firm in the building domain. It's an SME in Luxembourg made up by a dozen of employees.

Its activity is based around the production of construction plans for factories and buildings. *@rchimed* calculates building structures, 3D mock-ups for clients and design technical plans for contractors. The firm follows also the progress of the building construction and updates, if necessary, the plans and calculations. Its business objectives are especially based on producing high quality documents and 3D visual representations.

Its objective is now to improve the quality of its products and efficiency of its activities through the use of original ICT tools. The company targets national and international projects and would like to improve its IS for answering as quickly as possible to project proposal.

Organisation structure

The organisation is composed of five departments (Figure 1.7):

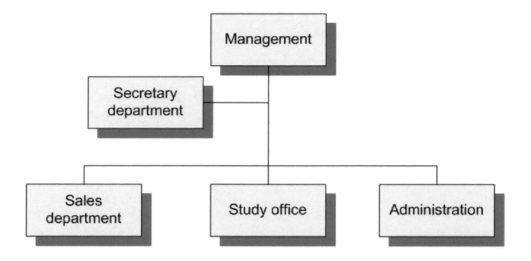

Figure 1.7: *@rchimed*'s organisation

- Management:
  The management is composed by the director and its assistant. The assistant has an architectural background, but plays also the role of IT manager.

- Secretary department:
  The secretarial staff is composed of a secretary, performing the secretarial work and the phone desk. She works with a computer for doing office work and email.

- Sales department:
  The sales department is composed of two employees creating and managing clients' records. They are mainly working on defining estimates for clients. This service is the one mainly communicating with external people. He supports so the corporate image of the company. It communicates a lot with the study office that provides many documents (3D mock-ups, technical plans, etc), with the administration for the prices and with external peoples and clients (requirements document, plans and estimates, technical information for architects, etc.)

- Study office:
  It is based on 4 engineers and 3 drawers performing the following activities:
  - Design technical plans for building workers
  - Design 3D mock-ups for clients that should be as precise and nice as possible
  - Establish structure calculations for material resistance

- Administration:
  In this service, one people is working as an accountant and is also responsible of managing administrative stuff like obtaining building permits, provided by the relevant authorities.

Clients

The range of *@rchimed*'s clients is large, ranging from private sector to public administration and concerning also building professionals. Statistics show that the main activity period is from October to May and that the current economic situation is good. However *@rchimed* is subject to high competition, needing to be quick, precise and original in its projects.

1.6.2 *@rchimed*'s IS infrastructure

The IS architecture of *@rchimed* can be summarised as:

- Hardware and network:
  The study office has 7 computers, the sales department 2 computers, the administration 1 computer and finally the secretary department 1 computer. The management owns 2 laptops and the commercial service has also 2 laptops available for presentations. All of these computers are connected on a local Ethernet network. A printing server and a file server are available for the whole company. Every service is connected to Internet: the sales department to communicate with clients, the study office to be able to find technical information and the management, administration and secretary department for emails.

- Software:
  A software called ARC+ is used for defining 3D mock-ups, a software called SIFRA is used for working on a tablet PC and finally the SPOT software is used for structure calculation with a database containing materials assumptions and results obtained. An office software is used on each computer.

1.6.3 IS development objectives

@rchimed aims now to be able to communicate more easily with its clients and suppliers. The company would like to introduce ICT components like groupware to improve the efficiency of the communication between the different people involved in a project (architects, contractors, public authorities, etc.) The tool should first improve documents sharing (plans, calculations, etc.) between the actors. Mechanisms for version and conflict management are necessary. Then the building construction follow-up should also be improved and the tool should manage the workflows and the tasks between the involved actors. For this purpose, tools like shared calendar will be put in place. This new IS naturally involves security concerns. The information each actor will have access to must respect confidentiality agreements. The integrity of sensitive documents like plans or structure calculations must be respected. Finally, the availability of the whole system is essential to have access instantaneously to the documents necessary for the construction.

1.7 Structure

This thesis is organised in four parts and eight chapters (Figure 1.8):

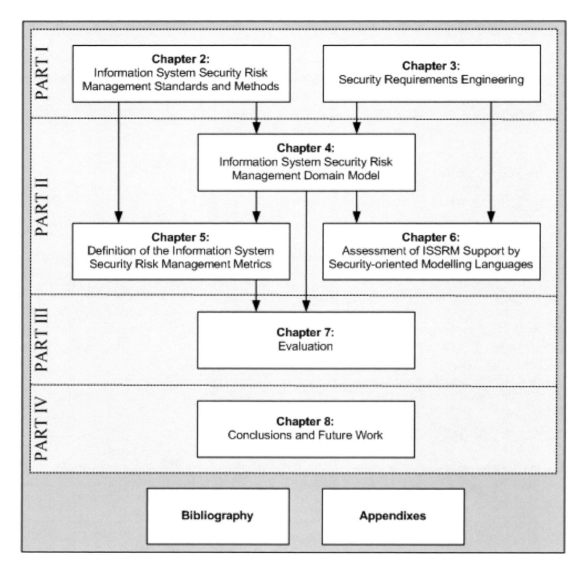

Figure 1.8: Structure of the work

PART I, State of the art contains two chapters related to the review of the current practice and research in ISSRM and security RE.

- **Chapter 2:** *Information System Security Risk Management Standards and Methods* presents an overview of the ISSRM process and its related tasks. Then, it surveys the different RM standards, security standards, security RM standards, and security RM methods.

- **Chapter 3:** *Security Requirements Engineering* deals first with the security RE frameworks. Second, it provides an overview of existing security-oriented modelling languages.

PART II, An Information System Security Risk Management Modelling Framework is about the contribution of this thesis, which consists of the definition of the ISSRM domain model, its metrics, and its comparison with existing security-oriented modelling languages.

- **Chapter 4:** *Information System Security Risk Management Domain Model* introduces the domain model of ISSRM. The research method applied for its construction and the different steps performed are explained.

- **Chapter 5:** *Definition of the Information System Security Risk Management Metrics* enriches the ISSRM domain model with metrics. A research method is again proposed and its application, combining two complementary approaches, is described.

- **Chapter 6:** *Assessment of ISSRM Support by Security-oriented Modelling Languages* proposes a comparison between existing modelling languages and the ISSRM domain model. The languages compared are KAOS extended to security [vL04], Misuse cases [SO05] and Secure Tropos [GMZ05]. For Secure Tropos, an adaptation is proposed, in the aim to better cover the ISSRM domain.

PART III, Applications shows how the results were applied on a concrete experiment.

- **Chapter 7:** *Evaluation* is about the concrete experimentation of the domain model and its related metrics. Both were used in the frame of the ISO/IEC 27001 certification of a luxembourgish SME.

PART IV, Conclusion summarises the major findings and discusses the future work.

- **Chapter 8:** *Conclusions and Future Work* presents the conclusions of the research problem and states the claimed contribution of this work. Identified limitations and future works are also proposed.

The document ends with the *Bibliography*, which recapitulates all the references used and cited throughout the thesis. Finally, appendices present some research material used in this research work.

- **Appendix A** gathers useful extracts and definitions, used for the concept alignment of Chapter 4.

- **Appendix B** is a table summarising the concept alignment.

- **Appendix C** reports the extraction of relationships between the concepts identified for ISO/IEC Guide 73. It is used as an example of how relatioship identification is performed.

- **Appendix D** collects the metrics used in the different ISSRM approaches that perform concept estimation

Part I

State of the art

Chapter 2

Information System Security Risk Management Standards and Methods

T he state of the art of this PhD is composed of two complementary parts. The first one aims at presenting the ISSRM literature, composed of standards and methods. The second one is about security RE, proposing frameworks and modelling languages related to security and taking place during RE. The objective of this chapter is to present the first part of the state of the art, about ISSRM standards and methods. During the last decade, ISSRM has been a very active domain and is still quickly evolving. Practitioners have developed ISSRM methods to help estimate the relative importance of security risks and the cost-effectiveness of solutions to tackle them. The methods are mainly driven by standards and professional best practices in the domain of security and risk management, defining the related concepts and processes to apply.

First of all, this chapter begins with Section 2.1 proposing an overview of the traditional ISSRM process. Then Section 2.2 starts the review of the literature by presenting RM standards. Section 2.3 is about the security standards. Section 2.4 describes standards already standing in the security RM domain. Section 2.5 shows a representative subset of security RM methods. The chapter ends with Section 2.6 about conclusion and comparison of the literature surveyed.

It is necessary to note that in this chapter, for each described approach, we use the terminology proposed by the approach. The different standards and methods are not presented with a unified terminology.

2.1 Introduction to the ISSRM process

ISSRM activities usually follow an overall process composed of classical steps generally found in traditional ISSRM methods (e.g., [AS/04, SGF02, DCS04b], etc.). Nevertheless, the reader should note that the different methods do not put the same weight on the activities performed and this is one of the main particularities of each method/standard. Some methods, for example, are more focused on risk assessment [DCS04b, CLU07b, AD01b] whereas others [ISO05c, Bun05b] suggest standard security controls (or countermeasures) to be applied in order to reach a satisfactory security level. The whole ISSRM process is summarised in Figure 2.1, under the form of a UML activity diagram [Obj04], and is illustrated with the help of the running example introduced in Section 1.6.

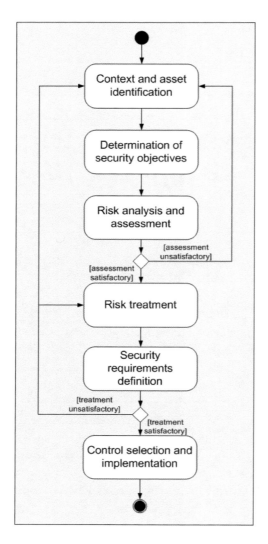

Figure 2.1: ISSRM process

Step (a): Context and asset identification

The process starts with a study of the organisation's context and the identification of its assets. In this step, the organisation and its environment are described, focusing on the sensitive activities related to information security. An overview of the IS, when already in place, is made.

Example: The @rchimed activities has been presented in Section 1.6. Within all of its activities, the design of technical plans is an asset that should be protected. At the IS level, the technical plans are created by drawers and engineers on computers connected to the Internet.

Step (b): Determination of security objectives

The security needs of the organisation are then defined. Based on asset identification, one needs to determine the security objectives to be reached. Security objectives are often defined in terms of confidentiality, integrity and availability properties of the assets.

Example: During their design, the technical plans should be kept confidential.

Step (c): Risk analysis and assessment

The main step of the process is risk analysis, eliciting which risks are harming assets and threatening security objectives. This step consists in identifying risks and estimating their level in a qualitative or quantitative manner. We speak about risk assessment [ISO02b] only when the level of analysed risks has been evaluated against the security needs, which are determined during the second step of the process (cf. Step (b)). It could be necessary at this step to fully review the context and asset identification, if the risk assessment is considered as unsatisfactory.

Example: A rival of @rchimed can try to use common operating system and network protocol weaknesses to penetrate on the personal computer of an employee, where are stored some confidential technical plans. This risk has an estimated level that is sufficiently high to be considered.

Step (d): Risk treatment

Once risk assessment is performed, decisions about risk treatment are taken. Risk treatment measures can include avoiding, reducing, transferring or retaining risk [ISO02b]:

- Risk avoidance is the decision not to become involved in, or action to withdraw from, a risk situation (e.g., don't use the risky functionality of the IS and so disable the risk).

- Risk reduction consists of taking actions to lessen the probability, negative consequences, or both, associated with a risk (e.g., select and implement some security requirements for mitigating the risk).

- Risk transfer consists of sharing with another party the burden of loss for a risk (e.g., take an insurance for covering the consequence of the risk).

- Risk retention is the acceptance of the burden of loss from a particular risk (e.g., accept the risk as is because its probability and consequence are low enough).

The decision is generally based on cost-effectiveness evaluation between risks and risks treatment.

Example: The decision of reducing the preceding risk with some security controls to implement in the IS seems to be the most appropriate.

Step (e): Security requirements definition

Security requirements on the IS can thus be determined as security solutions to mitigate the risks, mainly if the risk reduction treatment has been chosen. However, security requirements can emerge from other treatments, like for example risk transfer needing generally some requirements on the third party. At the end of the risk treatment step, followed by the security requirements definition, if they are considered as unsatisfactory, the risk treatment step can be revised, or all of the preceding steps can be revised from the definition of the context and the assets.

Example: The following security requirement has been selected to be applied on the

@rchimed's IS: Procedures for monitoring the use of information processing facilities should be established and the results of the monitoring activities reviewed regularly [ISO05c].

Step (f): Control selection and implementation
Requirements are finally instantiated into security controls, i.e. system specific countermeasures, that are implemented within the organisation.
Example: A firewall and an Intrusion Detection System (IDS) are selected and implemented within the @rchimed's IS.

As highlighted by the two decision points of the process, the process is iterative. It should be performed as many times as necessary until reaching an acceptable level for all risks, taking also into account new risks emerging after security control determination. The level of risk remaining after applying the security measures is called 'residual risk' [ISO02b]. Only the main decision points [ISO08] are represented on this process, but some others are possible and proposed within the different methods [DCS04b, CLU07b, AD01b]. Moreover, each time such a RM process is started, some parallel actions are also generally recommended. A *risk communication* process should be undertaken to guarantee an effective communication among stakeholders. The different stakeholders and decision-makers should be informed throughout the process about the RM activities and risk evolution. This helps them to have a permanent understanding of the organisation's ISSRM process and its results. A *risk monitoring and review* process is also recommended. Even after reaching an acceptable level for all risks, the ISSRM process should be monitored and regularly reviewed. Risks are obviously not static and should be monitored. Each modification in the organisation's business, in its context, in its IS, each emerging vulnerability, etc. can produce modifications on risks and/or their level. In an ideal way, the ISSRM process should in fact be continuously performed, in order to keep the organisation's business and its associated security needs aligned with the measures taken and the ensuing security level.

2.2 Risk management standards

RM standards are high-level references presenting RM in general and standing over domain-specific RM approaches. This section presents two RM standards: ISO/IEC Guide 73 [ISO02b] and AS/NZS 4360 [AS/04]. They are selected because they are the only two standards currently standing in this domain. Moreover, they are often an input in terms of concepts and terminology for other standards or methods [ISO04b, ISO05b, ISO08, DCS04b, VML+07].

2.2.1 ISO/IEC Guide 73

The aim of ISO/IEC Guide 73 [ISO02b], entitled "*Risk management - Vocabulary - Guidelines for use in standards*" and whose current version is of 2002, is to provide a terminological basis and generic definitions for RM, in order to develop common understanding amongst organisations across countries and amongst ISO and IEC members.

The guide is focused on RM in general, whatever the concerned domain. It is similarly applicable to risk in finance, environment, project management, information security risk, etc. It thus deals with RM from both the positive and negative perspectives (a risk taken for example in the financial domain can have positive consequences). This guide is especially used as an input for the definition or the revision of each other ISO standard dealing with RM in a specific domain. However, according to the Guide, it may be sometimes necessary to deviate from the exact wording proposed in the Guide to meet the needs of a specific domain.

The core of the ISO/IEC Guide 73 standard is a list of definitions on RM concepts including RM tasks. The terms defined cover the complete field of RM, including basic terms, terms related to people or organisations affected by risk, terms related to risk assessment, and terms related to risk treatment and control.

2.2.2   AS/NZS 4360

AS/NZS 4360 [AS/04] is a joined Australian/New Zealand standard. Its current version dates back to 2004 and the first was published in 1999. This standard is entitled *"Risk management"* and its purpose is to provide a generic framework for establishing the context, identifying, analysing, evaluating, treating, monitoring and communicating risk. As for the ISO/IEC Guide 73 [ISO02b], this standard is generic and can be applied to any RM domain, as well as to any sector or organisation.

The standard starts by proposing a glossary, generally compliant with the ISO/IEC Guide 73. The core of the standard is focused on an overview of the RM process (Figure 2.2). AS/NZS 4360 provides the following iterative RM process:

- Establish the context:

    - Definition of the (internal and external) context of the organisation
    - Definition of the criteria against which risk will be evaluated
    - Define the structure for the rest of the process

- Identify risks

    - Identify sources of risks and events that might have an impact on the organisation
    - Identify how they can occur

- Analyse risks

    - Evaluate existing security controls that already minimise risks
    - Estimate the magnitude of the consequences and the likelihood of the event of risks

- Evaluate risks

    - Take decisions about risks, based on the outcome of risk analysis

- Treat risks

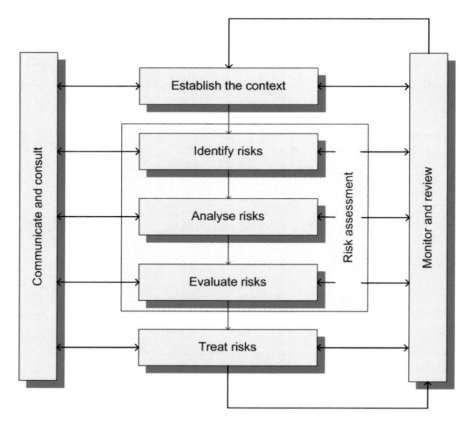

Figure 2.2: Overview of the RM process (as appears in [AS/04])

- Identify options for the treatment of risks (having positive or negative consequences)
- Select the most appropriate option, balancing costs of implementing against benefits obtained
- Define and implement a treatment plan

Two other parallel tasks should be performed all along the preceding process:

- Communicate actively and regularly with stakeholders about risks and the process to manage them, and consult stakeholders during the different tasks in the aim of being able to take the best decisions

- Monitor and review risks, to insure that they are up-to-date, as well as risk treatment, to guarantee its effectiveness

The standard ends with recommendations to establish effective RM.

2.3   Security standards

In this section we present two standards dealing with security, but not specifically focused on RM activities: ISO/IEC 13335 [ISO04b] and Common Criteria [Com06a].

These standards are selected because they are international, often used and referenced in various methods or other standards [ISO05b, DCS04b, Bun05a, SHF04, Ins03, VML⁺07] and presenting in particular the concepts at stake.

2.3.1 ISO/IEC 13335

The objective of the ISO/IEC 13335 standard is to define the basis for the information security management [ISO04b]. The ISO/IEC 13335 standard was first published between 1996 and 2001 as a set of Technical Reports (TR) entitled "*Guidelines for the Management of IT Security*" (GMITS), before becoming an international standard. It was composed of a set of guidelines for the management of IT security:

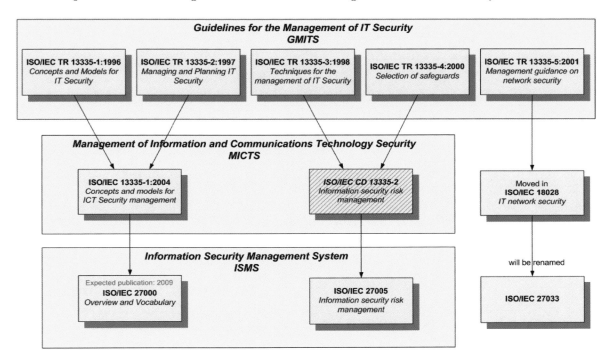

Figure 2.3: The ISO/IEC 13335 standard and its evolutions

- ISO/IEC TR 13335-1 (1996) "*Concepts and models for IT Security*" contains definitions applicable to all parts of the standard, and introduces various concepts and models of IT security that may be applicable to different organisations.

- ISO/IEC TR 13335-2 (1997) "*Managing and Planning IT Security*" contains information about management of IT security, security policy, risk analysis, security awareness, and several other issues to tackle for defining an IT security program.

- ISO/IEC TR 13335-3 (1998) "*Techniques for the management of IT Security*" portrays RM methods suitable for people concerned with management actions to be taken during a project's life-cycle. This may include planning, designing, implementing, testing, acquisition, or operations.

- ISO/IEC TR 13335-4 (2000) *"Selection of safeguards"* helps in the selection of safeguards (meaning technical security controls) taking into account business needs and security concerns.

- ISO/IEC TR 13335-5 (2001) *"Management guidance on network security"* provides guidelines for managing networks and communications, without suggesting any advice on the design and implementation aspects which are out of the scope of this document.

In 2004, the ISO/IEC 13335 series has become an international standard entitled *"Management of Information and Communications Technology Security"* (MICTS), with the publication of the ISO/IEC 13335-1 about *"Concepts and models for information and communications technology security management"* [ISO04b]. This standard supersedes (merges and an updates) ISO/IEC TR 13335-1:1996 and ISO/IEC TR 13335-2:1997 (cf. Figure 2.3). Its content is focused on definitions of security concepts and information about the management of ICT security. It is currently considered as the up-to-date standard about ICT security management definition.

Just as ISO/IEC 13335-1, ISO/IEC 13335-2 was intended to supersede the technical reports ISO/IEC TR 13335-3:1998 and ISO/IEC TR 13335-4:2000. However this new project of standard has been stopped and replaced by the ISO/IEC 27005 standard [ISO08] about *"Information security risk management"*. Finally ISO/IEC TR 13335-5 is moved to ISO/IEC 18028-1, becoming now ISO/IEC 27033.

The current objective of the ISO members is now to extend ICT security to information security, enlarging the scope previously focussed essentially on hardware, software and network aspects to information management in general. The material contained within ISO/IEC 13335-1 is proposed to be included in the ISO/IEC 2700x series, mainly in the vocabulary standard. It is expected that ISO/IEC 13335-1 will be withdrawn once ISO/IEC 27000 and ISO/IEC 27003 will be published.

2.3.2 Common Criteria for Information Technology Security Evaluation

The Common Criteria (CC) standard [Com06a] results from joint work between USA, United Kingdom, Netherlands, France, Germany and Canada, unifying three standards: the European standard ITSEC (Information Technology Security Evaluation Criteria), the Canadian standard CTCPEC (Canadian Trusted Computer Product Evaluation Criteria) and the United States Government Department of Defense standard TCSEC (Trusted Computer System Evaluation Criteria). CC provides tools for defining a set of security requirements and for evaluating the security specification of a product or a system. These requirements are divided into two categories: security functional components and security assurance components. Functional components define functional requirements for the system-to-be. Assurance components help to guarantee that the chosen security requirements correspond to the measures selected and that they are correctly implemented. CC is currently in version 3.1 and is also an international standard (ISO/IEC 15408) related to IS security. However, being focused on IT security of products, CC is not completely aligned with our research scope, i.e. IS security (Section 1.4). The requirements proposed by the standard are product-oriented (i.e., adapted for an IT product like an operating system, a firewall, etc.) but not IS-oriented (i.e., adapted for a whole IS within an organisation) (Section

1.5.2). Despite of this, CC is considered in this research work, because it is a major and well-known standard whose terminology and concepts are generally well accepted and represent the foundations for many ISSRM methods.

CC is based on three main concepts:

- **Protection profile**
  A Protection Profile (PP) is a set of security requirements aiming at reducing IT security risk in a given context. A PP is defined from the user's viewpoint (identifying the desired properties of a product). It is implementation-independent and meant to be reusable. A user can write his own PP or select an existing one in a catalog. A PP is composed of the specific security requirements the user is expecting for the product. He can then provide this PP as specifications to a developer or use it to evaluate and compare existing Commercial Off-The-Shelf (COTS) products.

- **Security target**
  A Security Target (ST) is a set of security requirements for a given product, generally from the developer's viewpoint. A ST is specific to a given product or system. It is a means for a product editor to specify the security characteristics of his product. The ST may claim conformance to one or more PPs, and forms the basis for an evaluation.

- **Target of Evaluation**
  The two preceding tools (PP and ST) are generally used to evaluate existing products or systems. In this case, the term Target of Evaluation (ToE) denotes the evaluated product or system.

CC is built around three main documents:

- *Part 1: Introduction and general model* [Com06a]
  This part defines the terminology, the general concepts and presents an overview of the underlying model for evaluation: evaluation of PP, ST and ToE. This part also provides the description of the content of a PP and of a ST.

- *Part 2: Security functional components* [Com06b]
  This part defines a collection of generic security functional requirements divided into classes, themselves broken down into families of components, which for example cover access control, identification, authentication, physical protection, etc. The developer selects the best adapted requirements for his product and instantiates them in the ST. CC also allows stating requirements for families of products within PP.

- *Part 3: Security assurance components* [Com06c]
  This part defines the assurance requirements, both for the development environment and for the product itself, as well as the tasks for the evaluator. These assurance requirements are organised in classes, then in families of components, which cover functional specification and design descriptions, like testing, life cycle management, delivery procedures, security of the development environment,

vulnerability analysis, etc. Developers can either build up their own consistent assurance package or use one of the seven predefined Evaluation Assurance Levels (EAL). EAL1 to EAL7 provide an increasing scale that balances the level of assurance obtained on the product security with the cost and feasibility of acquiring that degree of assurance. Each of these levels can be augmented with one or more additional components in order to meet specific objectives.

The Common Evaluation Methodology [Com07] is a complementary document presenting the principles and processes whereby evaluations are conducted using CC. It describes the tasks to be carried out by an evaluator for checking each assurance requirement. CC proposes three different but complementary kinds of evaluation:

- PP evaluation: evaluating whether a PP is complete, consistent, technically sound, and hence suitable for use in developing a ST.

- ST evaluation: evaluating whether a ST meets the requirements of one or more PPs.

- ToE evaluation: evaluating if a ToE is conform to the security requirements of its associated ST.

The main advantage of an evaluation following the CC model is that every evaluation will be done based on the same reference. This leads to comparable and reproductible results. Typical products or systems (ToE) evaluated with CC are operating systems, network components (switch, hub, VPN, etc.) or security products (firewall, IDS, authentication system, etc.). The current drawbacks of CC evaluations are the cost of the whole evaluation process including the effort and time necessary to prepare an evaluation and associated documentation.

2.4 Security risk management standards

This section presents standards dealing with security that are specifically focused on RM activities. The ISO/IEC series of standard [ISO05b, ISO05c, ISO08] is focussed on this field, as other national standards like NIST standards [SHF04, SGF02] and the German BSI standards [Bun05b]. We selected naturally the international standards of this field, but also the NIST and BSI standards that are well known and used outside of the standard's country [ENI06].

2.4.1 The ISO/IEC 2700x series of standards

The ISO/IEC 2700x series of standards deals with information security management. It is composed of a set of standards providing information for setting up an Information Security Management System (ISMS).

Introduction to ISO management systems

The ISO standards providing requirements and guidance about best management practices are part of the most well-known standards. The most popular management system series of standards are the ISO 900x series about quality management systems

[ISO00] and ISO 1400x series about environmental management systems [ISO04a]. Many other domains have followed this initiative and have proposed an adapted management system based on the same generic model (Table 2.1).

Table 2.1: Management standards and related sectors

Sector	Standard or series of standards
Automotive	ISO/TS 16949:2002
Education	IWA 2:2007
Environment	ISO 14001:2004
Food safety	ISO 22000:2005
Health care	IWA 1:2005
Information security	ISO/IEC 27001:2005
IT service management	ISO/IEC 20000:2005
Local government	IWA 4:2005
Quality	ISO 9001:2000
Medical devices	ISO 13485:2003
Petroleum and gas	ISO 29001:2003
Ship recycling	ISO 30000
Supply chain security	ISO 28000:2007

A *management system* is defined as the framework of processes and procedures used to ensure that an organisation can fulfill all tasks required to achieve its objectives [Wik08b]. Within the set of common principles shared by the management systems, the main one is the application of the "Plan-Do-Check-Act" paradigm, also called "Deming wheel" or "PDCA cycle" [LNN⁺96]. This cycle is composed of the four following steps to be performed iteratively [ISO05b, ISO00, ISO04a]:

- *PLAN*
  Establish the objectives and processes necessary to deliver results in accordance with the specifications.

- *DO*
  Implement the processes.

- *CHECK*
  Monitor and evaluate the processes and results against objectives and specifications.

- *ACT*
  Apply actions to the outcome for necessary improvement.

The main purpose of a management system is always to put the organisation in a continuous improvement for the concerned domain.

Overview of the ISO/IEC 2700x series of standards

The ISO/IEC 2700x series of standards is currently expected to be composed of 8 main standards (Figure 2.4), dedicated to information security. Some other standards,

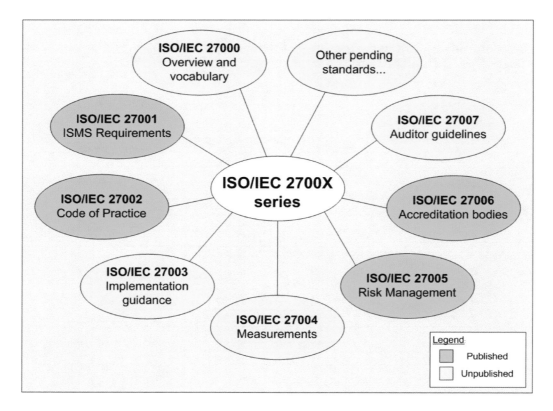

Figure 2.4: The ISO/IEC 2700x series of standards

numbered ISO/IEC 27001x, are reserved to sector-specific requirements or guidelines standards. The following are expected: *Information security management guidelines for telecommunications* based on ISO/IEC 27002, and *Sector-Specific ISMS Standards for the World Lottery Association* and for the *Automotive Industry* based on ISO/IEC 27001.

ISO/IEC 27000: Overview and vocabulary. This first standard defines the basic principles and the terminology concerning an ISMS. It will supersede the first part of ISO/IEC 13335 [ISO04b]. Publication is expected for 2009.

ISO/IEC 27001: ISMS Requirements. The ISO/IEC 27001 standard [ISO05b] provides the requirements necessary to establish and manage an ISMS. It was the first standard of the ISO/IEC 2700x series to be published (October 2005) and the whole series is built around this standard. Organisations can obtain an ISO/IEC 27001 certification with regards to their compliance with the requirements of this standard. The standard comes from a British Standard (BS 7799-2) that is now obsolete.

ISO/IEC 27002: Code of Practice for Information Security Management. The ISO/IEC 27002 [ISO05c] standard is only the renaming (in April 2007) of the already existing ISO/IEC 17799 standard. ISO/IEC 17799 was the first ISO standard dealing with information security and its objective was to define a set of good practices for insuring information security management. This standard published in 2000 was then reviewed in 2002 and 2005. The content of ISO/IEC 27002 is currently similar to the one of ISO/IEC 17799:2005 and the security controls it proposes are part of the ISO/IEC 27001 requirements.

ISO/IEC 27003: ISMS implementation guidance. The ISO/IEC 27003 standard aims at providing implementation guidelines for establishing and implementing an ISMS. It is focused on how to effectively perform the PDCA cycle and complete the requirements of an ISMS. Publication is expected for 2009

ISO/IEC 27004: Information security management measurements. Amongst the ISO/IEC 27001 requirements, some require to measure the efficiency of the ISMS. The ISO/IEC 27004 standard provides guidelines for helping organisations to observe and measure the efficiency of their ISMS implementation. Publication is expected for 2009

ISO/IEC 27005: Information security risk management. The ISO/IEC 27005 standard [ISO08] proposes a process to follow for performing security risk management, required by the ISO/IEC 27001. It was published in June 2008. It is an evolution of ISO/IEC 13335 part 3 and 4.

ISO/IEC 27006: Requirements for bodies providing audit and certification of ISMS. The ISO/IEC 27006 standard specifies requirements and provides guidance for bodies providing audit and certification of an ISMS. It is primarily intended to support the accreditation of certification bodies providing ISMS certification. It was published in February 2007.

ISO/IEC 27007: ISMS Auditor Guidelines. The ISO/IEC 27007 standard is providing guidance on conducting ISMS audits. A part is dedicated to the competences needed by ISMS auditors. This guide will be complementary with the ISO 19011 [ISO02a] standard, providing guidelines for quality and environmental management systems audit (and generic enough to be used as a reference for an ISMS audit). No publication date has currently been suggested.

ISO/IEC 27005: Information security risk management

The objective of the ISO/IEC 27005 standard is to describe the information security risk management process and its tasks. As mentioned in the scope of the standard, it supports the general concepts specified in ISO/IEC 27001 and is designed to satisfy the requirement of having an information security based on a risk management approach. Indeed ISO/IEC 27001 requires a systematic approach to information security risk management. For each task of the process, the inputs and outputs are given by the standard. Then, the action describing the task is defined and some implementation guidance is provided. The process proposed is an evolution of the one proposed in the AS/NZS 4360 standard (Figure 2.2).

The ISO/IEC 27005 information security risk management process consists of context establishment, risk assessment, risk treatment, risk acceptance, risk communication, and risk monitoring and review. This process should be iterative and continuous.

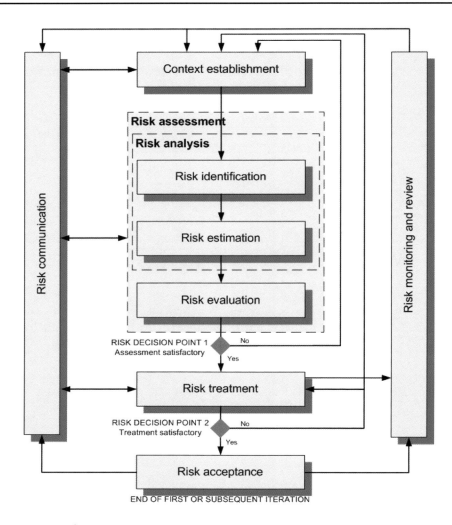

Figure 2.5: The ISO/IEC 27005 information security risk management process (as appears in [ISO08])

Once context establishment and risk assessment have been conducted, it is necessary to evaluate if sufficient information is available to take decision about risk treatment. If not, a new iteration (maybe partial) with updated context and risk assessment, is conducted. Otherwise, risk treatment task is performed (cf. Figure 2.5, Risk Decision Point 1).

Several iterations of the risk treatment task could be needed to reach the best state in terms of residual risk and ROSI. Moreover, since the effectiveness of the risk treatment depends on the results of the risk assessment, it is possible that no acceptable level of residual risk can be reached. In this case, a revision of the process starting from the context establishment can be necessary to update the different parameters (cf. Figure 2.5, Risk Decision Point 2).

After risk treatment, the risk acceptance task has the objective to ensure that residual risks are explicitly accepted by the managers of the organisation. Finally, risk communication is a task to be performed throughout the process, to be sure to have all of the relevant information at each task of the process. Thereby, the whole process should be clearly documented.

2.4.2 NIST Special Publication 800-27 Rev A and 800-30

The NIST (National Institute of Standards and Technology) is a federal technology agency founded in 1901 within the U.S. Department of Commerce. Its mission is to develop and promote measurement, standards, and technology in order to increase productivity in the U.S. and facilitate business.

The NIST SP (Special Publication) 800-27 Rev A [SHF04] and NIST SP 800-30 [SGF02], published respectively in June 2004 and July 2002, are part of the SP in the '800' series of NIST standards. This series was established in 1990 with the aim of providing documentation about computer security in general. The main targets of NIST 800-27 Rev A and NIST 800-30 are federal organisations that process sensitive information. However, the documents make clear that the use of these guidelines is not subject to copyright and that they can be applied by non-governmental organisations.

NIST 800-27 Rev A is a guide about *"Engineering Principles for Information Technology Security"*. It presents a list of system-level security principles to be considered in the design, development, and operation of an IS. The document presents 33 security principles and defines their applicability in the IS development life-cycle, i.e. Initiation Phase, Development/Acquisition Phase, Implementation Phase, Operation/Maintenance Phase, Disposal Phase. This IS development life-cycle is described in depth in the *"Generally Accepted Principles and Practices for Securing Information Technology Systems"* (SP 800-14). Finally, this standard comes with a set of security concepts, detailed in a glossary, on which the NIST SP 800-30 is based.

NIST SP 800-30 is entitled *"Risk Management Guide for Information Technology Systems"*. Its objective is to provide a baseline for conducting an efficient risk management. This guide is especially based on (and compliant with) the NIST 800-27 Rev A. After some preliminary elements about risk management, the document proposes two complementary processes: the "Risk Assessment" process and the "Risk Mitigation" process. These two processes completely cover the risk management process presented in Section 2.1, from context and asset identification to control implementation. For each step of both processes, the inputs, the outpouts, and the tasks to perform are described under the form of guidelines. However it is necessary to note that these two processes are presented at a high-level of granularity, with few details concerning the implementation of the different tasks. The "Risk Assessment" process determines the potential risks associated with an IS and helps to devise appropriate controls to mitigate them. It is composed of the 9 following steps, as depicted in the standard:

- Step 1: System Characterization

- Step 2: Threat Identification

- Step 3: Vulnerability Identification

- Step 4: Control Analysis

- Step 5: Likelihood Determination

- Step 6: Impact Analysis

- Step 7: Risk Determination

- Step 8: Control Recommendations

- Step 9: Results Documentation

The second process of risk management for NIST SP 800-30 is called "Risk Mitigation". It involves prioritising, evaluating, and implementing the appropriate controls coming from the risk assessment process. This process is composed of the 7 following steps, as depicted in the standard:

- Step 1: Prioritize Actions

- Step 2: Evaluate recommended Control Options

- Step 3: Conduct Cost-Benefit Analysis

- Step 4: Select Controls

- Step 5: Assign Responsibility

- Step 6: Develop Safeguard Implementation Plan

- Step 7: Implement Selected Controls

The document ends with some good practices and keys for success.

2.4.3 The IT-Grundshutz

The IT-Grundshutz is a set of German standards, based on a security management method. It is produced and maintained by the German Federal Office for Information Security (BSI - Bundesamt für Sicherheit in der Informationstechnik). This federal office is in charge of managing computer and communication security for the German government. The IT-Grundshutz is composed first of 3 standards and second of knowledge bases on assets, threats and safeguards, called catalogues (Figure 2.6).

BSI Standard 100-1: Information Security Management Systems (ISMS) [Bun05a]
This first standard defines the general requirements for an ISMS. The requirements are compatible with ISO/IEC 27001 [ISO05b] and, moreover, take the recommendations of ISO/IEC 13335 [ISO04b] and ISO/IEC 27002 [ISO05c] into consideration. The objective of this document is to facilitate the comprehension of these ISO/IEC standards and to help user to implement the requirements through the IT-Grundschutz, by providing greater details.

BSI-Standard 100-2: IT-Grundschutz Methodology [Bun05b]
The IT-Grundshutz Methodology deals with IT security management and proposes successive steps to effectively manage security (how to produce a security plan, how to select safeguards, how to implement them, how to maintain and improve IT security, etc.). The standard provides a very pragmatical approach and this document is mainly based on examples and background expertises. The methodology relies on the IT-Grundshutz Catalogues, providing the user with knowledge bases needed to apply the methodology. The final objective of the methodology is to reach a standard level

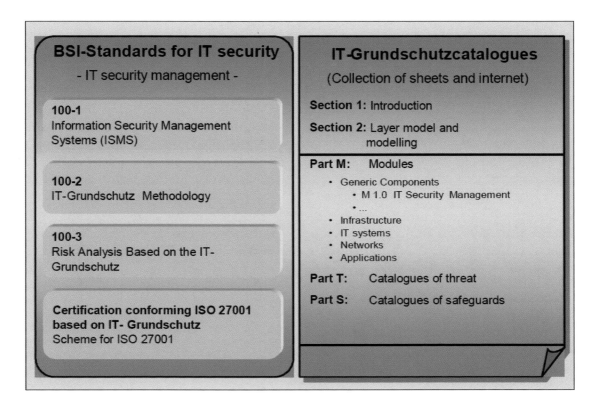

Figure 2.6: Overview of BSI publications on IT security management (as appears in [Bun05a])

of security.

BSI-Standard 100-3: Risk Analysis based on IT-Grundschutz [Bun05c]
The IT-Grundshutz Methodology together with its associated catalogues aims at proposing measures for a standard security level. However, feedback from the IT-Grundshutz users has shown that it is sometimes necessary to go further and provide techniques when the needed security level is higher. This standard proposes a method for analysing risks, complementary with the IT-Grundschutz Methodology, to be used for additional security analysis. It is generally used only on a particular set of assets.

The IT-Grundshutz Catalogues [Bun05d]
The IT-Grundshutz Catalogues are knowledge bases for 3 security components: IT assets, threats and safeguards. Based on these catalogues, a user could pick the IT assets of his IS, and the catalogues directly make the link with the associated threats and the safeguards to implement. The granularity level proposed is very detailed, it provides implementation aspects for safeguards.

These standards are freely available and have been designed to be continuously updated and extended to include new items on the basis of user surveys. The catalogues are revised every six months to incorporate suggestions for improvements, additional material and reflect the latest IT developments. A software tool (GSTOOL) supporting the IT-Grundshutz is available. It is also possible to be certified on the basis of the IT-Grundshutz [Bun05a].

2.5 Security risk management methods

This section is about security risk management methods. In 2004, a CLUSIF (Club de la Sécurité de l'Information Français[1]) study registered more than 200 security RM methods [Clu04a]. Among those, we selected a representative subset based on some recent conferences and studies, like the report *"Inventory of risk assessment and risk management methods"* [ENI06] from ENISA, surveying the methods known by the security experts of this european agency. The availability and quality of the documentation are also first-class selection criteria considered in this selection. Methods that are private and/or specific to a company or methods with few documentation are not selected in our study. The set of selected methods is finally a representative panel regarding the characteristics of the methods:

- History and background of the method;

- Method's country (France [DCS04b, CLU07b], United Kingdom [Ins03], USA [AD01b], etc.);

- Domain of origin (industry [CLU07b, AD01b, Ins03], military [DCS04b], scientific [VML$^+$07]);

- Based (or not) on knowledge bases [DCS04b, CLU07b, Ins03];

- Risk approach (analytic definition of risk [DCS04b, Ins03, VML$^+$07], based on risk scenario [CLU07b], based on brainstorming [AD01b]);

- Qualitative [DCS04b, CLU07b, AD01b, VML$^+$07] or quantitative [Ins03] concept estimation.

The methods surveyed are EBIOS [DCS04b], MEHARI [CLU07b], OCTAVE [AD01b], CRAMM [Ins03] and CORAS [VML$^+$07].

2.5.1 EBIOS

Under the authority of the Secretariat-General for National Defence, the Central Information Systems Security Division (DCSSI - Direction Centrale de la Sécurité des Systèmes d'Information) is the French national authority for IS security. The EBIOS (Expression des Besoins et Identification des Objectifs de Sécurité) method [DCS04b] has been created in 1995 by the DCSSI. It is currently in version 2. The EBIOS method is used to assess and treat risks related to IS security. It can also be used to communicate information about risk within the organisation and to partners. Therefore, it supports the whole ISSRM process. Its use is recommended for the analysis of French military and governmental IS, but EBIOS is also commonly used in industry and other organisations. The method is composed of 5 sections. A case study [DCS04a] explaining the method on an example has been designed. Additionally, an open-source software tool aiming at facilitating the use of the method is now available.

---

[1]http://www.clusif.asso.fr/en/clusif/present/

This tool is especially used for collecting data of an EBIOS study and for producing summary documents.

EBIOS has been widely used in France, but also in Europa. The method is particularly interesting because it has an analytic approach to risk: risk is incrementally built, based on knowledge bases of each atomic element of risk (as it is defined in EBIOS). The documentation is publicly available and well structured.

The general principle of the method can be summarised as: identify the assets requiring protection, analyse the consequence of incidents on assets, analyse at the same time the threats and vulnerabilities of the IS and finally choose the most appropriate security solutions to mitigate the risks. The method is composed of 5 steps (Figure 2.7):

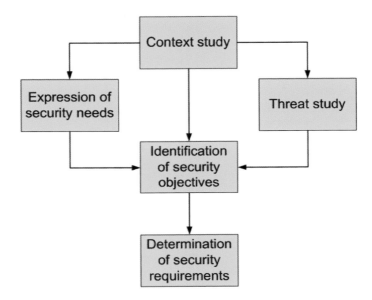

Figure 2.7: EBIOS global approach (as appears in [DCS04b])

Step 1 - Context study In the first step, the organisation is studied, by analysing its missions, its business, its own values, its constraints, its structure, the regulatory references applicable to the organisation, etc. The outcome of this step is first a description of the essential elements of the organisation (functions or information security sensitive) and second the determination of the entities or components of the underlying IS. A mapping is done between both of them.

Step 2 - Expression of security needs The purpose of this step is to allow IS users to express their security needs for the functions and information they handle, independently of any technical solution. A (so called) scale of needs is first defined for each security criteria (i.e. confidentiality, integrity, availability) to grade security needs in the form of levels. Then, every relevant impact is assigned to one of these levels for each security criteria. Finally a summary of the results obtained is produced.

Step 3 - Threat study This step aims at determining the threats affecting the IS. These threats are formalised in EBIOS by identifying the following components:

the attack methods to which the organisation is exposed, the threat agents that may use them, and the vulnerabilities exploitable on the IS components. A knowledge base proposing a complete list for each of these components is used as a reference for this step (cf. Section 1.5.2). Then, the attack potential of threat agents combined with attack methods and the level of vulnerabilities are estimated. The outcome of this step is the list of threats specific to the IS of the organisation, but independently from the security needs, information processed and functions supported.

Step 4 - Identification of security objectives In this step, the organisation's security needs are compared with the identified threats. The risks are thus highlighted and can be treated by some security objectives. These security objectives constitute the security specifications for the target system and its environment. They must be consistent with all of the assumptions, constraints, regulatory references and security rules identified during the first step of the method. The coverage level of security objectives with regards to risks can also be determined during this step.

Step 5 - Determination of security requirements The security requirements are finally selected to achieve the defined security objectives. EBIOS proposes to define first the security functional requirements, describing the required security behavior and designed to satisfy the security objectives as formulated in the previous step. A knowledge base compliant with ISO/IEC 17799 (updated now in ISO/IEC 27002 [ISO05c]) and CC [Com06a] is proposed. The security assurance requirements, providing the confidence that the product or system satisfies its security objectives, can also be selected based on the requirements of CC.

The techniques presented in the EBIOS documentation are only suggestions and the users should choose the most appropriate techniques for their context, i.e. the culture and users in their organisation, as well as the tools they prefer to use. For example the level of detail given in the method can be adjusted if necessary.

2.5.2 MEHARI

MEHARI (MEthode Harmonisée d'Analyse du Risque Informatique) is a security RM method [CLU07b] elaborated since 1996 by the CLUSIF, a french association composed of IS security professionals. It has been updated in 2007. MEHARI builds upon two older methods called MARION [CLU98] (Méthodologie d'Analyse de Risques Informatiques Orientée par Niveaux) and MELISA [Dir89] (Méthode d'Evaluation de la Vulnérabilité Résiduelle des Systèmes d'Armement). These two methods are now obsolete and not maintained anymore. The MEHARI method is composed of several guidelines presenting the concepts and the methodological part. Moreover, some knowledge bases are available to help to use the method. A case study has also been built for illustrating the method. Finally, a software tool (*Risicare*) that can be bought has been developed in support of the method.

MEHARI is selected because it is one of the most used ISSRM method in France, particularly in the industry. At the opposite of EBIOS, it is based on risk scenarios to identify relevant risks related to an organisation. Even the conceptual aspects are not extensively studied, the documentation is complete and publicly available.

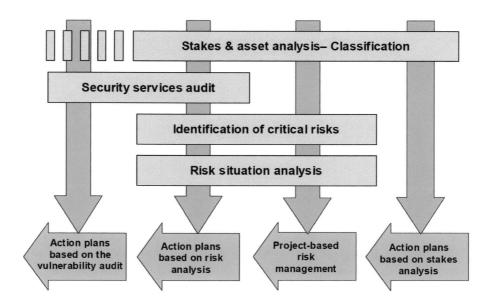

Figure 2.8: Using MEHARI modules for different outcomes (as appears in [CLU07a])

MEHARI is defined as a toolbox specifically designed for security management. Depending on the organisation's needs and circumstances, it ensures that an appropriate security management solution can be designed. The method is presented under the form of a set of so called "modules" [CLU07a], centered around risk assessment and management. Each module can be used independently or in combination and leads generally to an action plan (Figure 2.8[2]). The modules are the following:

1. Security Stakes Analysis and Classification
This first module allows analysing what are the assets of the studied organisation and, more generally, what is at stake regarding security. This module proposes to start by defining a malfunction value scale, by first identifying the main activities and their objectives, and then by identifying and evaluating potential malfunctions and their seriousness. A second step consists of classifying resources of the IS by identifying elements needed to be classified and rank them based on classification criteria (i.e. confidentiality, integrity, availability) and on the malfunction scale. This first module can be used as input for other modules, providing an impact table.

2. Evaluation Guide for security services
The objective of this module is to assess the security level of the IS by comparison with the state of the art of security by means of knowledge bases. It highlights the main weaknesses of the system. By performing an audit of security services, their quality is evaluated. This review helps to produce an action plan for enhancing the security services that have an insufficient level.

3. Risk Analysis Guide

---

[2]Despite this figure is extracted from the MEHARI documentation, the labels of the modules in this figure are not compliant with the current names of the modules.

The risk analysis guide is used for identifying critical risks and analysing the risk situations. Guidelines are provided for identifying risks with the help of the method knowledge bases, proposing standard risk scenarios. Then some automated procedures are given for analysing the identified risks, based on evaluation of potentiality and impact of risk. The outcome of risk analysis is the definition of security requirements that need to be applied on the IS.

2.5.3   OCTAVE

OCTAVE (Operationally Critical Threat, Asset, and Vulnerability Evaluation) is a risk-based strategic assessment and planning technique for security. It has been developed by the Software Engineering Institute of the Carnegie Mellon University in Pittsburgh. The current version of the method is 2.0 and it was published in 2001.

OCTAVE is a method from the USA, having a public and very detailed documentation. The current version of the method is a bit old regarding the other methods, however it remains relevant and has therefore been selected. The method especially has an interesting approach to risk, based on brainstorming.

OCTAVE aims at being self-directed, led by a small and flexible team of people internal to the organisation. The OCTAVE method [AD01b] is based on the OCTAVE criteria [AD01a], which define a standard approach for a risk-driven, asset- and practice-based information security evaluation. An adaptation of the method has been made for smaller organisations and is called OCTAVE-S. The OCTAVE method is a guide of 18 volumes showing how to implement the method. The method is built around three main phases (Figure 2.9) aiming first at examining organisational and technological issues and second at defining an organisation's security strategy and plan. The phases are, as depicted in OCTAVE, the following:

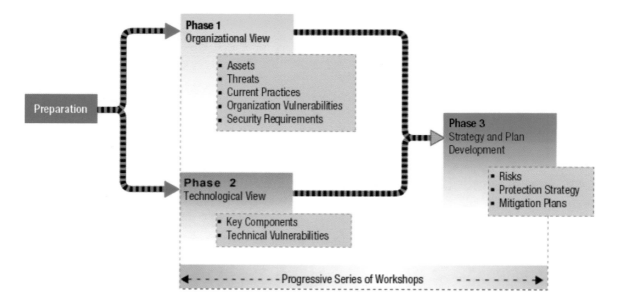

Figure 2.9: OCTAVE phases (as appears in [AD01b])

Phase 1: Build Asset-Based Profiles

The first phase aims at identifying critical assets and the threats to those assets. At each level of the organisation (senior management, operational area management and staff), some people are interviewed during workshops. The objective is to collect their knowledge in terms of assets, security requirements, threats, current security practices and organisational vulnerabilities. The last task of the phase is to summarise the information collected and consolidate it by defining for next phases: assets to be taken into account, security requirements in terms of security criteria (confidentiality, integrity and availability), threat profiles and main vulnerabilities.

Phase 2: Identify Infrastructure Vulnerabilities
This phase aims at identifying the vulnerabilities, both organisational and technological, that expose those threats, creating risks to the organisation. In this phase key components of the IS are identified and then evaluated with the help of vulnerability evaluation tools.

Phase 3: Develop Security Strategy and Plans
This phase aims at developing a practice-based protection strategy and risk mitigation plans to support the organisation's missions and priorities. It starts with conducting a risk analysis. Risk impacts are described and evaluated and risk profiles are built, bringing together impacts and threat profiles. A protection strategy plan is finally defined based on risk profiles, organisational vulnerabilities and protections already in place. The different action plans are finally reviewed and approved by the management.

2.5.4 CRAMM

The CRAMM (CCTA[3] Risk Analysis and Management Method) method was developed since 1985 by the Central Computer and Telecommunications Agency of the UK government [Ins03]. The method, currently owned by SIEMENS and developed by Insight Consulting [cra], is in version 5 and is mainly built around a software tool. The tool provides guidance for the user to exploit the method and has naturally the capability to collect the data needed.

CRAMM is selected because it is one of the first widely used ISSRM methods. Its use is worldwide. Therefore, it has the benefit of a lot of experience. Another key characteristic is that it is one of the rare method recommending quantitative risk estimation. Its weak point is that the method documentation is based on the software tool user's guide.

The methodological part of CRAMM is composed of three steps (Figure 2.10):

1. Asset identification and valuation
In CRAMM, assets are generally divided into 3 classes: physical assets (e.g., file server, workstation), software (e.g., application packages) and data (e.g., the information held on the IS). Their valuation is generally done in terms of replacement cost for physical assets and in terms of the impact coming from information potentially being unavailable, destroyed, disclosed or modified for software and data. This estimation of assets

---

[3]Central Computer and Telecommunications Agency

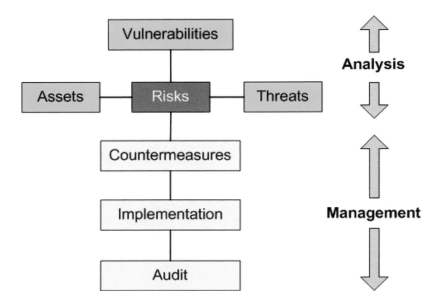

Figure 2.10: Overview of CRAMM (as appears in [cra])

can be done in a quantitative way, i.e. by valuing them in financial terms. Valuation of data assets is performed by interview of the 'data owners' (e.g., the business unit managers).

2. Threat and vulnerability assessment
The analysis part of CRAMM is completed by identifying and estimating level of threats and vulnerabilities. Threats and vulnerabilities are investigated against selected asset groups. Some mapping between threats and assets and between threats and impacts is provided. Concerning vulnerabilities, as usual in ISSRM methods, CRAMM is targeting high-level vulnerabilities. Technical or system specific vulnerabilities, which may be identified for example by vulnerability scanners, are thus not addressed by the method. Threats and vulnerabilities are assessed with the help of scales of values: threats on the five points scale "Very Low, Low, Medium, High or Very High" and "Low, Medium or High" for vulnerabilities. Finally, CRAMM calculates risks with the information provided for assets, threats and vulnerabilities. Risks are estimated on a scale from 1 to 7, with the help of a risk matrix.

3. Countermeasure selection and recommendation
The management part of CRAMM starts with countermeasure selection and recommendation. With the results of the preceding step, CRAMM produces a set of countermeasures applicable to the IS that are considered as necessary to manage the identified risks. CRAMM has a large set of countermeasures (over 3000) organised in logical groups and sub-groups. The countermeasures in each sub-groups have a hierarchical structure, from high-level security objectives to security functions until implementation examples.

2.5.5 CORAS

The CORAS consortium consists of three commercial companies: Intracom (Greece), Solinet (Germany) and Telenor (Norway); seven research institutes: CLRC/RAL (UK), CTI (Greece), FORTH (Greece), IFE (Norway), NCT (Norway), NR (Norway), and SINTEF (Norway); as well as one university college: Queen Mary University of London (UK). The CORAS project ran from January 2001 to July 2003. CORAS (Risk Assessment of Security Critical Systems) was a European project (FP5 - Fifth Framework Project) developing a tool-supported framework, exploiting methods for risk analysis, semi-formal methods for object-oriented modelling, and computerised tools, for a precise, unambiguous, and efficient risk assessment of security critical systems [FKG+02]. Two security critical application domains identified were telemedecine and e-commerce. Since the end of the project, several other uses of the CORAS framework have been made [VLM+05, VdBLS05, HS05].

CORAS is one of the rare method originating from scientific research. A lot of scientific articles are available, proposing an in-depth presentation of method. We selected it also because our interest is motivated by the fact that the method is based on modelling. CORAS could thereby be presented in the section dedicated to security-oriented modelling languages (Section 3.2). However, CORAS remains an ISSRM method and thus we chose to present it in this section.

The main focus of CORAS is security critical systems in general, but CORAS puts more emphasis on IT security. IT security includes all aspects related to defining, achieving, and maintaining confidentiality, integrity, availability, non-repudiation, accountability, authenticity, and reliability of IT systems [ISO04b]. An IT system in the sense of CORAS is not just technology, but is also including the humans interacting with the technology and all relevant aspects of the surrounding organisation. The scope of CORAS is therefore equivalent to the one we have defined in Section 1.4. CORAS is generally used for the assessment of existing IS, as seen in the case studies [RDGS02, SSH+03]. However, its integration with the Rationale Unified Process (RUP) [JBR99] should allow CORAS to be suited for IS development or system improvement. Unfortunately this aspect has not been extensively studied in the research work.

The main output of the CORAS project is a framework for model-based risk assessment having four anchor points:

- A risk management process based on the AS/NZS 4360 [AS/04].

- A risk documentation framework based on the ISO/IEC standard RM-ODP [ISO98].

- An integrated risk management and development process based on the RUP [JBR99].

- A platform for tool-inclusion based on XML.

During the CORAS project, two case studies were carried out:

- A case study about a B2C commerce platform and particularly the authentication mechanism and the Secure Payment mechanism [RDGS02].

- A case study about a telemedecine application [SSH+03].

A risk management process based on the AS/NZS 4360

AS/NZS 4360 [AS/04] provides a process for RM composed of context identification, risk identification, risk analysis, risk evaluation, and risk treatment. Two continous sub-processes are played throughout this main process: risk communication and risk monitor and review, giving rise to an iterative risk management process (cf. Section 2.2.2). The CORAS methodology proposes guidelines about models to be used for each sub-process, and how they should be expressed. CORAS proposes also several existing methods to perform risk assessment, mainly in the safety domain (HAZard OPerability study (HAZOP), Fault Tree Analysis (FTA), Failure Mode and Effect Criticality Analysis (FMECA), Markov analysis methods, etc.) but also in the security domain (CRAMM [Ins03] or Misuse cases [SO05]).

Models supporting the different risk management steps

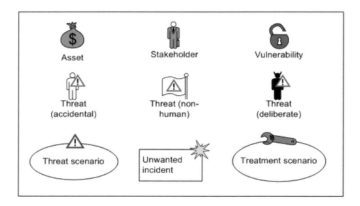

Figure 2.11: The CORAS modelling framework

Semi-formal modelling is used for three different purposes:

- To describe the target of evaluation at the right level of abstraction;

- To facilitate communication and interaction between different groups of stakeholders;

- To document risk assessment results and the assumptions on which these results depend to support reuse and maintenance.

CORAS has developed its own modelling framework (Figure 2.11) with its own concepts. The concepts proposed by CORAS are the following [VML+07] (an in-depth study is shown in Section 4.3.3):

Assets: Assets are the parts or features of the target which have value to the client of the analysis, such as physical objects, know-how, services, software and hardware, and so on.

Stakeholders: those people and organisations who may affect, be affected by, or perceive themselves to be affected by a decision, activity or risk.

Vulnerability: A vulnerability is a weakness of the system or organisation.

Threat: A threat may exploit a vulnerability and cause an unwanted incident.

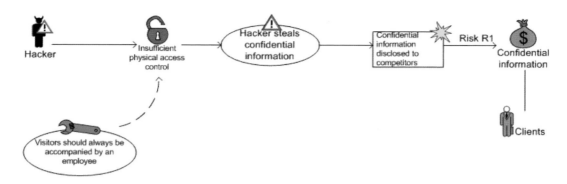

Figure 2.12: An example of use of the CORAS modelling framework

Threat scenario: A sequence of events or activities leading to an unwanted incident.
Unwanted incident: An unwanted incident is an event which reduces the value of one or more of the assets.
Risk: A risk is an unwanted incident along with its estimated likelihood and consequence values.
Treatment: Treatments represent various options for reducing risk.

An example of use of the framework (Figure 2.12), illustrated on our running example, is a *hacker* (threat) that may exploit the *insufficiency of physical access control* (vulnerability). Then could *the hacker steal confidential information* (threat scenario) leading to *confidential information disclosed to competitors* (unwanted incident). The asset targeted is *confidential information* (asset) owned by the *clients* (stakeholders). This risk is called 'R1'. The risk could be reduced by constraining the *visitors to be always accompanied by an employee*. More examples are provided in the CORAS literature [VML$^+$07, RDGS02, VLM$^+$05, HS05, SSH$^+$03, FKG$^+$02, VdBLS05].

2.6 Conclusion

In this chapter, the process and the tasks underlying ISSRM are first explained (Section 2.1). ISSRM standards and methods are then discussed (Section 2.2 to 2.5). The first conclusion we can draw from ISSRM standards and methods is that they provide different tools and techniques for reaching generally the same goal: protecting an IS by defining suited security requirements/controls with the help of a RM approach. However, the ISSRM approaches perform their tasks in different manners (based on interviews [AD01b], based on knowledge bases [DCS04b], based on a software tool [Ins03], etc.) and have different coverage level of the generic ISSRM process (some methods are not concerned by control selection and implementation [DCS04b, ISO08], some are high-level and just providing guidelines [SGF02], etc.). Each method thus has its own strengths and weaknesses, and the users may potentially need to resort to two (or more) complementary approaches. The conceptual differences and the lack of interoperability between the methods is thus a gap in the ISSRM domain. Moreover, for standard compliance purposes, some methods may need to prove their alignment with a standard [ISO05b] and show that the tasks required by the standard are effectively performed by the method. The lack of interoperability between the approaches and the difficulty to manage the different terminologies used are in this case once again a weakness. This problem of lack of interoperability between ISSRM approaches is discussed in Chapter 4.

Table 2.2: Summary of the ISSRM standards and methods state of the art

Reference	Security oriented	Risk-based approach	RE approach	Model-based approach
ISO/IEC Guide 73	-	++	-	-
AS/NZS 4360	-	++	-	-
ISO/IEC 13335	++	+	-	-
Common Criteria	++	+	-	-
ISO/IEC 2700x	++	++	-	-
NIST 800-27 RevA NIST 800-30	++	++	-	-
The IT-Grundschutz	++	++	-	-
EBIOS	++	++	-	-
MEHARI	++	++	-	-
OCTAVE	++	++	-	-
CRAMM	++	++	-	-
CORAS	++	++	-	++

Legend:
++: Completely covered and at the core of the document
+: Partially covered or not playing a central role
-: Not covered

Coming back to our objectives fixed in Section 1.1, most of the standards and methods studied cover the two first, that are delivering secure IS and using a risk-based approach (Table 2.2[4]). However, these approaches are generally designed to be used on an existing IS: they are not well suited to be used during IS development. Despite sometimes proposing additional guidelines to use the method for IS development, current ISSRM methods are not really connected to RE activities and reasoning from the early phases of IS development. We claim that one can benefit from performing RM tasks and IS development in parallel (Section 1.3). Another drawback of current ISSRM methods is that the documents produced as output are generally informal, most often in natural language, sometimes only structured with the help of tables. This leads to gaps in automation, at the level of reasoning, evolution, monitoring or traceability. CORAS [FKG+02] is the only exception, proposing models as product of the different risk-related tasks. However, CORAS is not clearly connected to RE activities: the relation between CORAS and the RUP has not been a major focus area. Moreover, the risk management process proposed by CORAS remains the one from AS/NZS 4360 [AS/04], not dedicated to IS development. Another weak point of CORAS is that it is clearly disconnected from standard terminology (cf. Section 4.3.3).

---

[4]By "Completely covered" for "Risk-based approach", we don't mean the concept of "risk" is only considered in the approach, but really that the underlying process/method is based on a risk management approach. For example, the concept of risk is mentioned in CC, but the underlying proposed approach doesn't propose any risk analysis/assessment/management process to define the security requirements.

For a long time, the RE community has used *models* as a way to achieve a better formality and quality. To allow a better integration of RM tasks throughout the IS development life cycle, we have decided to also study security RE engineering, and more specifically modelling languages concerned by security aspects. They are the topics of the next chapter.

2.7 Chapter summary

In this chapter, an overview of the ISSRM process was proposed and each task needed to be performed was presented. The core of this chapter was dedicated to a survey of the different RM standards, security standards, security RM standards, and security RM methods. A conclusion was finally drawn with regards to this survey.

In the next chapter, we investigate security RE, and particularly security RE frameworks and security-oriented modelling languages.

Chapter 3

Security Requirements Engineering

T he importance of addressing security concerns from the very beginning of IS development is now widely acknowledged [LYM03, DS00]. Early consideration of security allows IS developers to envisage threats, their consequences and countermeasures before a system is in place, rather than as a reaction to a possibly disastrous attack. To cope with these issues, researchers have recently proposed various frameworks to deal with security during RE (Section 3.1). In parallel, conceptual modelling languages supporting security with dedicated constructs have been developed. Those languages are actually security-oriented extensions of preexisting "general-purpose" RE modelling languages: Misuse cases [SO05] and Abuse cases [MF99] extend Use cases [Obj04, Coc01, Fow03] complementarily with Mal-activity diagrams [Sin07] which extend Activity diagrams [Obj04, Fow03]; Abuse frames [LNI+03b, LNIJ04, LNI+03a] derive from Problem frames [Jac01]; Secure Tropos [MG09, MGMP02, GMZ05] originates from Tropos [BGG+04] and $i*$ [Yu96]; and KAOS [vLL00] was also extended [vL04]. Moreover, a generic risk-based modelling framework has also been developed: the Tropos Goal-Risk framework [AG06] (Section 3.2). It is necessary to note that in this chapter, for each described approach, we use the terminology proposed by the approach. The different frameworks and modelling languages are not presented with a unified terminology.

3.1 Security requirements engineering frameworks

This section introduces RE approaches focused on security. They are approaches introducing methods and concepts that are security-specific and thus of primary importance regarding our research works.

3.1.1 Information security and safety models by Firesmith

In December 2003, Firesmith published a technical report entitled *"Common Concepts Underlying Safety, Security, and Survivability Engineering"*, that presents a set of interrelated information models that provide the conceptual foundation underlying safety, security, and survivability engineering [Fir03]. He then published various publications extending the former, focussed on safety [Fir04] and security [Fir05]. These publications are finally reinforced by some recent tutorials [Fir07a, Fir07b], presenting his work in-depth about security and safety engineering, which are part of "defensibility engineering".

The work of Firesmith relies on the so called "information models", i.e. UML class diagrams defining key concepts and relationships between them, for identifying and defining the foundational concepts underlying (mainly) safety and security engineering. Precise definitions of each concept come with the graphical models. The objective of this work is to make clear what are the conceptual similarities and particularities of safety and security, and how they are related. In a tutorial [Fir07a], he also proposes a process to effectively deal with both safety and security engineering. However the proposed process does not rely on a risk-based approach.

Firesmith defines these domains in [Fir07a]:

Safety engineering as the engineering discipline within systems engineering concerned with lowering the risk of *unintentional unauthorized harm* to valuable assets to a level that is acceptable to the system's stakeholders by preventing, detecting, and reacting to such harm, mishaps (i.e., accidents and incidents), hazards, and safety risks.

Security engineering as the engineering discipline within systems engineering concerned with lowering the risk of *intentional unauthorized harm* to valuable assets to a level that is acceptable to the system's stakeholders by preventing, detecting, and reacting to such harm, misuses (i.e., attacks and incidents), threats, and security risks.

Firesmith distinguishes particularly harm coming from intentional and unintentional source. He then introduces the concept of defensibility that is defined as the composition of both safety and security (also with survivability, which protects valuable military assets [Fir05]), and that is therefore closely related to the scope of our work (cf. Section 1.4).

3.1.2 A framework for representation and analysis of security requirements engineering by Haley *et al.* and Moffet and Nuseibeh

This research work is based on several research papers and technical reports from the Open University [HLMN08, HMLN06a, MHN04], also in collaboration with University of York [MN03]. The aim of this research work is to define a framework to determine adequate security requirements, i.e. leading to IS security goals being satisfied. The framework emphasises three aspects:

- *definitions*: the framework must rely on clear definitions, mainly for the concept of security requirement;

- *assumptions*: the framework must consider the assumptions made by the analyst on the IS and its environment for defining security requirements;

- *satisfaction*: the framework must provide ways to determine if the security requirements satisfy the security goals and if the IS satisfies the security requirements.

The framework implements those requirements through three contributions [HLMN08]:

- A practical definition of the concept of security requirement helping to define precisely if the requirements are satisfied by the IS,

- An explicit role for assumptions in the process of security requirements definition and their satisfaction in the IS,

- The use of formal and informal proofs to validate that a system can satisfy its security requirements.

Coming back to the definition part of the framework, it was published in [MHN04] and later refined in [HMLN06a]. These research papers are focussed on the definition of security requirement and some closely related concepts. The background of this work is presented in [MN03] that is an earlier research work. It introduces more concepts that are considered and studied for the definition of the framework. The concept of risk is, for example, not introduced within the final framework [HLMN08], because the outcome of the framework is not to define another risk management approach. However, the concept of risk is considered during the framework elicitation and explained in [MHN04]. The framework so defined could be part of an ISSRM method, helping to determine the security requirements in a more structured way.

On the other hand, trust assumptions were defined in [HLMN04, HLMN06]. Finally the research work on security satisfaction arguments was published in [HMLN06b, HMLN05]. Problem Frames [Jac01] are used within the framework as the notation for modelling the IS and its related assumptions and then the chosen security requirements (cf. Section 3.2.4). The whole framework was successfully applied on an air traffic control system [HLMN08].

3.1.3 The Department of Defense Information Technology Security Certification and Accreditation Process automation framework

The DITSCAP (Department of Defense Information Technology Security Certification and Accreditation Process) is the standard certification and accreditation process for the Department of Defense of the USA. It proposes a process and a management structure to certify and accredit IS, with regards to information security.

The basis statement of this research work is that this certification and accreditation process generally provides not comparable and inconstant results [GL07]. Moreover, the information provided is usually inadequate, and it is thus difficult for the stakeholders to understand security risks and take the right decisions. Finally, the process is generally long and needs many resources to conduct the different necessary activities. The objective of this research work is therefore to improve this process of certification and accrediation.

The result is the DITSCAP automation framework. Its objective is to be integrated, well-defined and comprehensive with respect to the DITSCAP [LGA05]. A key component of the framework is a problem domain ontology, built from regulatory documents, aiming at explicating the requirements with the help of DITSCAP domain concepts. Each requirement is explicated based on attributes that capture the goals, scenarios, viewpoints and other domain-specific concepts. A model is proposed to explain the relationships between security requirements and risk components, for certification and accreditation purpose. It is used for identifying the risk components, and map them to concepts in domain-specific taxonomies (e.g., of threats, assets, vulnerabilities, countermeasures) defined within the approach. This model is an extension of the Common

Criteria model [Com06a], including security requirements and its relationships with the risk factors required to be considered in risk assessment [LGA05, GL07].

3.1.4   The SQUARE methodology

The SQUARE (Security Quality Requirements Engineering) methodology was published in 2005 [MHI05, MS05] by the Networked Systems Survivability program at the Software Engineering Institute, Carnegie Mellon University. It is defined as a stepwise methodology for eliciting, categorising, and prioritising security requirements for information technology systems and applications. A lighter version of SQUARE called SQUARE-Lite was also developed. A CASE tool to support the SQUARE process is also currently developed.

SQUARE is based on the assumption that, in software engineering, it is largely more costly to recover errors once the system is implemented compared to tackling them during RE phases. Errors in requirements lead generally to increase the budget of projects, to delay the project schedule, to deliver poor-quality or non-relevant products, and even sometimes to cancel the project. Naturally, security requirements are concerned by these assumptions. Moreover, security requirements are often ignored during the requirements elicitation process and added later, incurring higher costs. SQUARE proposes to carry out security during the early stages of software engineering and specify security requirements in similar ways as system functional requirements.

The SQUARE methodology is based on 9 steps summarised in Table 3.1. They are generally performed by a RE team with security expertise in conjunction with stakeholders of the project:

Step (1) Agree on definitions: the RE team and the stakeholders agree on the terminology and on the definitions to be used during the whole process.

Step (2) Identify security goals: based on business goals, the security goals to be reached are defined; they are required to identify the priority and relevance of security requirements.

Step (3) Develop artifacts: it is necessary to collect or create some artifacts to support the next steps and mainly the security requirements definition, like system architecture diagrams, use/misuse cases, attack trees, etc.

Step (4) Assess risks: risks are assessed, mainly by identifying threats and vulnerabilities of the system and evaluating the likelihood of their occurrence.

Step (5) Select elicitation technique(s): a security requirements elicitation technique should be selected, taking into account the number and expertise of stakeholders.

Step (6) Elicit security requirements: the security requirements are elicited by using the chosen elicitation technique(s); this step is considered to be the heart of the SQUARE process.

Table 3.1: The nine steps of the SQUARE process (as they appear in [MHI05])

Num.	Step	Input	Techniques	Participant	Output
1	**Agree on definitions**	Candidate definitions from IEEE and other standards	Structured interviews, focus group	Stakeholders, requirements team	Agreed-to definitions
2	**Identify security goals**	Definitions, candidate goals, business drivers, policies and procedures, examples	Facilitated work session, surveys, interviews	Stakeholders, requirements engineer	Goals
3	**Develop artifacts to support security requirements definition**	Potential artifacts (e.g., scenarios, misuse cases, templates, forms)	Work session	Requirements engineer	Needed artifacts: scenarios, misuse cases, models, templates, forms
4	**Perform risk assessment**	Misuse cases, scenarios, security goals	Risk assessment method, analysis of anticipated risk against organisational risk tolerance, including threat analysis	Requirements engineer, risk expert, stakeholders	Risk assessment results
5	**Select elicitation techniques**	Goals, definitions, candidate techniques, expertise of stakeholders, organisational style, culture, level of security needed, cost benefit analysis, etc.	Work session	Requirements engineer	Selected elicitation techniques
6	**Elicit security requirements**	Artifacts, risk assessment results, selected techniques	Joint Application Development (JAD), interviews, surveys, model-based analysis, checklists, lists of reusable requirements types, document reviews	Stakeholders facilitated by requirements engineer	Initial cut at security requirements
7	**Categorize requirements as to level (system, software, etc.) and whether they are requirements or other kinds of constraints**	Initial requirements, architecture	Work session using a standard set of categories	Requirements engineer, other specialists as needed	Categorized requirements
8	**Prioritize requirements**	Categorized requirements and risk assessment results	Prioritization methods such as Triage, Win-Win	Stakeholders facilitated by requirements engineer	Prioritized requirements
9	**Requirements inspection**	Prioritized requirements, candidate formal inspection technique	Inspection method such as Fagan, peer reviews	Inspection team	Initial selected requirements, documentation of decision making process and rationale

Step (7) Categorize requirements: the elicited security requirements are classified based on a standard set of categories.

Step (8) Prioritize requirements: using a prioritisation technique, priorities are defined for the security requirements, that could be based on a cost-benefit analysis.

Step (9) Inspect requirements: the security requirements are inspected to obtain accurate and verifiable security requirements.

3.2 Security-oriented modelling languages

Tackling security during the early phases of RE has been motivated in Section 1.3. This study of security-oriented modelling languages thus focuses on approaches dealing with early requirements. Some existing security-oriented modelling languages are thus explicitly not considered in this work. SecureUML [LBD02] is a modelling language helping to define access control policies. UMLsec [Jö4, Jö2] introduces a UML profile for security, including activity diagrams, statecharts, sequence diagrams, static structure diagrams, deployment diagrams, and subsystems. Both of these UML extensions are dedicated to late-RE and mainly design phase, and hence they are out of our scope.

This study is mainly focused on the modelling language part of the approaches. The process aspects are quickly overviewed, with respect to the modelling parts that are explained in greater details. As an illustration, each modelling language is presented based on (part of) the running example (Section 1.6).

3.2.1 KAOS and its security extension

The KAOS (Knowledge Acquisition in autOmated Specification) approach consists of a modelling language, a method, and a software environment [vLL00]. It starts in 1990 from a joint project between University of Louvain (Belgium) and University of Oregon (USA). The objectives of KAOS are [CED03]:

- to fit problem descriptions by allowing to define and manipulate concepts relevant to problem description,

- to improve the problem analysis process by providing a systematic approach for discovering and structuring requirements,

- to clarify the responsibilities of all the project stakeholders,

- to let the stakeholders communicate easily and efficiently about the requirements.

The main purpose of KAOS is to ensure that high-level goals are identified and progressively refined into precise operational statements [vL03, Let01]. These are then assigned to component agents of the software-to-be and its environment, both forming the so-called (composite) system-to-be. Along this process, various alternative goals and responsibility assignments are considered until the most satisfactory solution is chosen (Figure 3.1).

The KAOS modelling language

A global KAOS model includes four models: goal, object, agent and operation models. The *goal model* is the driver of the language and it defines and refines the goals of the system-to-be until requirements attributable to agents are found. The *object model* declares the objects of interest in the application domain. It plays the same role as the class diagram in UML [Obj04]. Then the responsibilities of agents for goals are defined in the *agent responsibility model*. Complementary to the preceding model, the *agent*

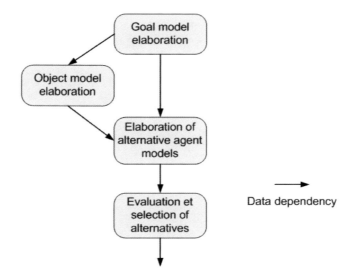

Figure 3.1: The goal-driven requirement elaboration process (as appears in [Let01])

interface model declares which objects are monitored and controlled by each agent. Finally, the *operation model* defines the state transitions in the application domain [Let01]. We illustrate KAOS goal and operation model through some snapshots relative to *@rchimed* (Figure 3.2). We focus on the goal model, since it is the most relevant for early requirements, and complement it with the operation model to have a more complete view of our example. On these two diagrams, we also introduce some key elements of the agent and object models. More information about the different kinds of models in KAOS can be found in [Let01].

Figure 3.2 illustrates the different concepts of the KAOS modelling language on the running example and more specifically on the establishment of structure calculation by the study office. In KAOS a *goal* is a prescriptive assertion that captures an objective that the system-to-be should meet. In Figure 3.2, examples of goals are `Achieve[BuildingValidated]`, `Avoid[StructureCalculationModifiedByCrook]`, and `Avoid[LoginInformationKnownByCrook]`. A goal can belong to one of four patterns: *maintain, avoid, achieve* and *cease*, which declare the temporal behaviour categories corresponding of a goal change [Let01]:

- Achieve goals: goals requiring that some property eventually holds

- Cease goals: goals requiring that some property eventually stops to hold

- Maintain goals: goals requiring that some property always holds

- Avoid goals: goals requiring that some property never holds

In addition, goal categories provide a further goal classification helping in goal acquisition, definition and refinement (e.g., *Satisfaction goals* are Achieve goals concerned with satisfying agent wishes; *Safety goals* are Maintain goals concerned with avoiding hazardous states; *Security goals* are Maintain goals concerned with avoiding threats to the system, etc.).

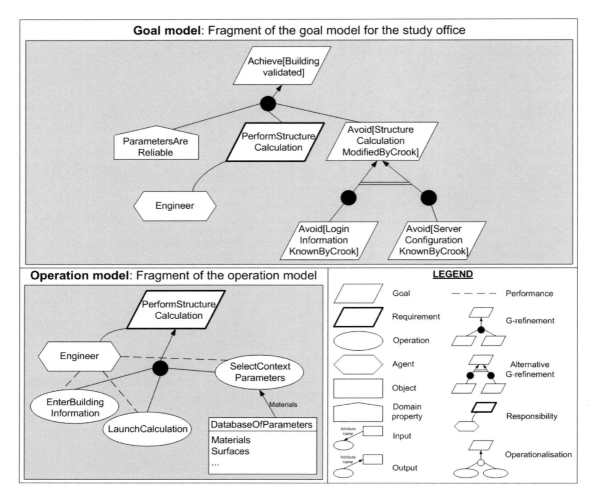

Figure 3.2: Fragment of the goal and operation model for the study office of @rchimed

A goal can be refined through *G-refinement*, which relates it to a set of subgoals whose conjunction, possibly together with domain properties, contributes to the satisfaction of the goal. For example, in Figure 3.2 the goal `Achieve[BuildingValidated]` is refined to two subgoals `PerformStructureCalculation`, `Avoid[StructureCalculation-ModifiedByCrook]`, and one *domain property* `ParametersAreReliable`. A goal can have alternative G-refinements (e.g., `Avoid[StructureCalculationModifiedByCrook]`), which result in different designs of the system-to-be.

An *object* (e.g., `DatabaseOfParameters`) is a (kind of) thing(s) of interest in the system[1]. Its instances can be distinctly identified and may evolve from state to state. Objects have *attributes* (e.g., `Materials`, `Surfaces`, etc.), which characterise the states of the system-to-be.

An *agent* (e.g., `Engineer`) plays a role towards a goal's satisfaction by controlling object behaviour. Goals are refined until they are assigned to individual agents. A goal effectively assigned to a software agent (in Figure 3.2: `PerformStructure-Calculation`) is called a *requirement*. A goal effectively assigned to an environment agent is called an *expectation*.

---

[1]The notions of object and class seem to be merged in KAOS [vL03, Let01].

An *operation* (in Figure 3.2: `EnterBuildingInformation`, `LaunchCalculation`, and `SelectContextParameters`) is an *input-output* relation over objects. Operations are characterised textually by *domain* (DomPre, DomPost) and *required* (RegPre, ReqTrig, and ReqPost) conditions [MHO06]. Whenever the required conditions hold, performing the operations satisfies the goal. If a goal is operationalised and has a responsible agent (e.g., `PerformStructureCalculation`), the latter *performs* the operations.

KAOS extended to security

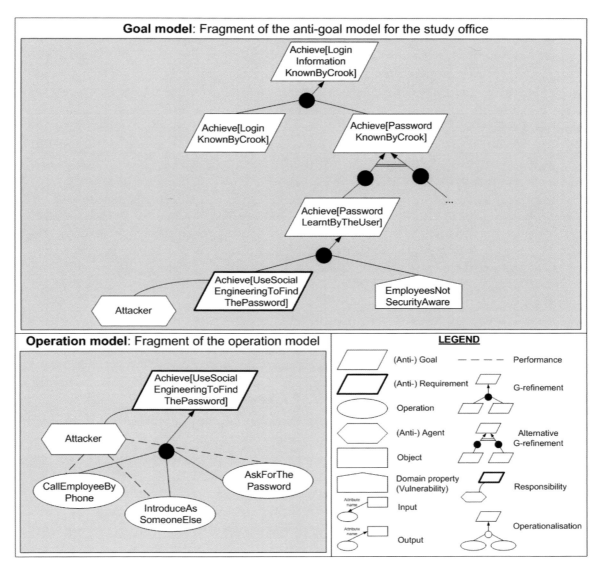

Figure 3.3: Fragment of the anti-goal and attack method model for the study office of @rchimed

In KAOS, the concept of *obstacle* was first introduced [vLL00]. An obstacle to some goal is defined as a condition whose satisfaction may prevent the goal from being achieved. However standard obstacle analysis approach has been assessed as too limited to deal with malicious obstacles [vL04]. An interest has been highlighted to clearly show the goals underlying malicious obstacle, and to model attacker agents, their capabilities, and the vulnerabilities of the system-to-be. The reasoning behind building such intentional models about malicious goals has also been evaluated as relevant in order to be more exhaustive in the analysis [vL04].

KAOS extended to Security (KeS) has thus been introduced in [vL04]. Security of the system-to-be is defined in the traditional goal model using *security goals*, which concern sensitive objects. In the example (Figure 3.2) `Avoid[LoginInformation-KnownByCrook]` concerns `DatabaseOfParameters` that could be threatened if the goal is not respected. To identify the goals of the attacker, an *anti-model* composed of *anti-goals* is built showing the attacker's own goals (Figure 3.3). An *attacker* is defined as a malicious agent in the environment. Examples of anti-goals are `Achieve[Login-InformationKnownByCrook]` and `Achieve[PasswordLearntByTheUser]`. *Anti-requirements* which are terminal anti-goals assigned to the attacker (e.g., Achieve[UseSocial-EngineeringToFindThePassword]) and *vulnerabilities* (represented as *domain properties*) assigned to the attackee (e.g., EmployeesNotSecurityAware) are also identified. Associated object and agent anti-models can be built too.

Once the intentional anti-goal model has been built, the next step is to consider *countermeasures* to the identified *anti-requirements* and *vulnerabilities*. Categories of countermeasures are for example *goal substitution*, *agent substitution*, *goal weakening*, *goal restoration*, *anti-goal mitigation*, *anti-goal prevention*, *vulnerability protection*, or *vulnerability avoidance* [vL04]. The selected countermeasure decisions yield new security goals to be integrated in the models. For example, countermeasures for the example in Figure 3.3 include vulnerability avoidance: the following security goals `Avoid[EmployeesAreNotSecurityAware]` shall be added (not represented in Figure 3.2). The new *security goals* need to be refined until *requirements* and *expectations* are reached. A new anti-model may be further created for new emerging security goals, if necessary.

3.2.2 Misuse cases and Abuse cases extending Use case diagrams

Presentation of use case diagrams

Use case diagrams are part of the standard object modelling language UML defined by the Object Management Group[2] (OMG). The objective of this kind of diagram is to capture the functional requirements of an IS, by describing the typical interactions between the users of the system and the system itself [Fow03]. Use case diagrams are a notation suited for early requirements, because they can be used before defining any internal structure of the IS. It represents external behavior of the system-to-be. In a nutshell, a use case diagram describes *what* the system should do and it does not specify *how* it carries it out.

A use case diagram represents a set of scenarios tied together by a common goal, like in Figure 3.4 about the running example. The figure illustrates an excerpt of the production of construction plan. Within a use case diagram, the first concept is the one of *actor*. An actor is a role that a user plays with respect to the IS. Two actors are represented in Figure 3.4: `Engineer` and `Drawer`. Actors are related to use cases with

---

[2]http://www.uml.org

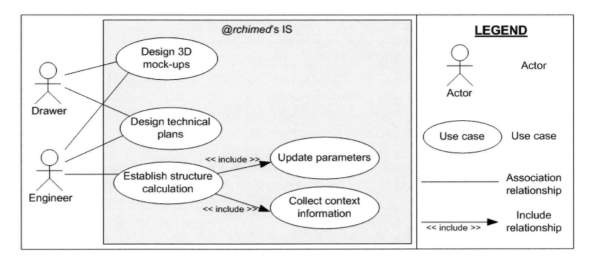

Figure 3.4: Use case diagram representing a fragment of the production of construction plan

association relationships, showing an interaction between an actor and a use case in which (s)he participates. A *use case* is a set of actions performed by the system and requested by the actors. It represents an objective to be fulfilled by the system-to-be, motivated by the need of one (or several) actors. Examples of use cases are `Design 3D mock-ups`, `Design technical plans` and `Establish structure calculation`. A use case can be related to another use case by an *include relationship*. It indicates that the source use case is composed among other things of the destination use case. `Establish structure calculation` is related in this way to `Update parameters` and `Collect context information`. Two other relationships between use cases exist [Pen03] (not represented in Figure 3.4). First, the *extend relationship* proposes an alternative use case (end of the graphical link) of an initial one (start of the graphical link). Its selection depends on a condition needed to be expressed. This relationship is equivalent to the extensions of the textual descriptions of use cases, as depicted below. Second, the *generalisation relationship* identifies an inheritance relationship between actors or between use cases.

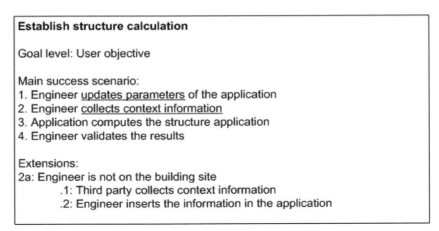

Figure 3.5: Example of use case textual description on the structure calculation establishment (inspired from [Fow03])

Textual descriptions are associated with a use case diagram[3]. They are meant to further describe the use cases and therefore the system functionalities, but also the interaction with the actors [Coc01]. Various textual formats exist and a typical one is proposed in Figure 3.5, inspired from [Fow03]. It illustrates the `Establish structure calculation` use case. The information provided is the *goal level* and the typical steps to follow for the *main success scenario*. Other alternative scenarios can be considered and are written in the *extensions* part. An extension within a use case names a condition (`Engineer is not on the building site`) resulting, if satisfied, in different steps from those described in the main success scenario to be performed sequentially (`Third party collects context information` and `Engineer inserts the information in the application` should be performed instead of `Engineer collects context information`). Finally, the include relationship represented in the graphical use case is expressed in the textual description by underlined words, which suggest a hyperlink[4].

Misuse cases

Use cases are as suited for identifying functional requirements. However, they are generally neglect non-functional requirements, like security requirements. In such a context, Misuse cases is introduced in 2000 [SO00, SO01], aiming at extending 'traditional' use cases with negative use cases specifying the behaviors not wanted in the proposed IS. A misuse cases diagram can be seen as a use case from the point of view of an actor hostile to the system [Ale02]. It also has two representations: a graphical diagram (Figure 3.6) and a textual specification (Figure 3.7). Misuse cases come with a *security requirements process*, which outcome is the elicitation of suited security requirements. The process consists of the 5 following steps [SO05]:

1. Identify critical assets

2. Define security goal

3. Identify threats

4. Identify and analyse risks

5. Define security requirements

Graphical misuse cases

Misuse cases reuse the main concepts existing in use cases diagrams: *actors* and *use cases*, coming with the associated relationships: *association relationship, includes relationship* and *extends relationship*. Figure 3.6, representing a misuse cases diagram, is therefore built on the same basis as the use case diagram from Figure 3.4. Misuse cases introduces new concepts related to security. The main one is *misuse case* (e.g., `Steal login information`) which describes "a sequence of actions, including variants, which a system or other entity can perform, interacting with misusers of the entity and causing harm to some stakeholder if the sequence is allowed to complete"

---

[3]Use cases are also often complemented with other (behavioural) models in addition to text.
[4]In many tools it is really a hyperlink

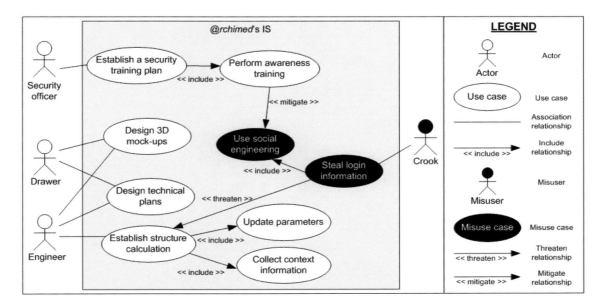

Figure 3.6: Example of misuse cases diagram

[SO05]. A *misuser* (e.g., `Crook`) is "an actor that initiates misuse cases, either intentionally or inadvertently" [SO05]. Two relationships may be defined between use cases and misuse cases. A *threatens relationship* targets a use case (`Establish structure calculation`) that a misuse case (`Steal login information`) wants to harm. A *mitigates relationship* characterises how some security use cases (e.g., `Perform awareness training`) can be defined as countermeasures against the misuse cases.

Textual template

Textual descriptions also play an important part when representing misuse cases [SO01, SO05]. Two ways of expressing misuse cases textually are suggested: a lightweight description and an extensive description. A *lightweight* description is an embedded description of a textual use case (such as suggested in [KG00, Coc01, BDG05]) by extending them with an entry called *Threats*. An *extensive* description supports a detailed determination and analysis of security threats [SO01, SO05] based on a template of fields. Figure 3.7 is an example of the entries of the extensive template as proposed and described in [SO05].

Abuse cases

Abuse case models were proposed in 1999, motivated by the gap existing between security specialists and software developers, having both their own supporting models [MF99]. Like Misuse cases, it is an adaptation of the use case modeling technique aiming at capturing and analysing security requirements in a simple way. As use cases, abuse cases are described using use case diagrams and use case textual descriptions. They are considered as helpful during the requirements, design and testing phases of a security engineering process and have been used in the context of building security assurance arguments [McD01].

Abuse case models and misuse cases diagrams are very close approaches. However,

Name:	Steal login information
Summary:	A crook steals some login information allowing him to access to internal applications
Basic path:	**bp1:** Crook calls an employee by phone
	bp2: Crook introduces as someone else
	bp3: Crook uses social engineering techniques for asking login information
	bp4: Employee discloses his personal login information
	bp5: Crook logs into the system
Mitigation points:	**mp1:** Employees are aware of security and know the social engineering techniques
Extension points:	**ext1:** Includes misuse case "Use social engineering"
Trigger:	Always true, this can happen at any time
Assumption:	**as1:** No fingerprint logon is used
Preconditions:	**pc1:** The crook is able to find employees phone numbers, either because they are publicly available, or because an accomplice can provide them to him
Worst case threat:	Someone unauthorised modifies structure calculation
Mitigation guarantee:	The employees never disclose their personal login information (see mp1)
Related business rules:	Only authorised people should be able to connect to internal applications
Misuser profile:	Skilled. Knowledge of social engineering techniques.
Stakeholder and risks:	**Engineer:** Structure calculations modified, leading to waste of time by establishing the calculations again.
	Client: Loss of reputation and danger for human life if not detected.
Scope:	Entire business
Abstraction level:	Misuser goal
Precision level:	Focussed

Figure 3.7: Example of the misuse cases template on the 'Steal login information' misuse case

abuse case is considered as complementary to misuse cases because [SO05]:

- Abuse case models focus specifically on security requirements and their relation to design and testing (not illustrated in Figure 3.8 and 3.9), whereas misuse cases diagrams focus on elicitation of security requirements in relation to other requirements.

- Abuse cases do not show "use cases" and "abuse cases" in the same diagram, contrarily to Misuse cases which also show the relations between "misuse cases" and "use cases".

- Abuse cases provide more details concerning actors in their textual descriptions, whereas misuse cases descriptions are more complete than abuse case description.

The proposed process for building an abuse case model is:

1. Identify the actors

2. Identify the abuse cases

3. Define abuse cases

4. Check granularity (to be sure to have neither too many nor too few abuse cases)

5. Check completeness and minimality (to be sure each abuse case results effectively in harm to the system and none of the critical abuse cases has been omitted)

Graphical abuse cases

An *abuse case* is defined as "a specification of a type of complete interaction between a system and one or more actors, where the results of the interaction are harmful to the

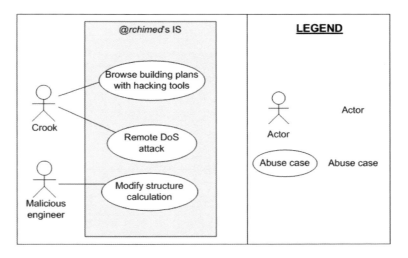

Figure 3.8: Example of abuse case model

system, one of the actors, or one of the stakeholders in the system" [MF99]. Examples of abuse cases are `Browse building plans with hacking tools`, `Remote DoS`[5] `attack` and `Modify structure calculation` (Figure 3.8). An abuse case model thus represents (one or more) interactions between an *actor* (e.g., `Malicious engineer` or `Crook`) and the system resulting in harm to a resource associated with one of the actors, one of the stakeholders, or the system itself. About the representation of actor and related abuse cases, the standard UML notation of actor and use case is used, in the aim to be compliant with the existing software supporting UML (cf. Figure 3.8).

Actor description	**Abuse case description**
Crook	**Browse building plans with hacking tools**

Resources: The Crook operates alone. He has hardware, software, and an Internet connection that can be funded by a competitor of *@rchimed*. Our model assumes that the Crook will try during several days to break into the study office's IS.	*Harm*: The Crook will be able to access confidential building plans by penetrating into the IS.
	
	Privilege range: The Crook might carry out this abuse using privileges in the following range:
	    1. Installation of software with root/administrator privileges on a computer of the study office
	    2. Control of a root/administrator account on a computer of the study office
	    3. Installation of a malicious software with user privileges on a computer of the study office

Skills: The Crook has good technical skills. He has an advanced knowledge of network protocols and operating systems.	
Objectives: The Crook is interested by the financial aspect of accessing to the building plans. His objective is to gain some money by selling the plans to a competitor.	*Abusive interaction*: Exploiting an operating system flaw on a computer of the system office, the Crook installs a malicious software on the computer. Once ran and using again flaws in the operating system, the malicious software allows the Crook to have a root/administrator access to this computer. He then is able to install new software helping him to view and browse through the building plans of the study office.

Figure 3.9: Example of textual descriptions for the Crook actor and the 'Browse building plans with hacking tools' abuse case

---

[5]Denial of Service

Textual description

Abuse case models are completed by two textual description: actor description and abuse case description. Concerning actors, three key characteristics have been defined as relevant to correctly understand the abuse case model: *resources* (e.g., hardware and software, available time, financial resources, etc.), *skills* (e.g., technical skills related to network protocols, cryptography, operating systems, etc.) and *objectives* (e.g., vandalism, theft, terrorism, etc.). An example of textual description is proposed for Crook in Figure 3.9. Concerning abuse cases textual description, it provides information about potential *harm* that will occur as a result of the abuse, *privilege range* allowing the attacker to carry out this abuse, and *abuse interaction* proposing the scenario underlying the abuse case. The textual description of the abuse case `Browse building plans with hacking tools` is presented in Figure 3.9. This description could also come with a diagram illustrating the path to be used by the actor to fulfil the abuse case [MF99].

3.2.3   Mal-activity diagrams extending Activity diagrams

Presentation of Activity diagrams

Activity diagrams are also part of the UML language. The objective of this kind of diagram is to describe procedural logic, business process, and workflow [Obj04, Fow03]. They can be used at different stages of the IS development process, including early requirements. Activity diagrams are often compared to flowcharts, although activity diagrams support the modelling of parallel behavior. A complete introduction to the syntax and semantics of activity diagrams is not necessary as a background to present mal-activity diagrams. Figure 3.10 is a simple activity diagram introducing the basics components.

An *initial node* indicates the initial state of each activity diagram. An *activity* is shown as a box with round corner containing the description of the activity. `Find client`, `Evaluate costs` and `Design 3D mock-ups` are examples of activities performed during the process of estimates definition. The activity following a completed activity is shown by an arrow. The arrows thus represent the *flow* of activities. Each activity can be assigned to his owner, like done in Figure 3.10. Three actors are playing a role in this process: the `Sales department`, the `Study office` and the `Management`. A *merge* diamond with multiple incoming arrows is used when only one of the incoming activities shall be completed to go to the next activity. When activities shall be played in parallel, a *fork* with several outgoing arrows is inserted. A *join* with several incoming arrows shows the end of parallel activities and all of them shall be completed before leaving the merge. In our example, if a client is found by the `Sales department`, then `Evaluate costs` and `Design 3D mock-ups` should be done in parallel. The `Validate costs and mock-ups` activity could only be started once both of these activities are completed. A diamond with multiple labeled outgoing arrows represents a *choice*. The expression on each arrow is the condition that should be true to be able to select this arrow as the outgoing one. Considering the `Validate costs and mock-ups` activity performed by the *Management*, if it is considered as `satisfactory`, the next activity

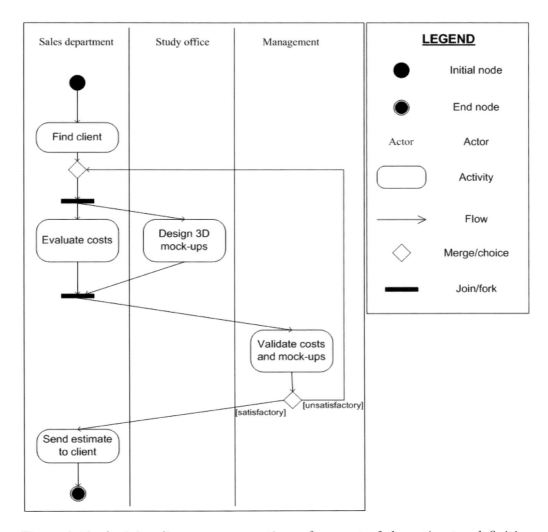

Figure 3.10: Activity diagram representing a fragment of the estimates definition

will be `Send to client`. Otherwise, activities of `Evaluate costs` and `Design 3D mock-ups` will be revised. Finally, the end of an activity diagram is represented by an *End node*. It is necessary to note that generally, textual descriptions are provided in activity diagrams to complete the graphical notation.

Mal-activity diagrams

Mal(icious)-activity diagrams were proposed in 2007, completing the Misuse cases notations, by a way of modelling the behavioral aspects of security problems [Sin07]. The general way of building a mal-activity diagram is to build the normal process and then to add the potential mal-activities against this process. It is also possible to further add defensive processes (i.e. mitigation activity) to the diagram (cf. Figure 3.11). The syntax and semantics of ordinary activity diagrams is kept, and some extra-concepts are added:

- **Malicious activities**, represented with black filled activity icons;

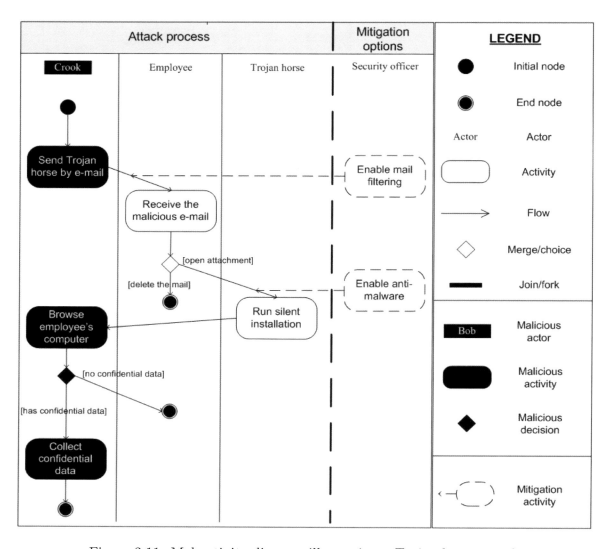

Figure 3.11: Mal-activity diagram illustrating a Trojan horse attack

- **Malicious actors,** represented as the inverse of normal actors (i.e. white text on black background);

- **Malicious decision boxes,** shown as black diamonds and used when a decision is made with a malicious purpose.

Figure 3.11 is an example of a mal-activity diagram inspired by those of [Sin07]. It represents the process performed for a `Crook` (i.e. the *malicious actor*) to attack the organisation with the help of a Trojan horse. The first *malicious activity* of the attacker is to `Send Trojan horse by e-mail`. Then an `Employee` will `Receive the malicious mail` and based on his decision to open or to delete the e-mail, the malware will be installed if the latter is chosen. The `Crook` is then able to `Browse employee's computer`. Depending on the presence of confidential data on the employee's computer, the *malicious decision* indicates the ability of the `Crook` to `Collect confidential data`. A way of representing mitigation options is also proposed in the mal-activity approach. On the right hand side of Figure 3.11, the mitigations are shown in a column separated from the mal-activity process by a dotted line and inserted into the attack process with dashed arrows. A new actor, the `security officer`, is added, and the proposed *mitigation activities* are to `Enable mail filtering` before `Receive the malicious e-mail` and to `Enable anti-malware` before `Run silent installation`.

3.2.4   Abuse frames extending Problem frames

Problem frames were introduced in 1995 in the book "Software Requirements & Specifications" [Jac95]. The purpose of the problem frames is to provide an approach to understand and describe real world software-intensive problems [CHR05]. It emphasises problems over solutions and provides tools that support the understanding of a problem. This graphical notation is used for structuring a system development problem as a set of sub-problems with each sub-problem represented as a problem frames diagram. Through the problem frames notation, each sub-problem can be analysed individually. Problem frames are especially used within the framework of Haley *et al.* and Moffett and Nuseibeh, presented in Section 3.1.2. A complete description of the problem frames approach and its notation is provided in [Jac01].

The Problem frames modelling language

A *context diagram* represents the context of a problem by capturing the characteristics and interconnections of the parts of the world the problem is concerned with [CHR05]. Context diagrams typically include domain descriptions (*the world*) that describe the environment of the system to be built, and descriptions of their *shared phenomena*. Problem domains are represented by plain rectangles and phenomena shared between two domains are represented by an annotated line connecting the two domains. Phenomena can be, for instance, events, states or commands. Domains are generally (but not necessarily directly) in contact with the *machine* to be built, and shared phenomena may exist between domains and the machine. A rectangle with two double vertical stripes represents the machine to be developed. The machine to be built in Figure 3.12 is a `Mock-ups displayer`. `Maps` and `Monitor` are part of the problem domain. The Maps share with the `Mock-ups displayer` the data necessary to build a movie, played on the `Monitor`.

A *problem frames diagram* is built by the addition of a *requirement* to the context diagram, represented by a dashed oval. Figure 3.12 gives a simple example of a problem frame diagram by adding the requirement `Display mock-ups`. The dashed lines connecting the oval to a problem domain represent a requirement reference; that is, the requirement refers to certain phenomena of the problem domain. It is necessary to note that no distinction is made between a problem frame expressing a security requirement and those expressing other kinds of requirements.

Abuse frames

The Abuse frames approach emerged from the observation that most of the techniques developed by the security engineering community have mainly focused on design and implementation issues. However it seems to be as important to precisely define and

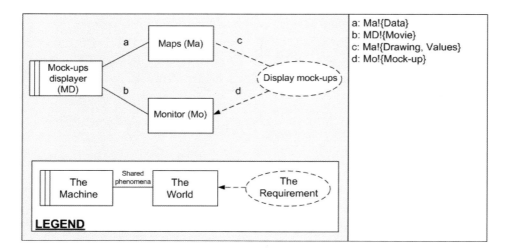

Figure 3.12: Problem frames diagram representing a Maps displayer

analyse the security requirements, coming with a systematic approach to define suitable problem boundaries in order to provide a focus for early security threat analysis [LNI+03b]. Abuse frames aim at supporting the reasoning on security during the early stages of the development process, mainly by correctly defining the system boundaries. This helps in 1) finding non-trivial security vulnerabilities and 2) analysing security threats and derive security requirements [LNIJ04].

Abuse frames build on the principles of Problem frames to analyse security threats and vulnerabilities and derive security requirements in a bounded context. This approach introduces two new concepts: *anti-requirements* [CILN02] and *abuse frames*. An anti-requirement is defined as "the requirements of users with malicious intent, that is, an anti-requirement specifies the undesirable phenomena in the system that must be prevented from happening". The concept of anti-requirement is thus close to the one of anti-goal in KAOS. Anti-requirements are incorporated into abuse frames "to represent the notion of a security threat imposed by malicious users in a particular problem context" [LNI+03b, LNI+03a, LNIJ04]. The notation of Problem frames is adopted in the abuse frames, although each domain is now associated with a different meaning (Figure 3.13):

- The *Machine* domain contains the vulnerabilities that the malicious user exploits to achieve the attack (although, of course, other kinds of attacks on other domains are possible).

- The *Asset* domain identifies the asset under attack.

- The *Malicious user* domain having an anti-requirement defines the threat agent.

- The *phenomenon* represented by the dashed arrow describes the undesirable phenomenon in the asset domain during an attack [LNI+03b].

In Figure 3.13, the example shows a `Trojan horse` used by an `Attacker` harming the `Mock-ups displayer`. The anti-requirement `Movie interception` indicated by the dashed oval, specifies the observable and undesirable phenomena acting on the asset as the result of the interaction between the `Trojan horse` and the `Mock-ups displayer`.

In cases where the threat is realised without the active participation of a malicious user, the malicious user domain may be omitted in the diagram. To show that a threat is realisable, an abuse frame argument is constructed. It should demonstrate that the anti-requirement is satisfied by a sequence of interactions of domain phenomena.

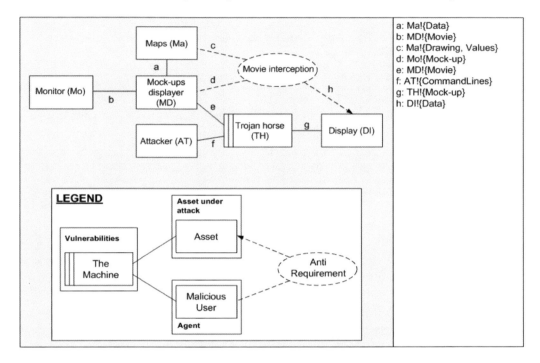

a: Ma!{Data}
b: MD!{Movie}
c: Ma!{Drawing, Values}
d: Mo!{Mock-up}
e: MD!{Movie}
f: AT!{CommandLines}
g: TH!{Mock-up}
h: DI!{Data}

Figure 3.13: Example of abuse frames diagram

The process applied for abuse frames elaboration is composed of four main steps [LNIJ04]:

1. Scoping the problem and identify the subproblems: from the initial problem statement, identify the sub-problems and define their problem frames diagrams. The security concerns are described as security constraints on the functionality to be achieved in each problem frame diagram.

2. Identifying the threats and constructing abuse frames: the initial anti-requirements can be obtained by negating the security constraints on the problem frames. The identified anti-requirements are then captured in abuse frames to represent the threat to the system context bounded by the problem frame diagram.

3. Identifying security vulnerabilities: from the abuse frame diagram, identify the security vulnerabilities as the properties in terms of the behaviours of the domains for which the anti-requirement can be 'existentially' satisfied. An anti-requirement only needs to occur once for the system to be insecure.

4. Addressing security vulnerabilities: security vulnerabilities identified will need to be addressed appropriately by design decisions that should preserve the security properties.

It is recommended to play this process in a "twin-peaks" style [Nus01], i.e. to iteratively review vulnerabilities of the architecture emerging from new security requirements proposed (and hence provide new problem descriptions), thereby progressively increasing the requirements and architectures level of detail.

3.2.5   Secure Tropos and Tropos Goal-Risk framework

The *i** framework

Work on the *i** framework started in the first half of the 90's at the University of Toronto. Its motivation came from the observation that most of the existing modelling framework tend to focus on processes, and thus concentrate on answering the "what" or the "how" of the processes (e.g., *what* are the different steps of the process, *how* to perform them, etc.). The objective of the *i** framework is to have an understanding of the "why" questions underlying the IS requirements. It provides a view of the organisational environment, helping to make tradeoffs among the alternatives based on the motivations and interests of process participants, before going further in detailed specification of "what" the system should do. *i** is thus meant to support early phases of RE [Yu96, Yu97]. It is necessary to note that, according to [LSS+08, ACC+05], several definitions of the language have been formulated. For example, we can cite GRL (Goal-oriented Requirement Language) [LY01] influenced by the NFR framework [CNYM00], or Tropos (summarised in the next section) that are both strongly based on *i**, but varying in the modelling language. The *i** framework defined in this section is the one proposed by Yu [Yu96, Yu97]. Not all of the existing *i** modelling constructs are presented, but only these that are necessary to have a global understanding of the framework and that are relevant with regards to our work.

Two modelling components are part of *i**. The first one, called *Strategic Dependency* (SD) model, describes a process in terms of intentional dependency relationships among agents [Yu96]. Note that the *i** models are usually incomplete; only items of strategic interest regarding the concern of the model are included. The top part of Figure 3.14 shows first a SD model illustrating the "estimates definition" activity. The different departments playing a role in estimates definition (i.e. `Study office`, `Administration`, `Sales department` and `Management`) are represented as *actors*. Moreover, the `Clients`, even external to the company, are represented in the model because playing a role in terms of dependency relationships for the represented activity. These actors have dependencies between them, in terms of *goals* to be achieved, *tasks* to be performed, and *resources* to be provided. For example, the `Sales department` (depender) depends on the `Study office` (dependee) for achieving `Calculate structure`, and furnishing `Technical plans` and `3D mock-ups`. On the other hand, the `Study office` depends on the `Sales department` for `Manage project`. Note that a task is selected (and not a goal) only when the depender has already made decisions about how the task is to be performed. The last type of dependency is the *softgoal* dependency. It differs from the goal dependency because a softgoal does not have clear-cut criteria of satisfaction (goals are said to be *satisfied* while softgoals are said to be *satisficed* according to the terminology introduced in [MCY99, CNYM00]). Here the `Management` depends on the `Study office` to have `Documents of quality` that is a non-functional goal requested by the management.

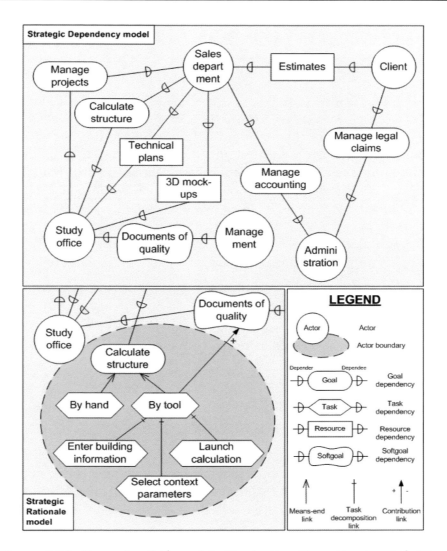

Figure 3.14: Example of *i** models illustrating the estimates definition

The second modelling component of *i** is called *Strategic Rationale* (SR) model [Yu96]. It describes the reasoning that each (inside) actor makes about its goals and its relationships with other actors. The bottom part of Figure 3.14 shows the internal activities of the `Study office` to achieve the `Calculate structure goal` (that is only part of the complete associated SR model). First, two different means of achieving this goal are proposed: to perform calculation `By hand` or `By a tool`. They are linked to the parent goal by *means-end links*, expressing the multiple and alternative ways of achieving it. For the second proposal, the task is further decomposed into sub-tasks with *task decomposition links*. Finally *contribution links* (which can be negative or positive) describe the impact that one element has on another. In our example, we claim that structure calculation performed by a tool will improve the quality of the documents.

With regards to security, Liu *et al.* propose to analyse security and privacy with *i** models [LYM02, LYM03]. First, security concerns are represented through softgoals, attacker through actors and their attacks through tasks. Then, countermeasures are represented through tasks.

The Tropos methodology

The motivation behind Tropos was that no work had been done on requirements analysis for agent-oriented systems. Tropos has proposed a software development methodology aiming at bridging this gap and helping to describe both the organisational environment of a multi-agent system and the system-to-be. It builds on the i^* framework for modelling early and late requirements, architectural and detailed design. Tropos brings also a formal specification language called Formal Tropos. Formal verification and validation techniques, such as model checking, are used to validate the adequacy and accuracy of i^* models [FMPT01].

The proposed methodology covers the four steps below [BGG+04, CKM02]. The implementation stage can then take place, generally (but not necessarily) based on an agent-oriented programming platform:

- **Early requirements**, concerned with the understanding of a problem by studying its organisational setting. The output of this phase is an organisational model which includes relevant actors, their respective goals and their interdependencies.

- **Late requirements**, where the system-to-be is described within its operational environment, along with relevant functions and qualities. The system is represented as an actor which has dependencies with the actors identified during the previous step.

- **Architectural design**, where the system's global architecture is defined in terms of sub-systems, interconnected through data, control and other dependencies. Sub-systems are represented as actors and data/control relationships as dependencies.

- **Detailed design**, where behavior of each architectural component is defined in further detail. In this step, elements of the Agent UML formalism [BMO00] are used to complement the i^* features.

It is necessary to note that some concepts are modified or added to the initial i^* modelling language (e.g., *task* is sometimes called *plan*; *capability* of the actors and *belief*, which represents actor knowledge of the world, are added; etc.). For further details the reader can refer to [LSS+08, ACC+05].

Secure Tropos

Although the Tropos methodology partially allows to tackle security by modelling non-functional requirements (like security requirements) as softgoals, some limitations have been highlighted regarding the support of security by Tropos [Mou04]:

- The concepts available in Tropos have been considered as not suited to capture constraints imposed to some actors of the organisation, like security constraints. Moreover, the use of softgoals for representing all of the non-functional requirements does not allow to distinguish the security requirements from other types of requirements of the system.

- The Tropos process remains vague regarding the definition of security requirements and how they influence the steps of the process. Moreover, the relations between security requirements definition and the modelling activities are not expressed.

- Tropos fails to provide a process that allows developers to evaluate the proposed design regarding security.

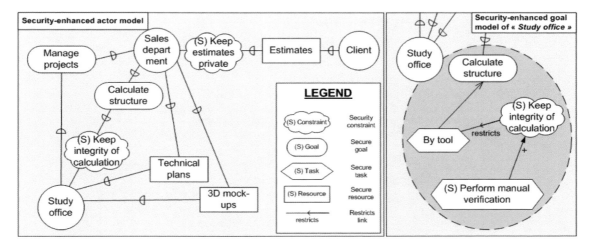

Figure 3.15: Example of Secure Tropos diagrams illustrating the "Estimates" definition

Considering these limitations, some concepts and modelling activities related to security have been added to Tropos under the form of an extension called Secure Tropos [GMZ07, MG09, MG04, MGMP02, MGM03a, MG07a]. Regarding the modelling language, Figure 3.15 summarises the main extensions brought by Secure Tropos in the strategic dependency and strategic rationale models, called now security-enhanced actor model and security-enhanced goal model. For simplicity, we have restricted our example to the analysis of the `Study office`, `Sales department` and `Client` actors and their respective dependencies identified in Figure 3.14.

The first concept added is *security constraint*. A security constraint is defined as "a restriction related to security issues, such as privacy, integrity and availability, which can influence the analysis and design of the system under development by restricting some alternative design solutions, by conflicting with some of the requirements of the system, or by refining some of the system's objective" [MGM05]. As examples, we have proposed in Figure 3.15 two security constraints related to our running example. The first one is for the `Sales department` to `Keep the estimates private`. The second one states that the `Study office` should `Keep integrity of calculation` (related to structure calculation). A *secure dependency* is defined as a dependency involving a security constraint between two actors. The security constraint must be satisfied either by the depender, the dependee, or both of them (in this case we speak about *double secure dependency*). In our example, `Keep the estimates private` must be satisfied by the `Sales department` and `Keep integrity of calculation` by the `Study office`.

During further actor analysis, the security constraints internal to each actor are related to these goals/tasks/resources by the use of *constraint link*. In the example, during the analysis of the `Study office` actor, we have related to this actor the security constraint `Keep integrity of calculation` (cf. right part of Figure 3.15). It is a security constraint that restricts the task `By tool`, specialising the goal `Calculate structure`. To satisfy security constraints, we use *secure entities*. Secure entities are secure goals, tasks or resources of the system that can be defined as traditional goals, tasks and resources, but related to the security of the IS [MG09]. In the example, we have introduced the secure task `Perform manual verification`, that has a positive contribution to the identified security constraint. Regarding the modelling framework, security constraints and secure entities are specified by a "(S)" label before the name of the entity (Figure 3.15). Finally, *secure capabilities* can be identified for each actor/agent to achieve a secure goal, carry out a secure task and/or deliver a secure resource. In our example, the study office should have someone able to manually check the structure calculations to perform the secure task.

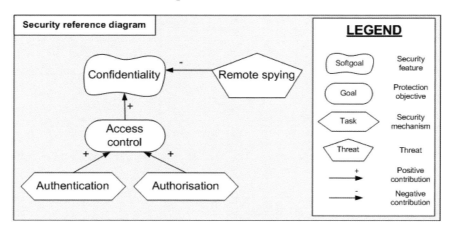

Figure 3.16: Example of security reference diagram

Identifying the security requirements during the early phases of RE being a difficult task, the *security reference diagram* has also been introduced to help the developers. First of all, the *security features* or protection properties of the system-to-be are considered. In our example (Figure 3.16), we select the `Confidentiality` security feature. The security features are represented under the form of softgoals. Then the *protection objectives* are identified as goals. They are defined as "a set of principles or rules that contributes towards the achievement of the security features" [MG09, MG07a]. `Access control` is a protection objective having a positive contribution to `Confidentiality`. The protection objectives are further satisfied through *security mechanisms*. For example, `Authentication` and `Authorisation` help to fulfill the `Access control` objective. Finally, *threats* represent circumstances that have the potential to cause loss or problems related to the security features of the system-to-be. `Remote spying` is an instance of threat, associated to `Confidentiality` by a negative contribution.

Considering the process provided by Tropos, security constraints and secure entities modelling are generally done during the early requirements phase for the actors, and during late requirements for the system-to-be [MG09]. However, the designer can decide himself which activity must be employed at which stage of the IS development [MG07a]. The security reference diagram is also constructed during the initial stages of the IS development [MG07a]. However, it can be used as a reference throughout the development process proposed by Tropos.

Within Secure Tropos, a last relation called *attacks* link is introduced in the modelling framework. This relation is not used during the RE phases of Tropos, but used during the design phase of the system under development, within the *Security attack scenario* diagram. It is a kind of model representing the actors of the IS with possible attackers. The attacks link starts from an attacker's goal and ends to the attacked entity. Finally, Secure Tropos also introduces a set of concepts related to trust (e.g., delegation, ownership, etc.) [MG07a, GMZ07] but they are not studied in depth in our research work.

Tropos Goal-Risk framework

The Tropos Goal-Risk (GR) framework is another Tropos extension that considers the concept of 'risk' [AG06, AGMZ07, AGMS07, ABG07]. Its objective is to assess the risk of uncertain events over organisation strategies and to evaluate the effectiveness of treatments [AMSZ08]. Regarding our scope, it is necessary to note that the range of risks supported by Tropos GR framework is not focused on IS security. It is open to risk in general, taking place in different domains at the level of an organisation, like risk in project management or financial risk. Compared to risk management processes proposed by standards [AS/04, ISO08], the Tropos GR framework mainly focusses on risk assessment and treatment steps [AMSZ08].

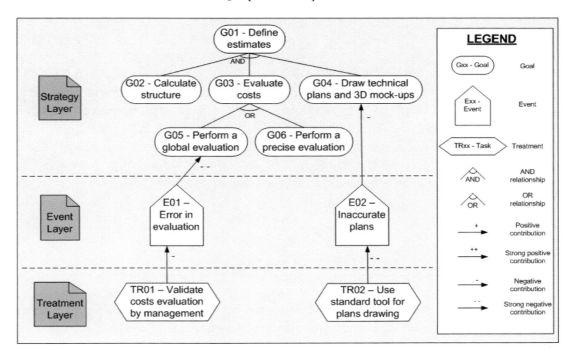

Figure 3.17: Example of Goal-Risk model

The framework first adds three layers to the Tropos modelling framework: *goal, event* and *treatment* [AGMZ07, AMSZ08]:

- The **Strategy** (or Goal) **layer** analyses strategic interests of the stakeholders;

- The **Event layer** analyses uncertain events along with their impacts to the strategy layer;

- The **Treatment layer** analyses treatments to be adopted in order to mitigate risks.

Two new entities are also proposed in the Tropos GR models: *event* and *treatment*. Events (depicted as pentagons) are used in the event layer to model uncertain circumstances that can affect goals or tasks in the strategy layer. *Treatments* are represented under the form of tasks and aim at mitigating such events, in order to make risks acceptable to all actors. Goals, events and treatments are decomposed by AND/OR relationships. They are also related with the help of four different kinds of contribution relations: strong positive (++), positive (+), strong negative (–) and negative (-) contribution.

With this framework, risk analyses can be performed at the level of an organisation, with its set of actors, and also further, beyond the rationale of single actors. The example of Figure 3.17 illustrates part of the global organisation of the running example, without specifying the actors (for simplicity), as it is allowed in GR models [AG06, ABG07]. In the *Strategy layer*, the root goal is `Define estimates`. This goal is composed of three sub-goals that should all be performed (*AND-relationship*): `Calculate structure`, `Evaluate costs` and `Draw technical plans and 3D mock-ups`. Two different and alternative manners (*OR-relationship*) of performing costs evaluation are proposed: `Perform a global evaluation` or `Perform a precise evaluation`. Two events are proposed in our example: `Error in evaluation` impacting `Perform a global evaluation` (strong negative) and `Inaccurate plans` impacting `Draw technical plans and 3D mock-ups` (negative). Finally two treatments are proposed (Figure 3.17): `Validate costs evaluation by management` mitigating `Error in evaluation` and `Use standard tool for plans drawing` strongly mitigating `Inaccurate plans`.

The outcome of a Tropos GR model is the assessment of the level of satisfaction or denial of goals. Each of the constructs of a model can have two attributes, *SAT* and *DEN*, representing respectively their satisfaction and denial value (not evaluated on our example). These values are qualitatively represented in the range of *Full, Partial, None*. Contribution relations represent the impact of a construct over another and propagate the SAT or DEN attribute (or both of them).

3.3 Conclusion

This chapter summarises contributions in software and security engineering related to our research work. First, we have investigated several frameworks dealing with security engineering during RE phases (Section 3.1). These frameworks introduce security concepts and terminology or are built upon a risk-based approach. In a second step, we have presented the set of security-oriented modelling languages, our focus being on the early phases of RE (Section 3.2).

The main conclusion is that the use of a risk-based approach for defining suited security requirements during IS development is still an open research question. Risk-based approaches have been introduced in computer science for a while [Boe91], but the

Table 3.2: Summary of the software and security engineering state of the art

Reference	Security oriented	Risk-based approach	RE approach	Model-based approach
Firesmith	++	+	++	-
Haley *et al.* and Moffet and Nuseibeh	++	+	++	-
DITSCAP automation framework	++	++	++	-
SQUARE	++	++	++	-
KAOS extended to security	++	-	++	++
Misuse cases	++	-	++	++
Abuse cases	++	-	++	++
Mal-activity diagrams	++	-	++	++
Abuse Frames	++	-	++	++
Secure Tropos	++	-	++	++
Tropos Goal-Risk Framework	-	++	++	++

Legend:
++: Completely covered and at the core of the document
+: Partially covered or not playing a central role
-: Not covered

connection between security risk management methods or standards and IS development is still an emerging domain. Some research work proposes conceptual frameworks that help to deal with security risk during RE [Fir03, HLMN08, GL07]. Others propose a RE process taking care of RM [MHI05]. Finally, many modelling languages are supporting security during the RE stages [SO05, MF99, Sin07, LNIJ04, MGMP02, vL04] but are not connected to RM. Tropos GR framework [AG06] is the only one that clearly considers the concept of risk. However, it remains a generic framework, not dedicated to security and its conceptual specificities. Our summary table (Table 3.2[6]) shows thus that no existing approach is tackling all of our four objectives (Section 1.1).

Moreover, security-oriented modelling languages generally have their own viewpoint of IS security and may thus be used in a complementary manner in an IS development project. However, they are built on different terminologies and conceptual models and it is thus difficult to switch from one to the other. It can be helpful to have a central ontology to make the link between all of these languages at the level of security.

The aim of the next chapter of this thesis is therefore to propose a domain model of ISSRM. It will first determine what are the concepts that should be present in a modelling language supporting ISSRM. Second it will help to introduce interoperability between the existing security-oriented modelling language. The domain model will indeed be used as a reference for aligning the concepts of each language.

---

[6]By "Completely covered" for "Risk-based approach", we don't mean the concept of "risk" is only considered in the approach, but really that the underlying process/method is based on a risk management approach. For example, the concept of risk is mentioned in Firesmith's or Haley's works, but the underlying proposed approach doesn't propose any risk analysis/assessment/management process to define the security requirements.

3.4   Chapter summary

In this chapter, we studied approaches related to security RE. First, we presented different security RE frameworks. Second, an overview of security-oriented modelling languages was proposed. We ended this chapter by conclusions with regards to this survey.

In the next chapter, we start our contribution on ISSRM modelling. We introduce a research method, and follow it, to define the ISSRM domain model. This domain model presents the concepts to be integrated in an ISSRM modelling language.

Part II

An Information System Security Risk Management Modelling Framework

Chapter 4

Information System Security Risk Management Domain Model

The various approaches related to our objectives have been presented in the previous part: first the ISSRM standards and methods, and second the RE frameworks and modelling languages related to security. Based on these sources, we now answer our first research question: *what are the concepts that should be present in a modelling language supporting ISSRM?* The outcome of this work is the ISSRM domain model. This domain model will first be used as the syntactic and semantic reference for the security-oriented modelling languages comparison, with regard to the ISSRM domain. Moreover, the introduction of an ISSRM domain model will help to provide an unified terminology between the different ISSRM approaches, and therefore will help to go towards a common understanding of the domain and its concepts. For example, a method like SQUARE [MHI05, MS05], needing to agree on ISSRM definitions as a preliminary work, can use our domain model as the artefact for catching and agreeing about the concepts of ISSRM and their definitions. Finally, the introduction of a model to present the concepts of ISSRM will improve the documentation usually provided in the literature, and will help to catch the different concepts.

Section 4.1 presents the research method applied to define the ISSRM domain model. The various sources considered relevant to this definition are summarised in Section 4.2. Section 4.3 presents the first step of the research method, about concept alignment, and its results; then Section 4.4 addresses the second step of the research method, and proposes the ISSRM domain model and its construction. The chapter ends with Section 4.5 discussing conclusions and limitations of the domain model.

4.1 Research method

In order to answer the research question in a structured way, we suggest a research method to follow. The research method is presented in Figure 4.1. It is inspired from the methods of conceptual graph construction, in the sense it is based on syntactic and semantics analysis [Sow76, LMFGL05, HD05]. Our research method consists of two steps:

Step 1 – *Concept alignment.* First, we investigate the state of the art in ISSRM.

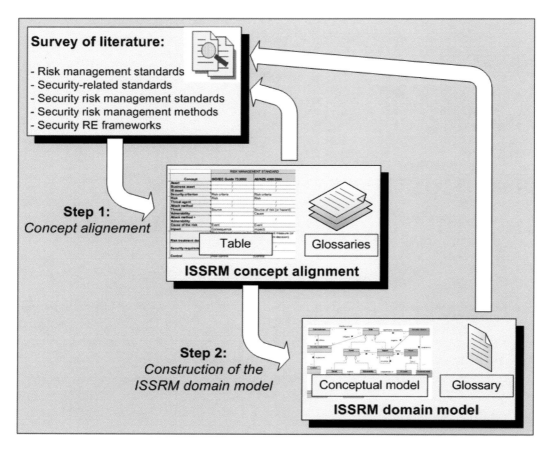

Figure 4.1: Research method applied for the ISSRM domain model definition

The main goal is to identify the core concepts of the domain and harmonise the terminology. Basically, we extract the relevant concepts through a systematic analysis of ISSRM sources, and then align them semantically. By systematic, we mean exhaustive and reproductible, in the sense we analyse all of the selected sources and in the same manner. The main results of this step are:

- A *concept alignment table* that highlights the core concepts of the various approaches and indicates synonymy or other semantic similarity relationships when approaches use different terms (cf. Section 4.3);

- *Glossaries* of the terms as found in the different sources. They are listed in Appendix A and classified according to the analysed source.

To get a comprehensive view of ISSRM approaches, we base this step on a survey of the literature (Section 4.2) consisting of five main families of sources:

1. Risk management standards (cf. Section 2.2),

2. Security-related standards (cf. Section 2.3),

3. Security risk management standards (cf. Section 2.4),

4. Security risk management methods (cf. Section 2.5),

5. Security Requirements Engineering (RE) frameworks (cf. Section 3.1).

Security-oriented modelling languages are not addressed in this step. In Chapter 6, we will apply our domain model to analyse them.

In each considered source, we only gather the (parts of) sentences that are 1) interesting regarding the semantic of the concept 2) non-redundant with regards to elements and information already gathered for this source. The concept alignment is not a streamlined process. This step is performed in an iterative and incremental manner with successive refinements of the table coming with deeper understanding of the semantics of the concepts.

Moreover, the relationships between the identified concepts are identified in this step too. Based on the survey of the literature, we used the same iterative elicitation approach as for concepts.

Step 2 – *Construction of the ISSRM domain model.* Based on the outcomes of step 1, we define a conceptual model of the ISSRM domain as a UML class diagram presented in Section 4.4. UML class diagram [Obj04] is chosen to represent our conceptual model, because this notation is widespread and expressive enough to represent the concepts and the relationships (with their properties) of our model. First, we choose a name for each identified concept. Then, for each concept is given a definition in a separate glossary. The definitions are obtained by reusing and, if needed, improving the most relevant definitions found in step 1. Last activity was the definition of the relationships between the concepts, derived from those observed in the analysed literature.

If a new source is needed to be taken into account, or in case of comments/feedbacks on the domain model, the process is started again from the survey of the literature. The concept alignment is thereby completed or revised, leading to potential updates of the ISSRM domain model.

4.2 Survey of the literature

The first step of the research method is grounded in a literature survey, including five families of sources that fully support our research scope – IS security risk management. All of them are presented in the first part of this thesis (Part I) and their studied version is the one presented in this state of the art. We quickly recall them in this section.

The first family is that of *RM standards*. They are high-level references presenting general RM upon which are built domain specific RM approaches.

- ISO/IEC Guide 73 [ISO02b]: This guide defines the RM vocabulary and guidelines for use in ISO standards. It mainly focuses on terminology, which is of great interest with respect to our research method.

- AS/NZS 4360 [AS/04]: This joint Australian/New-Zealand standard provides a generic guide for RM. The document proposes an overview of RM terminology and process.

The second family of sources consists of (IS/IT) *security-related standards*. The selected documents often contain a section that concerns security-specific terminology. Sometimes some RM concepts are also mentioned.

- ISO/IEC 13335-1 [ISO04b]: This standard is the first of the ISO/IEC 13335 guidelines series that deals with the planning, management and implementation of IT security. This part is about concepts and models of IT security that may be applicable to different organisations.

- Common Criteria [Com06a]: The Common Criteria (standardised in version 2.3 by ISO/IEC 15408) provides a common set of requirements for the security functions of IT products and systems and for assurance measures applied to them during a security evaluation. The first part entitled "Introduction and general model" is important with respect to our research scope.

The third family concerns *security RM standards*, thus dealing with standards precisely in our scope.

- ISO/IEC 27001 [ISO05b]: The objective of this standard is to provide a model for establishing, implementing, operating, monitoring, reviewing, maintaining and improving an ISMS, that is the part of the overall management system of an organisation concerned by information security. The terminology related to an ISMS is provided in this reference.

- ISO/IEC 27005 [ISO08]: This standard is a guideline associated to the ISO/IEC 27001 standard, explaining how to perform information security risk management with regards to the ISO/IEC 27001 requirements.

- NIST 800-27 Rev A [SHF04] / NIST 800-30 [SGF02]: Within the series of publications proposed by the NIST, the 800-series is about computer security. In this series of publications, NIST 800-27 and NIST 800-30 are relevant to the scope proposed in Section 1.4. Terminology and concepts are provided by these standards and are compliant with one another.

- The IT-Grundschutz [Bun05b, Bun05d]: This German standard is composed of several complementary documents aiming at managing security, from a "standard" security level to a more fine-tuned security management based on risks.

Security RM methods is the fourth family of sources. As explained in Section 2.5, we select a representative subset of ISSRM methods. Most of the methods are supported by a software tool, but we will focus only on their methodological part.

- EBIOS [DCS04b]: The EBIOS method is developed and maintained by the DCSSI in France.

- MEHARI [CLU07b]: MEHARI is a RM methodology developed by the CLUSIF and built on the top of two other RM methods: MARION [CLU98] and MELISA [Dir89], not maintained anymore.

- OCTAVE [AD01b]: OCTAVE is an approach to information security risk evaluations developed by the SEI at the Carnegie Mellon University.

- CRAMM [Ins03]: CRAMM is a RM method from UK originally developed by CCTA in 1985 and currently maintained by Insight Consulting.

- CORAS [VML+07]: CORAS is the result of a European project developing a tool-supported framework, exploiting methods for risk analysis and risk assessment of security critical systems.

Finally, the last family concerns *security frameworks* proposed in research publications. These publications are extracted from the RE domain, with a focus on safety and security.

- Firesmith [Fir03, Fir07b] presents a set of related information models that provides the theoretical foundation underlying mainly safety and security engineering. A process to effectively deal with both safety and security engineering is proposed.

- Haley *et al.* [HMLN06a, HLMN08] and Moffett and Nuseibeh [MN03] propose a framework for dealing with security requirements.

- The DITSCAP automation framework introduces a conceptual model about security requirements and risk factors [LGA05, GL07].

A last note is about SQUARE [MHI05], a stepwise methodology for eliciting, categorising, and prioritising security requirements for IT systems and applications. Although SQUARE is focussed on security RE and suggests to use an ISSRM approach to elicit security requirements, it is not selected in this research work, because the first step of SQUARE is about definition by the RE team and the stakeholders of the terminology to use. SQUARE is thereby not grounded on a pre-defined terminology we could study in this section.

4.3 ISSRM concept alignment

This section describes the first step of the research method presented in Figure 4.1. Based on the literature identified in Section 4.2, ISSRM concepts are identified and aligned in a table. The relationships linking the identified concepts are also identified. The section ends with conclusions about the concept alignment.

4.3.1 Concepts to consider

The first task of the concept alignment is to define the range of concepts to study. The core concept to consider is the one of risk, that is analysed in depth in the coming subsection. However, risk is dependent on, and related to, (i) security needs associated with the assets and (ii) risk treatments selected, as seen in Section 2.1. Therefore, these related concepts are naturally included into the set of concepts to consider. This range of concepts is only a first boundary for step 1. Note that this first step is performed iteratively, specifying incrementally the range of concepts to consider and transform them into a defined set of concepts.

The final set of concepts elicited will be the one listed in the table, which is the outcome of step 1. Nevertheless, the set of concepts can be reduced or increased afterwards, in case of specific needs or new concepts needed for consideration. Then other steps of the research method will be modified incrementally.

4.3.2 Analysis of the concepts

In this section we illustrate our approach by reporting on the analysis of the central concept – *risk* – as extracted from the sources surveyed in Section 4.2. An emphasis is placed on the definition of *risk* and the identification of its associated components. Other characteristics of risk presented in its various definitions [SGF02, DCS04b, Fir03], like, for example, its value, are not currently considered. At the opposite, risk sub-components or related concepts are directly involved in this step. In terms of object modelling [Obj04], the objective of this step is to identify the different 'objects' or 'classes' of the ISSRM domain model. The identification of the metrics, that will be the 'properties' or 'attributes' of these objects, is done in Chapter 5.

Considering the amount of sources and concepts to study, it is unrealistic to describe in a detailed manner the concept alignment, and every iteration performed for step 1. In this section, we present only the first iteration of step 1. Further activities involve other iterations, in order to review and improve the results.

Risk management standards

ISO Guide 73 gives the following definition of risk:

> **Risk**: *combination of the probability of an event and its consequence.* [ISO02b, p. 2]

The AS/NZS 4360 source proposes a very close definition in its glossary:

> **Risk**: *the chance of something happening that will have an impact on objectives.*
> *NOTE 1: A risk is often specified in terms of an event or circumstance and the consequences that may flow from it.* [AS/04, p. 4]

Both sources show that a risk is composed of two related elements: a cause, called *event* or *something happening*; and a *consequence*, also called *impact*. This consideration is valid to all the risk domains. Next we compare both definitions with the ones from the security domain. Our purpose is a further refinement of our analysis.

Security-related standards

In ISO/IEC 13335, risk is defined in the glossary in terms of three involved concepts:

> **Risk**: *the potential that a given threat will exploit vulnerabilities of an asset or group of assets and thereby cause harm to the organisation.* [ISO04b, p. 2]

The analysis of this definition shows that it is compliant with RM standards because risk is always composed of a cause and a consequence component. However the definition introduces some new concepts: the cause of the risk is presented as the combination of *threat* and *vulnerability*, and the consequence is called *harm* (cf. Table B.1 in Appendix B).

CC defines *risk* incrementally:

> *- These threats therefore give rise to **risks** to the assets, based on the likelihood of a threat being realised and the impact on the assets when that threat is realised. Subsequently countermeasures are imposed to reduce the risks to assets. These countermeasures may consist of IT countermeasures (such as firewalls and smart cards) and non-IT countermeasures (such as guards and procedures).*
> *- A threat consists of a threat agent, an asset and an adverse action of that threat agent on that asset.*
> *- Threat agents are entities that can adversely act on assets. Examples of threat agents are hackers, users, computer processes, TOE development personnel, and accidents. Threat agents may be further described by aspects such as expertise, resources, opportunity and motivation.*
> *- Adverse actions are actions performed by a threat agent on an asset. These actions influence one or more properties of an asset from which that asset derives its value.* [Com06a, p. 35,53]

Here, the emphasis is placed on the concept of *threat*. It is defined as consisting of sub-components: *threat agent* and *adverse action* acting on *assets*.

The use of the term *risk* in security-related standards shows that its definition is more precise than the one proposed in RM standards, but it is nevertheless compliant with the ones given in RM standards. *Risk* in security standards is the specialisation, in the context of security, of *risk* in RM standards. The concept of *risk* is therefore aligned between RM standards and security-related standards in the alignment table (Table B.1). With regards to CC, the concepts of *asset* and *countermeasure* are also introduced in the table, because they are related to risk.

Security risk management standards

In ISO/IEC 27001, the concept of *risk* is not present in the glossary, but in an excerpt of the standard presenting the risk identification step, we find:

> *Identify the **risks**.*
> *1) Identify the assets within the scope of the ISMS, and the owners of these assets.*
> *2) Identify the threats to those assets.*
> *3) Identify the vulnerabilities that might be exploited by the threats.*
> *4) Identify the impacts that losses of confidentiality, integrity and availability may have on the assets.* [ISO05b, p. 4]

Regarding ISO/IEC 27005, the definition of risk, proposed in the glossary, is:

> *information security **risk***
> *potential that a given threat will exploit vulnerabilities of an asset or group of assets and thereby cause harm to the organisation.*
> *NOTE: It is measured in terms of a combination of the likelihood of an event and its consequence.* [ISO08, p. 1]

These definitions are very close and compliant in terms of concepts involved in ISO/IEC 13335.

NIST standards also propose a different definition for risk:

> ***Risk**: The net mission/business impact considering (1) the likelihood that a particular threat source will exploit, or trigger, a particular information system vulnerability and (2) the resulting impact if this should occur.* [SHF04, p. A-2]

In terms of involved concepts, risk is once again defined with the help of three components that are *threat source*, *vulnerability* and *impact*. The concept of *threat* is defined as the combination of a threat-source, its motivation (for human threat) and threat-actions, like hacking, social engineering, or system intrusion [SGF02, p. 14].

The IT-Grundschutz [Bun05b] is less explicit in terms of concepts involved for risk. The emphasis is put on the value of risk.

> **Risk**
> *A risk is the prediction of possible damage, often based on calculation, in a negative case (danger), or in a positive case a possible advantage (chance). The definition of damage or advantage depends on the benchmark values.*
> *Risk is also often defined as the combination of the probability of the occurrence of damage and the extent of this damage.* [Bun05d, p. 45]

Like in security-related standards, security RM standards increase the precision of the components of risk. The consequence of the risk only differs in terms of associated "label" or name, sometimes called *consequence*, *impact* or *harm*, but the underlying semantic remains the same. However, the cause of the risk is presented as a composition of elements, which are different between the sources. We can see differences and equivalences in the alignment table (Table B.1). The concept of *asset* is often mentioned in the *risk* definition of security-related standards. However, it is sometimes associated with the threat [ISO05b], sometimes with the vulnerabilities [ISO04b, ISO08] and sometimes with the impact [Com06a]. A conclusion is that the concept of *asset* is playing a role in the definition of a risk and should be linked with it. But more investigation about *asset* is necessary to define precisely the relationship among risk, its components and the concept of *asset*. At this stage it is, therefore, not included in the alignment table. A new iteration of step 1 of the research method 4.1, focussed on *asset*, will help to understand this concept and its role in the ISSRM domain.

Security risk management methods

EBIOS defines the concept of *risk* as:

> **Risk**: *Combination of a threat and the losses it can cause, i.e.: of the opportunity, for a threat agent using an attack method, to exploit one or more vulnerabilities of one or more entities and the impact on the essential elements and on the organisation.* [DCS04c, p. 14-15]

This definition in terms of concepts and relationships between them is aligned with the one of an older version of CC (v.2.3) [Com05]. Here, the cause of the risk is called *threat* and it encompasses vulnerability unlike most of the ISO standards [ISO04b, ISO05b, ISO08] that define them as related, but separate concepts and at the same level (i.e. both composing *risk*). The threat in [DCS04b] is therefore composed of multiple subcomponents like *threat agent*, *attack method*, *attack*, etc. *Threat* in these standards has thus not the same sense as *threat* in EBIOS. *Threat* from these standards and *threat* from [DCS04b] are thus not aligned in Table B.1.

In MEHARI, the absence of a glossary is an obstacle to a clear comprehension and alignment of concepts. However, clues can be found for *risk* definition within the method.

> *A **risk scenario** is the description of a malfunction and the way in which the malfunction can happen. The malfunction states the potential damage, or the direct deterioration caused by the malfunction, and any indirect consequences. It is usual to speak of a risk situation, where it is understood that the organisation is potentially exposed to such a scenario. [...]*
> *Each scenario will therefore be described as follows:*
> *- The type of consequence (sometimes in relation with predefined value scale)*
> *- The type of assets implicated by the scenario (sometimes in relation with the predefined critical resources)*
> *- The types of causes that can lead to the risk situation. [CLU07b, p. 13-14]*

In MEHARI the term *risk* is used less often than the term *risk scenario* for expressing the concept of *risk*. The cause and the consequence parts of the risk are well respected. A link between risk and assets is also proposed.

OCTAVE provides the following risk definition:

> ***Risk**: [...] Risk refers to a situation where a person could do something undesirable or a natural occurrence could cause an undesirable outcome, resulting in a negative impact or consequence.* [AD01a, p. 46]
> *It breaks down into three basic components: asset, threat, and vulnerability.* [AD01b, p. 5]

The definition of risk and its components is the same as in CRAMM. In this source, the risk is defined using the Figure 4.2 and followed with the definition:

> *Security **risk**: The likelihood of a system's inherent vulnerability being exploited by the threats to the system, leading to the system being penetrated.* [Ins03, p. B-29]

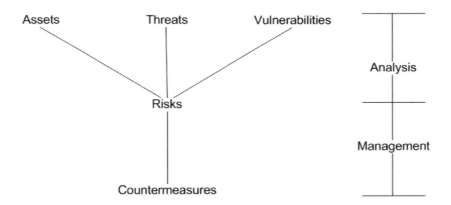

Figure 4.2: Risk representation in CRAMM (adapted from [Ins03])

Three components compose the risk for OCTAVE [AD01b] and CRAMM [Ins03]: *threat, vulnerability* and the consequence relative to *assets*. CRAMM gives a clue in its definition of *risk* for defining *attack* with respect to a risk. It is the concrete instantiation of the threat using the vulnerability on the target system. Attack is therefore not in the potential domain of RM. Attack is thus not playing a role in ISSRM. It is not taken into account in the ISSRM concept alignment table. Naturally this definition of *attack* may eventually only apply to CRAMM.

Finally, the CORAS RM method proposes a definition of risk, that is highly related to the concept of *unwanted incident*:

> **Risk:** *A risk is an unwanted incident along with its estimated likelihood and consequence values.* [VML+07, p. 313-314]
> *Unwanted incident: An unwanted incident is an event which reduces the value of one or more of the assets* [VML+07, p. 325]

The use of the term *event* should not be confused with the one used in other sources like [ISO02b, AS/04, ISO04b] designating the cause of the risk. Here *event* actually denotes the impact of the risk on the organisation. Examples of unwanted incidents are "design disclosed to competitor" or "customer loses trust in [the company]" that is characteristic of an impact. Here, the term *incident* is not used to depict an established safety problem, as it is usually the case in the literature [Fir04, Ins03]. A risk in CORAS is defined as an impact with an associated level of potentiality and consequence. Naturally the likelihood of the impact to occur is highly dependent on the cause of the risk. Further analysis of CORAS also introduces elements associated with the cause of the risk: *threat, threat scenario* and *vulnerability*.

Within security RM methods, the concept of risk is once again not universally agreed. First, the methods reinforce the conclusion obtained from RM standards that identify a cause and a consequence part in a risk. However a great diversity is provided in the fine-grained definitions of risk and its components. With the new elements obtained from the sources of security RM methods and security-related standards, a tendency is emerging: the cause (or event) part of the risk consists of two elements most often called *threat* and *vulnerability*.

RE security frameworks

The conceptual model introduced in the DITSCAP automation framework is an extension of the CC [Com06a] model. The concepts related to risk are assets, threats, vulnerabilities and countermeasures, and only very brief definitions are given [GL07], as the reader is referred to the CC. Thus, the added conceptual value of this model with respect to the preceding sources is deemed insubstantial.

In [Fir03], Firesmith proposes a very precise definition of *risk*, which is split into safety risk and security risk:

> **Safety risk** *is the potential risk of harm to an asset due to accidents. Safety risk is defined as the sum (over all relevant hazards) of the products of the following two terms: (1) the largest negative impact of the harm to the asset (i.e., its criticality, severity, or damage) times (2) the likelihood that the hazard will result in an accident [...]* [Fir03, p. 31]
> **Security risk** *is the potential risk of harm to an asset due to attacks. Security risk is the sum (over all relevant threats) of the negative impact of the harm to the asset (i.e., its criticality) multiplied by the likelihood of the harm occurring [...]* [Fir03, p. 35]

In [MN03], Moffet and Nuseibeh were inspired by CRAMM and propose the same figure to present risk and its components (cf. Figure 4.2) associated with the following definitions (their proposal is reinforced by Haley *et al.* [HMLN06a, HLMN08]):

> **Threat:** *Harm that can happen to an asset* **Impact:** *A measure of the seriousness of a threat*
> **Attack:** *A threatening event*
> **Attacker:** *The agent causing the attack (not necessarily human)*
> **Vulnerability:** *a weakness in the system that makes an attack more likely to succeed* [MN03, p. 6]

The combination of these two last definitions of risk makes clear that the two parts of a risk are characterised by *likelihood* for the cause (here, an emphasis is done on the 'value' or 'metric' of the cause, but this property is studied in Chapter 5) and *impact* or *harm* for the consequence. Investigation of definitions and associated information models of Firesmith shows that the likelihood of the risk depends on the likelihood of a threat (for security domain) or hazard (for safety domain) and the existence of a (safety or security) vulnerability.

Discussion about the concept of risk

We can draw some conclusions from this iteration of step 1 performed on the concept of *risk*. First of all, a risk is composed of a cause part, generally called *event*, and a consequence part, generally called *impact*. Second, an event is composed of a *threat* and a *vulnerability*.

Some other concepts have been identified as related to risk (e.g., *asset*) . Moreover, some information about other concepts have already been found in some *risk* definitions (e.g., in EBIOS [DCS04b], the definition of *risk* indicates some components of *threat*, like *threat agent* or *attack method*).

However, these conclusions come from only one iteration of step 1 on the concept of *risk*. It is necessary to perform other iterations of step 1 on other concepts, but also again on the concept of *risk*, to refine the preceding conclusions and elicit the other concepts related to risk.

4.3.3 Alignment table of ISSRM concepts

After gathering the different definitions of the ISSRM-related concepts (Appendix A), as done for the *risk* concept in the preceding section, alignment tables are defined iteratively. This means that, based on the definitions of the concepts, the concepts are semantically analysed and aligned with one another. Very often, during this alignment work, a new concept is emerging (like the concept of asset in the preceding section), or the definition of another concept is needed to completely understand the studied concept (as it is done in ISO/IEC Guide 73, e.g., for *event* and *consequence*, to understand what is *risk*). The new definition is added to the glossaries and the alignment is incrementally completed/modified based on this new element.

This section proposes the alignment tables for the different ISSRM concepts involved in the studied sources. The results are presented by family of source for clarity. The complete alignment table is available in Table B.1 in Appendix B. At last, 14 concepts have been identified and are thus proposed here. They are numbered from (1) to (14), but not labelled for the moment (cf. Section 4.4). The concepts are classified by category, as in Section 4.3.1: *Asset-related concepts*, *Risk-related concepts* and *Risk treatment-related concepts*. These categories have been defined with regards to the ISSRM process, presented in Section 2.1. Asset-related concepts are concepts focused around the asset concept and expressing what has value for the organisation and needs to be protected. Risk-related concepts are the set of concepts used to define the risk. Risk treatment-related concepts are the concepts used for countering the risk, generally at different level of granularity.

The concepts that are on the same line are concepts semantically equivalent. For example, in Table 4.1, the concept of *source* in ISO/IEC Guide 73 is equivalent to the concept of *hazard* in AS/NZS 4360. *Source* is defined as "item or activity having a potential for a consequence" and *hazard* as "a source of potential harm" (*consequence* and *harm* being also semantically equivalent). If several concepts are in the same cell, these concepts are semantically equivalent and from the same source. For example, as depicted in Table 4.1 for ISO/IEC Guide 73, *risk treatment measure* and *risk management decision* are two concepts of ISO/IEC Guide 73 that are semantically equivalent. *Risk treatment measure* is the decision of "avoiding, optimizing, transferring or retaining risk", and *risk control* is defined as "actions implementing *risk management decision*".

The reader shall note that the tables proposed in this section are the final ones, obtained after having performed every iteration of step 1. This explains why 14 lines are proposed in each table, that is equivalent to the final number of concepts identified in the ISSRM domain. Sometimes, some concepts have no equivalence in the sources. For example, in Table 4.1, the concept (1), named later *asset* (cf. Section 4.4), does not have any equivalence in ISO/IEC Guide 73 and in AS/NZS 4360.

Risk management standards

In RM standards, the concept of asset is not introduced (Table 4.1). Only *risk criterion* (4) is introduced for expressing how the significance of risk is assessed. As already mentioned, risk is composed of two sub-components in RM standards: an *event* and a *consequence*, differentiating the causal part of risk (6) from its consequence (7). The origin of the (cause of the) risk (8) is also identified by *source* or *hazard*. Finally, two levels of risk treatment are proposed: the first one for the decision of how to treat the risk (12) and the second one for the concrete controls applied on the IS (14), coming from the preceding decision.

Table 4.1: Alignment table for RM standards

Type	Concept	**ISO/IEC Guide 73**	**AS/NZS 4360**
Asset-related concepts	(1)	/	/
	(2)	/	/
	(3)	/	/
	(4)	Risk criterion	Risk criterion
Risk-related concepts	(5)	Risk	Risk
	(6)	Event	Event
	(7)	Consequence	Consequence Loss Harm
	(8)	Source	Hazard
	(9)	/	/
	(10)	/	/
	(11)	/	/
Risk treatment-related concepts	(12)	Risk treatment measure Risk management decision	Risk treatment measure
	(13)	/	/
	(14)	Risk control	Control

Security-related standards

Some new conclusions can be drawn from the analysis of security-related standards (Table 4.2). First, the concept of *asset* (1) is introduced in these security-specific standards. Then, a finer granularity is provided to define *risk*, i.e. new risk sub-components are introduced, like *vulnerability* (9) or *threat agent* (10). However, these risk sub-components are further and better explained in the next families of sources. Finally, a new granularity level of risk treatment is introduced with CC, that is, as explained in Section 1.5.2, equivalent to product-oriented *requirement* (13).

Table 4.2: Alignment table for security-related standards

Type	Concept	ISO/IEC 13335-1	Common Criteria
Asset-related concepts	(1)	Asset	Asset
	(2)	/	/
	(3)	/	/
	(4)	ICT security requirement	/
Risk-related concepts	(5)	Risk	Risk
	(6)	Event	/
	(7)	Impact	Impact
	(8)	/	Threat
	(9)	Vulnerability	Vulnerability
	(10)	/	Threat agent
	(11)	Threat	Adverse action
Risk treatment-related concepts	(12)	/	/
	(13)	/	Countermeasure Security objective Security (functional) requirement
	(14)	Safeguard Control	/

Security risk management standards

Concepts used in security RM standards (Table 4.3) are better defined and more complete with respect to security-related standards. In ISO/IEC 27001 [ISO05b] and ISO/IEC 27005 [ISO08], the general concept of *asset* is split in two categories: one related to the business of the studied organisation and the information and processes that should be protected (2), and the other for the IS components supporting the business activities (3). *Criteria* or *properties* are still applied on assets for allowing the significance of the assessed risks to be expressed. In general, *risk* is more precisely defined in security RM standards. There are still a causal part (6) and a consequence (7). However, the causal part is composed of what is most often called a *threat* (8) and a *vulnerability* (9). Sometimes, the threat is defined more finely, by differentiating the origin or source of the threat (10) and the action performed (11). Regarding risk treatments, two levels are generally proposed, compliant with the levels proposed in RM standards.

Table 4.3: Alignment table for security RM standards

Type	Concept	ISO/IEC 27001 ISO/IEC 27005	NIST 800-27 REV A NIST 800-30	The IT-Grundschutz
Asset-related concepts	(1)	Asset	/	Asset
	(2)	Primary asset	/	/
	(3)	Supporting asset	/	IT asset
	(4)	Property Criterion	Security goal	Basic parameter Basic IT security parameter
Risk-related concepts	(5)	Risk	(IT-related) Risk	Risk
	(6)	Event	Threat	Applied threat
	(7)	Impact Consequence	Impact Consequence	Damage
	(8)	Threat	Threat	Basic threat
	(9)	Vulnerability	Vulnerability	Vulnerability
	(10)	Threat source Origin of threat	Threat source	/
	(11)	/	Threat action	/
Risk treatment-related concepts	(12)	Risk treatment	Risk mitigation option	Decision
	(13)	Control	/	/
	(14)	Control	Control	Safeguard Security measure Control

Security risk management methods

There is a great diversity between the methods in terms of number of concepts used and name of the common concepts (Table 4.4). EBIOS and MEHARI are compliant with ISO/IEC 27005 at the asset level, with a clear distinction between assets at the business level and assets at the IS level. Regarding the other methods, their support of *asset* is slightly different, and more focused on the IS level for OCTAVE and CRAMM. Risk is a concept continually involved in the methods and as most of the preceding sources, a global cause of risk is expressed as wall as a consequence, here most often labelled *impact*. In each method, *vulnerability* is a sub-component of the cause of the risk. The concept of *threat*, exploiting the vulnerability for fulfilling the risk, is also often identified. However, in EBIOS and in some security RM standards [SHF04, SGF02], *threat* is used to represent the global cause of the risk, the event happening (concept (6)). These two meanings of *threat* are different. It explains the non-alignment of *threat* in different sources (i.e. in EBIOS, *threat* is equivalent to concept (6) and in OCTAVE or CRAMM, it is equivalent to concept (8)). In security RM methods, EBIOS also clearly distinguishes the origin of the threat, called *threat agent* and the action performed, called *attack method*. A specificity of security RM methods observed at the level of risk-treatment is that the emphasis is rather put at the level of security requirements definition (13) than at the level of decision of treating risk (12). The *control* concept (14) as expressed in the different standards [ISO02b, ISO04b, ISO05b, etc.] is kept, but its name is different, going from very generic names (e.g., countermeasure, security solution, etc.) to more technical ones (e.g., mechanism, protection strategic practice, etc.). A concept specific to EBIOS (i.e. not mentioned in any other source) has been found during our analysis. It is called *attack* and represents the use of an *attack method* through a *vulnerability*. This concept has no equivalence in the other sources and so we have considered it as non-representative of the domain. It has so been withdrawn from the analysis table.

Table 4.4: Alignment table for security RM methods

Type	Concept	EBIOS	MEHARI	OCTAVE	CRAMM	CORAS
Asset-related concepts	(1)	Asset	Asset	Asset	/	Asset
	(2)	Essential element	Primary asset	/	/	/
	(3)	Entity	Supporting asset	Key component	Asset	/
	(4)	Security criterion	Criterion / Classification criterion	Security requirement	Property	Security property
	(5)	Risk	Risk / Risk scenario	Risk	Risk	Risk
	(6)	Threat	Cause	Area of concern	/	/
Risk-related concepts	(7)	Impact	Consequence	Outcome / Impact	Impact	Unwanted incident
	(8)	/	/	Threat	Threat	Threat scenario
	(9)	Vulnerability	Vulnerability	Vulnerability	Vulnerability	Vulnerability
	(10)	Threat agent	/	Actor	/	Threat
	(11)	Attack method	/	/	/	/
	(12)	/	/	Risk mitigation plan	/	/
Risk treatment-related concepts	(13)	Security objective / Security (functional) requirement	Security service / Security function / Security sub-service / Security measure	/	Countermeasure / Security objective / Security function	Treatment
	(14)	Security measure	Mechanism / Security solution	Protection strategic practice / Countermeasure	Countermeasure / Implementation option / Examples	/

RE security frameworks

Finally, the RE security frameworks (Table 4.5) are compliant with the preceding analysis. At the asset level, the focus is on the business level for Moffet and Nuseibeh and Haley *et al.* [HLMN08, HMLN06a, MHN04] and at the general level for Firesmith [Fir03] and the DITSCAP automation framework [GL07]. *Security concerns* and *quality subfactors* are respectively used in the two former sources to assess the risks. The global cause of risk is not introduced in these sources, but *risk* is already split in three components: *threat* (or *danger*, *hazard* for Firesmith in [Fir03]), *vulnerability* (split in *safety vulnerability* and *security vulnerability* for Firesmith in [Fir03]) and *impact* or *harm* (not mentioned in the DITSCAP automation framework). For the origin of risk, the focus is put on human source in the two former frameworks and the so called *attacker* [HLMN08, HMLN06a, MHN04]. In Haley *et al.*, attacker performs *action*. Finally, these frameworks coming from the RE domain, *security* (and *safety*) *requirements* are at the core of these frameworks [HLMN08, HMLN06a, MHN04, GL07]. Firesmith goes further and explains the relationships between the requirements and what he calls *mechanisms*, *tactics*, *safeguards* or *countermeasures* helping to fulfill the requirements. In the DITSCAP automation framework, the concept of countermeasure is introduced with respect to the CC [Com06a] model.

Discussion about the alignment tables

After identifying the different terms used in each ISSRM source, our assumption that the terminology in the ISSRM domain is not unified has been validated. Many different terms are used to depict the same concept. More than a dozen of different names have been found for some concepts (concept (4), (13), (14), etc.). Sometimes, the same name is used to depict different concepts. For example, a *threat* in EBIOS [DCS04b] is composed of vulnerabilites, while a *threat* in some other sources composes with vulnerabilities a concept of higher level, called *event* [ISO02b, AS/04, ISO04b, etc.], *cause* [CLU07b], *area of concern* [AD01b], etc.

The alignment tables help to connect the different sources with one another. A practitioner can need to combine several methods in a study, in order to enhance his results. He can also need to use some methods in parallel to validate his results. Finally, for compliance purpose, he can use a method for fulfilling the requirements needed by a standard [ISO05b]. In all these cases, to be able to map the concepts of two (or more) approaches is necessary. The alignment tables are an artefact providing this capability.

4.3.4 Extraction of relationships between ISSRM concepts

After identifying and aligning concepts, it is necessary to identify the relationships existing between them. In this section, the literature (Section 4.2) is analysed to extract relationships between the concepts. The process used is similar to the one applied for the elicitation of ISSRM concepts (Section 4.1). Based on the excerpts of sentences used for concepts identification, and sometimes on some complementary information about relationships extracted from the documents, we define relationships between concepts.

Table 4.5: Alignment table for RE security frameworks

Type	Concept	Haley *et al.* Moffet and Nuseibeh		Firesmith	The DITSCAP automation framework
Asset-related concepts	(1)	/		Asset Valuable asset	Asset
	(2)	Asset		/	/
	(3)		/	/	/
	(4)	Security concern		Quality subfactor	/
Risk-related concepts	(5)	Risk		Risk Safety risk Security risk	Risk
	(6)		/	/	/
	(7)	Impact Harm		Harm	/
	(8)	Threat		Danger Hazard Threat	Threat
	(9)	Vulnerability		Safety vulnerability Security vulnerability	Vulnerability
	(10)	Attacker		Attacker	/
	(11)	Action		/	/
Risk treatment-related concepts	(12)		/	/	/
	(13)	Security requirement		Safety requirement Security requirement	Security requirement
	(14)		/	Safety mechanism Safety tactic Safeguard Security mechanism Countermeasure	Countermeasure

Elicitation of the relationship between two concepts

To illustrate the analysis of relationships, we show the definition of relationships between the concept (8) (most often called *threat* in the literature) and (9) (called *vulnerability*). The existence of a relationship between two concepts is not mandatory, but after the analysis of the definitions for the concept alignment (Section 4.3.3), we claim that these two concepts are related to one another.

In RM standards [ISO02b, AS/04], the concept of vulnerability does not exist. No relationship between the two analysed concepts is thus noticed. Regarding security-related standards, *threat* and *vulnerability* are related together in ISO/IEC 13335-1. A claim is found in the definition of *vulnerability*:

> *Vulnerability: a weakness of an asset or group of assets that **can be exploited** by one or more threats.* [ISO04b, p. 3]

However, *threat* in this standard is not equivalent to concept (8) but to concept (11). CC also mentions *vulnerability*, but this concept is not clearly related to the one of threat (cf. Figure A.1).

The relation between the two concepts is clearer in security RM standards. ISO/IEC 27001 and ISO/IEC 27005 relate them together respectively:

> *Identify the vulnerabilities that **might be exploited** by the threats.* [ISO05b, p. 4]

> *Vulnerabilities that **can be exploited** by threats to cause harm to assets or to the organisation should be identified (relates to ISO/IEC 27001, Clause 4.2.1 d) 3)).* [ISO08, p. 12]

In NIST 800-27, it is *threat source* (concept (10)) that is related with vulnerability:

> *IT-related risk / Risk: The net mission/business impact considering (1) the likelihood that a particular threat source **will exploit, or trigger**, a particular information system vulnerability and [...]* [SHF04, p. A-2]

At last for the security RM standards, in the IT-Grundschutz, vulnerability is defined as:

*A vulnerability **can result in the manifestation of** a basic threat [...]* [Bun05b, p. 46]

This last definition is quite different in terms of existing relationship to the ones already collected: it is the only one not mentioning the "exploitation" of vulnerabilities by a threat.

Regarding security RM methods, EBIOS relates *attack* and *vulnerability*:

> *Attack: **Exploiting** one or more vulnerabilities using an attack method with a given opportunity.* [DCS04b, p. 11]

In MEHARI [CLU07b], no equivalence to concept (8) has been identified and moreover, no binary relationship between any risk-related concept and *vulnerability* is found. The same applies for CRAMM [Ins03], in which *threat* and *vulnerability* are only linked by their aggregation in the risk concept (cf. Figure A.2).

OCTAVE proposes a definition for *vulnerability* that reinforces the link mainly identified in security RM standards:

> *Vulnerability: a weakness in an information system, system security practices and procedures, administrative controls, internal controls, implementation, or physical layout that **could be exploited by** a threat to gain unauthorized access to information or disrupt processing. There are two basic types of vulnerabilities (organisational and technology).* [AD01a, p. 126]

In CORAS, *vulnerability* is not related to concept (8), but to *threat* being considered as equivalent to concept (10):

> *A threat **may exploit** a vulnerability and cause an unwanted incident.* [AD01a, p. 313]

In the last family of sources, RE security frameworks, Firesmith relates through his information models [Fir03] (safety and security) vulnerability with danger/hazard/threat (that are considered as equivalent to concept (10)). They may ***exploit*** vulnerability to result in accident/attack. In [MN03], Moffett and Nuseibeh provide the same idea:

> *For each threat, the baseline is analysed in order to identify the vulnerabilities, i.e.* ***the means of***
> ***exploiting*** *a threat successfully.* [MN03, p. 8]

Finally, the link between *threats* and *vulnerabilities* in the conceptual model of DITSCAP automation framework is called **exploit**.

As a conclusion, the final tendency is that the vulnerability is generally *exploited* by one of the following concepts: (8), (10) or (11). Iterative reviews of relationships bring up that concept (10) and (11) are in fact aggregated in concept (8) (cf. Figure 4.4). This explains that they can all be related to vulnerability by an *exploit* relationship, as it is most often the case. Considering this aggregation, the most relevant to us appears to link concept (8) (called *threat* in Figure 4.4) and *vulnerability* with an *exploit* link.

Summary of the relationship elicitation

It is theoretically possible to define the same kind of alignment table for relationships between concepts, as it has been done for concepts (Section 4.3.3). The definition of such a table should indicate the multiplicities of each relationship. However, a first try of such a work [Gen07] highlights some limitations. The set of possible relationships between the concepts is huge. As seen in the preceding section, each source has its own point of view of the relationships existing between the concepts. This point is sometimes reinforced by the difficulty to interpret natural language. It was already a weakness for concept alignment, but even more for relationship elicitation between concepts. The experience [Gen07] has also shown that the utility of such a table is severely limited, because it is really difficult to read (concept alignment is more explicit than relationship alignment). The multiplicity introduction in such an alignment is complex too. The main problem remains the lack of sufficient information available regarding multiplicities. Finally, such a table is not considered as necessary for the definition of relationships. Most of the needed information can be found in the collected definitions, provided in Appendix A. Sometimes, it is necessary to collect some more information (like in Firesmith's information models [Fir03]), but this case remains rare.

In this context, a review of existing relationships has been considered as suited to define the relationships between the concepts of the ISSRM domain model. The review is done by analysing each source one by one and identifying every relationship existing between the concepts of the source. Based on the definitions of the source, every concept is analysed to see if it is linked (and how) with other concepts. The multiplicities are defined too. This review is done iteratively, for each source of the selected literature (cf. Section 4.2).

4.3.5   Conclusion about concept alignment and relationship identification

Regarding the outcome of the identification and the alignment of ISSRM concepts and relationships, this research work provides a bit more formality than the different informal sources studied. For each source, a conceptual model can now be defined based on the identified concepts and relationships. Figure 4.3 shows an example of such a model for ISO/IEC Guide 73. It represents the different concepts involved and relates them by the identified relationships. Appendix C presents the information allowing to define the relationships between the concepts. Since defining a conceptual model for each ISSRM source is neither an objective of our research work, nor a step toward the achievement of our objectives, the models are not built for each sources. However, based on the identified concepts (Section 4.3.3) and their associated relationships (Section 4.3.4), the different conceptual models can easily be built.

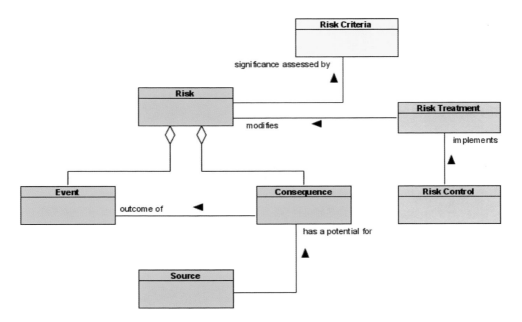

Figure 4.3: Conceptual model of ISO/IEC Guide 73

4.4 ISSRM domain model

Based on the survey performed, the first step of the research method (Figure 4.1) has resulted with the alignment of the ISSRM concepts and the elicitation of their relationships. The second step of the method includes the construction of the ISSRM domain model. It is a conceptual model represented under the form of a UML class diagram [Obj04], composed by the concepts identified and presented in the alignment table (Table B.1). For each of them, a name is chosen, inspired from their name in the literature (Section 4.4.1). A glossary is then provided with the model, giving a definition for each concept of the conceptual model (Section 4.4.2). Finally, the concepts are linked together based on the relationships identified (Section 4.4.3). This domain model is further the syntactic and semantic reference for the assessment of security-oriented modelling languages, with regards to their support of ISSRM (Chapter 6).

4.4.1 Names of the concepts

Each concept is currently represented by a number (and a line) of the alignment table (Table B.1). We now need to define a name for each of these concepts. The proposed names are given in Table 4.6.

The choice of names is based on different criteria. First of all, the number of occurrences of a name for a concept in the different sources is taken into account.

Table 4.6: Name of the concepts included in the ISSRM domain model

Type	Concept	Name
Asset-related concepts	(1)	Asset
	(2)	Business asset
	(3)	IS asset
	(4)	Security criterion
Risk-related concepts	(5)	Risk
	(6)	Event
	(7)	Impact
	(8)	Threat
	(9)	Vulnerability
	(10)	Threat agent
	(11)	Attack method
Risk treatment-related concepts	(12)	Risk treatment
	(13)	Security requirement
	(14)	Control

Then, the terminology coming from ISO standards [ISO02b, ISO05b, ISO08] has been considered as the most important, because it is generally the most accepted and used vocabulary. We have also considered the coming ISO/IEC 2700x series of standards and most specifically the ISO/IEC 27000 standard, bringing out the general tendency in terms of ISSRM terminology. Once published, it will indeed be one of the main reference regarding the domain and also naturally the most recent and up-to-date standard. Finally, when sometimes existing names are considered as insufficiently relevant or improvable, we have proposed original names. However, this case remains rare (concept (2) and (3)).

In the next section, these concepts are ordered and related to one another under the form of a UML class diagram. A precise definition is provided.

4.4.2 Concept definitions

The ISSRM domain model and concept definitions are ordered, as the alignment tables, following the three major groups of concepts: (i) *asset-related concepts*; (ii) *risk-related concepts*; and (iii) *risk treatment-related concepts*. Each concept is illustrated with the help of examples related to the running example (Section 1.6).

Asset-related concepts describe what are the assets important to protect, and what are the criteria to guarantee asset security. The concepts are:

<u>Asset</u> – anything that has value to the organisation and is necessary for achieving its objectives.
Examples: technical plans; project management process; architectural competences; operating system; SPOT software; Ethernet network; people encoding data; system administrator; air conditioning of server room.
NOTE: This concept is the generalisation of the business asset and IS asset concepts.

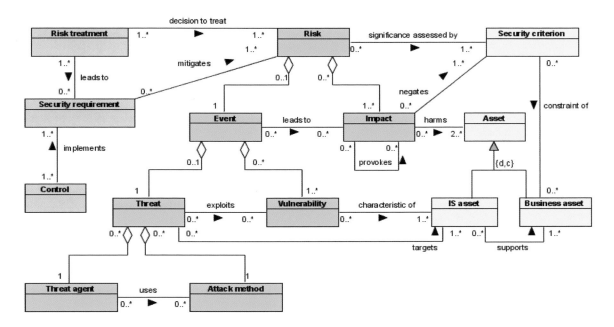

Figure 4.4: The ISSRM domain model

Business asset – information, process, skill inherent to the business of the organisation, that has value to the organisation in terms of its business model and is necessary for achieving its objectives.
Examples: technical plans; structure calculation process; architectural competences.
NOTE: Business assets are immaterial.

IS asset – a component or part of the IS that has value to the organisation and is necessary for achieving its objectives and supporting business assets. An IS asset can be a component of the IT system, like hardware, software or network, but also people or facilities playing a role in the IS and therefore in its security.
Examples: operating system; SPOT software; Ethernet network; people encoding data; system administrator; air conditioning of server room.
NOTE 1: IS assets are (except software) material.
NOTE 2: Sometimes, for conducting a macroscopic analysis, it is relevant to define as an IS asset a system composed of various IS assets, belonging to the other types described above (e.g., a computer (hardware) with its software).

Security criterion (also called security property) – property or constraint on business assets characterising their security needs. Security criteria act as an indicator to assess the significance of risk. Security criteria are most often confidentiality, integrity and availability, but sometimes, depending on the context, some other specific criteria might be added, like authenticity, non-repudiation or accountability.
Examples: confidentiality; integrity; availability.
NOTE: The security objectives of an IS are defined by using security criteria on business assets (e.g., confidentiality of the technical plans; integrity of the structure calculation process).

Risk-related concepts present how the risk itself and its components are defined, what are the major principles that should be taken into account when defining the possible risks. The concepts are:

Risk – the combination of a threat with one or more vulnerabilities leading to a negative impact harming one or more of the assets. Threat and vulnerabilities are part of the risk event and impact is the consequence of the risk.
Examples: a cracker using social engineering on a member of the company, because of weak awareness of the staff, leading to non-authorised access on personal computers and loss of integrity of the structure calculation process; a thief penetrating the company's building because of lack of physical access control, stealing documents containing sensitive information and thereby provoking loss of confidentiality of technical plans.

Impact – the potential negative consequence of a risk that may harm assets of a system or an organisation, when a threat (or an event) is accomplished. The impact can be described at the level of IS asset (data destruction, failure of a component, etc.) or at the level of business assets, where it negates security criteria, like for example: loss of confidentiality of an information, loss of integrity of a process, etc.
Examples: password discovery (IS level); loss of confidentiality of technical plans (business level).
NOTE: An impact can provoke a chain reaction of impacts (or indirect impacts), like for example a loss of confidentiality on sensitive information leads to a loss of customer confidence.

Event – the combination of a threat and one or more vulnerabilities.
Examples: a cracker using social engineering on a member of the company, because of weak awareness of the staff; a thief penetrating the company's building because of lack of physical access control.
NOTE: Event is a generic term, used in every risk management domain, defined as "occurrence of a particular set of circumstances" [ISO02b]. The definition provided in this glossary is specific to IS security.

Vulnerability – characteristic of an IS asset or group of IS assets that can constitute a weakness or a flaw in terms of IS security. It could be accidentally or intentionally exploited by a threat.
Examples: weak awareness of the staff; lack of physical access control; lack of fire detection.

Threat – potential attack or incident, carried out by an agent, that targets one or more IS assets and that may lead to harm to assets. A threat is usually composed of a threat agent and an attack method.
Examples: a cracker using social engineering on a member of the company; a thief penetrating the company's building and stealing media or document.
NOTE: Sometimes, it is more relevant to describe a risk with a global threat, without refining it into threat agent and attack method, like for a flood or a component failure.

Threat agent – an agent that can potentially cause harm to assets of the IS. A threat agent triggers a threat and is thus the source of a risk.
Examples: member of the personnel with little technical ability and time but possibly a strong motivation to carry out an attack; cracker with considerable technical ability, well equipped and strongly motivated by the money he could make.
NOTE: It can be characterised by its type (usually human or natural/environmental) and by the way in which it acts (accidental or deliberate). In the case of an accidental cause, it can also be characterised by exposure and available resources and in the case of a deliberate cause, it can also be characterised by expertise, available resources and motivation.

Attack method – standard means by which a threat agent carries out a threat.
Examples: system intrusion; theft of media or documents.

Risk treatment-related concepts describe what decisions, requirements and controls should be defined and implemented in order to mitigate possible risks. The different risk treatment-related concepts are different levels of design decisions on the IS. The concepts are:

Risk treatment – the decision of how to treat identified risks. A treatment satisfies a security need, expressed in generic and functional terms, and can lead to security requirements. Categories of risk treatment decisions include:

- Avoiding risk (risk avoidance decision) – decision not to become involved in, or to withdraw from, a risk. Functionalities of the IS are modified or discarded for avoiding the risk;

- Reducing risk (risk reduction decision) – action to lessen the probability, negative consequences, or both, associated with a risk. Security requirements are selected for reducing the risk;

- Transferring risk (risk transfer decision) – sharing with another party the burden of loss from a risk. A third party is thus related to the (or part of the) IS, ensuing sometimes some additional security requirements about third parties;

- Retaining risk (risk retention decision) – accepting the burden of loss from a risk. No design decision is necessary in this case.

Examples: do not connect the IS to the Internet (risk avoidance); take measures to avoid network intrusions (risk reduction); take an insurance for covering the loss of service (risk transfer); accept that the service could be unavailable for 1 hour (risk retention).
NOTE: Risk treatment is basically a shortcut for risk treatment decision, according to the state of the art.

Security requirement – a condition over the phenomena of the environment that we wish to make true by installing the IS, in order to mitigate risks.
Examples: appropriate authentication methods shall be used to control access by remote

users; system documentation shall be protected against unauthorised access.
NOTE 1: Risk reduction decisions lead to security requirements. Sometimes, risk transfer decisions need some security requirements about third parties. Avoiding risk and retaining risk do not need any security requirement.
NOTE 2: Each security requirement contributes to cover one or more risk treatments for the target IS.

Control (also called countermeasure or safeguard) – a designed means to improve security, specified by a security requirement, and implemented to comply with it. Security controls can be processes, policies, devices, practices or other actions or components of the IS and its organisation that act to reduce risk.
Examples: firewall; backup procedure; building guard.

4.4.3   Relationships and multiplicities of the ISSRM domain model

In this section, we highlight the relationships between the concepts of the ISSRM domain model (Figure 4.4).

A risk is *composed of* an event and one or more impacts. The same impact can be part of several risks, but an event identifies a given risk. A given event *leads* to zero (if no relevant impact is found; in this case the event does not produce a risk) to several impacts; an impact can be caused by many different events. Sometimes, a relevant impact can be caused by no relevant events of risk and thereby contained in none of the risks. For example, the disclosure of private information about users could be seen as a relevant impact for an organisation, but because of the absence of personal information gathering, no event leading to this impact could be realistic. Moreover, one or several impacts can *provoke* some other (indirect) impacts. For instance, an impact at the IS level of unauthorised access to a database, provokes confidential information disclosure at the business level, leading then to loss of customer confidence and legal penalties. In the context of IS security, the event is *composed of* a threat and one or more vulnerabilities. A given threat can only be related to a given event. The threat *exploits* zero to several vulnerabilities. If a threat is identified, but has no relevant associated vulnerability (e.g., "attack by network" on an offline IS), it will neither be part of an event nor a risk. A given vulnerability can be exploited by many different threats and therefore related to many different events, or be not exploited by any of them, if no relevant threat is found. A threat is *defined* in terms of a threat agent who *uses* an attack method. Each threat agent (respectively attack method) identified as relevant can be involved in several threats, or sometimes in none of them, if no relevant corresponding attack method (respectively threat agent) is found. For example remote spying (attack method) has no relevant corresponding threat agent in the context of a local network neither connected to Internet nor having other external access point. A given threat agent could thus use from zero to several attack methods, and an attack method can be used by zero to several threat agents.

Assets can be *specialised* in two different kinds: business assets and IS assets. The specialisation is disjoint and complete. An IS asset can *support* one or more business assets, but a business asset can have no support in the IS (e.g., the selling skills of the sales department are an asset of the company, but they are not part of the IS).

However, a usual situation is that a business asset is supported by several IS assets. A vulnerability is a *characteristic of* an IS asset or group of IS assets, and an IS asset can have from zero to several vulnerabilities (an IS asset can potentially always include a vulnerability, but at the level of a study, some IS assets can be considered as exempt from vulnerability). A threat *targets* one or more IS assets and an IS asset can be targeted by zero to several threats. The IS asset targeted by a threat is not necessarily the same as the one linked to the vulnerability exploited by this threat. For example, a vulnerability of employees who are not enough security-aware can allow a threat on a server. Each business asset can be *constrained* from zero (e.g., if the business asset has no support in the IS) to several security criteria. A security criterion can constrain several different business assets, or not constrain any of them. Impacts *harm* assets, at the business and also at the IS level. An asset can be harmed by zero (if no impact is considered as relevant) or several impacts, and an impact harms at least an IS asset and a business asset, but more than two assets are often harmed by an impact. At the level of business assets, an impact *negates* one or more security criteria, and a given security criteria can be negated by zero (if no relevant impact is concerned by this security criterion) or several impacts. One or several security criteria can be taken into account to *assess the significance* of a risk, but a security criterion can be concerned by none of the risks, in the case where there is no relevant impact for this criterion.

A risk treatment expresses the *decision to treat* one or more risk. Each identified risk has a risk treatment (even if the decision is to accept the risk) and sometimes several of them can be combined (they are not mutually exclusive). Risk treatments *lead to* one or more security requirements. However, the risk treatments of acceptance and avoidance lead to no security requirement. Each security requirement comes from one or many risk treatments. A security requirement *mitigates* one or more risks; a given risk can well not be mitigated by any security requirement (for example, when the risk is accepted), or mitigated by several of them, if they are necessary to reach an acceptable level of risk. Finally, a control *implements* one or more security requirements, and the same security requirement may be implemented by one or several control(s).

4.4.4 Validation of the ISSRM domain model

The validation of the domain model was performed through expert review, that led to iterations of the research method depicted in Figure 4.1, and incremental improvements of the domain model. The validation was already carried out by practitioners, scientists and standardisation experts. Three practitioners, three scientists and two standardisation experts were involved in this review. Each review was performed in a face to face workshop with the expert. They challenged the domain model with regards to their view of ISSRM and their knowledge of the ISSRM sources. First, the context of the project and the research method were presented to them. Second, the domain model was presented and explained. The evaluation was then based on open discussions and questions about the domain model. The discussions and questions were not based on a template, but focused on the issues highlighted by each reviewer. All of their comments were analysed and discussed together based on the information collected in the glossaries of Appendix A. The process ended once a consensus was reached on the domain model. The time spent for each interview was different from one person to the other, ranging from half an hour to several hours of presentation and discussion, stretching over several days by mail. The main comments of the reviewers were that 1) the research method is reliable and 2) the domain model is easy to validate, because of the glossaries and the alignment tables. From this validation, we did not have to reconsider the concepts and their relationships, but only their names, their definitions and the multiplicities.

The validation was completed by the application of the domain model on the assessment of a real IS, in the frame of an ISO/IEC 27001 certification [ISO05b]. This assessment is reported in Chapter 7. The domain model was used in this frame to introduce the ISSRM to the employees of the company. It was the central artefact to catch the different concepts taking place in the different steps of the performed approach. Despite most of the employees did not have any IS security background, they learned quickly the different concepts. Moreover, to present and explain the different concepts with the help of a model, instead of only text in natural language, was considered by them as efficient. By the way, the company has kept the domain model, to integrate it in their security training they should provide to every new employee, as required by the certification.

Finally, the domain model was used with master students, in order to teach them the ISSRM domain. The process of learning was faster and easier with the domain model, compared to the experience of preceding years where the lecture was based on methods and documents in natural language. The conceptual model helps to have an exhaustive view of the domain and to catch quickly the concepts.

The validation performed has some limits. First, eight experts were involved in the expert review. This only represents a limited set of advices on the domain model and the conclusions can therefore not be generalized. Moreover, expert review is subjective, dependent on her experience, knowledge, etc. Regarding the application of the domain model to the assessment of a real IS, this experiment was performed in the context of an ISO/IEC 27001 certification and with the guidance of the developers of the domain model. These limitations are further explained in Section 7.6. Finally, no fixed conclusion can be drawn from the use of the domain model with the students. Regarding future work, a controlled experiment is currently built with the aim of further validating the domain model with master students. The controlled experiment will consist in comparing the effort needed and the success obtained in understanding the domain by two groups of students, one having to learn the domain through the domain model, and the other through documents in natural language.

4.5   Conclusions about the ISSRM domain model

This section highlights the benefits and the limitations of the ISSRM domain model.

4.5.1   Benefits of the domain model

The ISSRM domain model provides several benefits for different users: for ISSRM practitioners, for researchers, or for both of them.

General/terminological level

The ISSRM domain model contributes to establish a standard terminology for the ISSRM community. As shown in Section 2.4.1, there are several efforts run by standardisation bodies, but today they are still work in progress. Our work has raised the interest of the national body of Luxembourg and has actually been selected as a reference for the review of the coming ISO/IEC 27000 standard, about the fundamentals and vocabulary of ISMS. It has also been considered in the revision of the EBIOS method [DCS04b].

ISSRM approaches are also increasingly introduced and learnt in different academic and professional curricula. Due to the absence of a global terminology, each teacher has to reinvent her/his own or use a specific one. As a consequence, we observed that students, when they become risk managers, experience communication problems when discussing about risk-related concepts. We think that the results of our research can help in a desired harmonisation at this level.

Finally, some approaches, like SQUARE [MHI05, MS05], require as a preliminary work to define the terminology to be used. The domain model provides such a terminology.

Practitioner level

Although we have constructed the ISSRM domain model based on the existing literature on RM and security frameworks, the developed model can serve as the guidelines to investigate new emerging references, e.g., a new method or standard. The ISSRM domain model might suggest the contextual information, which should be screened in the new sources. Further, the ISSRM domain model itself might evolve when new important sources are determined. In this case, a new iteration of the research method (Figure 4.1) should be performed, taking the new source into account.

However, the multitude of existing ISSRM methods leads often to confusion concerning their scope and their strengths. They have generally a different coverage of the RM process, as discussed in Section 2.6, and thus of the underlying concepts. The alignment tables provided in Section 4.3.3 help us to provide interoperability between the different sources. It shows the equivalence of concepts between sources. The definition of the ISSRM domain model with its associated glossary is one step further toward interoperability between ISSRM sources. It could be used as the common reference between several sources, with a traceability provided by the alignment table between the ISSRM domain model and the sources.

Research level

We hope that the proposed ISSRM domain model can help the scientific community to better understand the scope of ISSRM and therefore achieve a better integration of security risk-related concepts in security-oriented modelling languages. Also, in case where several languages are put together in order to cover the IS lifecycle, the domain model can be used as the basis for the traceability framework that will support the mapping between the different models produced (as, for example, the traceability needed between a business and an IS model).

Moreover, the ISSRM domain model is used as an input to Chapter 6 for the assessment of security-oriented modelling languages. The ISSRM domain model serves as guidelines to find out about the support for ISSRM provided by the existing security-oriented modelling languages [MMM+08, MMH08]. In Chapter 6, we will illustrate this comparison between the ISSRM domain model and the following security-oriented modelling languages: KAOS extended to security [vL04], Misuse cases [SO05] and Secure Tropos [MGMP02].

4.5.2 Limitations of the domain model

Successful experiences have been reported in using formal and ontology-based approaches to define and compare the semantics of modelling constructs [MHO07, HST+07, SHTB07, SHTB06]. In the current context and based on the feedback of these experiences, we have decided to first follow an approach based on conceptual models, natural language descriptions and common sense to analyse ISSRM sources. The reasons are the following:

- the analysed sources are neither simple, nor already sufficiently formalised (in the sense of what is discussed in [HR04]), to let us apply a formal comparative semantics method in a realistic timeframe;

- similarly, the core concepts of the ISSRM domain can realistically be formalised as a conceptual model complemented with natural language definitions. However, further formalisation of semantics [HR04], although eventually desirable (cf. Chapter 6), has been currently deemed too risky. Indeed, complete semantics would require a significant effort that might just be a waste of time, regarding our objectives, if consensus on the partial formalisation is not reached first;

- automated semantic similarity analysis (see e.g., [RB01]) pays off when domains are too complex to be handled by domain experts or the amount of information to be compared is unmanageable by humans. We do not meet these conditions here.

Regarding the construction of a domain model, several techniques are proposed in software product lines and feature-oriented system development. These techniques are generally the domain analysis part of domain engineering. Domain analysis should specify the basic elements of the domain, organise an understanding of the relationships among these elements, and represent this understanding in a useful way [RBSS05]. In this context, we find approaches like FODA (Feature-Oriented Domain Analysis) [KCH+90], DARE (Domain Analysis and Reuse Environment) [FDF98] or ADOM (Application-based Domain Modeling) [RBSS05]. Although we are not directly using these techniques (our objective is not to develop product lines), the method we used for defining the ISSRM domain model is actually compliant with these approaches. In particular, we have produced the three main artefacts required for domain analysis: a domain definition, a domain lexicon and a concept model.

As discussed in Section 4.4.4, the validation can still be improved. Although our validation through expert review and teaching results observation has some limitations, it has been assessed as the most efficient and relevant regarding our objectives (Section

1.1). The validation by other experts is still open. Moreover, an experiment is currently built, to assess with students the efficiency of the domain model for teaching purpose.

4.6 Chapter summary

In this chapter, the ISSRM domain model was defined, composed of a conceptual model, represented under the form of a UML class diagram, and the definitions of its different concepts and relationships.

First, a research method was presented, which aimed at defining in a structured way the domain model. This research method relied on a survey of the ISSRM literature. The application of the first step of the research method leaded to an ISSRM concept alignment. Definitions of terms, as found in the sources studied, were collected, and an alignment table was built, indicating synonymy or semantic similarity when approaches use different terms. Once concepts were identified, relationships between the concepts are also elicited in the same manner. The ISSRM domain model was then build, first by assigning a name to each concept, and second by defining each concept and each relationship. The chapter ended by conclusions and limitations of the domain model.

This chapter was focussed on definition and identification of concepts and relationships pertaining to ISSRM, as made clear in Section 4.3.2. However, estimation and evaluation are also at the core of ISSRM approaches. The topic of the next chapter is therefore to improve the domain model with various metrics commonly used in security risk estimation and evaluation, and often found in the literature, like the risk level or the event likelihood.

Chapter 5

Definition of the Information System Security Risk Management Metrics

$\mathbf{I}$n the preceding chapter, we have defined the ISSRM domain model, through a conceptual model and an associated glossary. The conceptual model is represented under the form of a UML class diagram, composed of a set of classes (the concepts of the ISSRM domain) and their relationships. However, no attributes (or properties) of these classes have currently been defined [Pen03]. By the way, a core of our concerns is to link business security needs and security measures applied on the IS. ISSRM approaches are usually considered as a tool for managing this business/IT (or IS) alignment [SGF02]. To help in this alignment, a core part of ISSRM approaches is risk measurement, coming with an evaluation of the different concepts of ISSRM. In the literature, different sets of metrics are proposed in the existing approaches [ISO08, DCS04b, CLU07b, AD01b, Ins03]. However, they are generally different with one another. Moreover, they are difficult to catch by the users, because presented within a documentation in natural language. The objective of this chapter is to add to the domain model, as its attributes, the metrics of ISSRM.

It is generally agreed that the two main factors of ISSRM, with respect to the business/IS security alignment, are the security level and the value of the assets, as shown, for example, in the definition extracted from the CISA Review Manual [ISA06]: "*Risk management is the process of identifying vulnerabilities and threats to the information resources used by an organisation in achieving business objectives, and deciding what countermeasures, if any, to take in reducing risk to an acceptable level, based on the value of the information resource to the organisation.*" We therefore aim to improve and automate ISSRM for reaching the best Return On Security Investment (ROSI). The underlying research question addressed here is: *what are the metrics relevant to perform ISSRM and to reason about ROSI?* The domain model improved with metrics is, first, a guideline helping anyone to understand which concepts need to be measured in ISSRM, and using which metric. As for ISSRM concepts, the introduction of a model to present the different metrics will improve the documentation generally provided in the literature, and will help to catch the different metrics. Second, anyone wanting to define his/her own set of concrete metrics in order to include in his/her method or tool can use the domain model as a guideline to do so. It is necessary to notice that, at this time, we do not want to define directly a new concrete risk assessment framework with precise metrics, as done in existing ISSRM methods [DCS04b, CLU07b, AD01b, Ins03]. Our objective is limited to the identification of what are, at the abstract level, the relevant metrics for ISSRM. This is mainly motivated by the fact that each user may still want to choose his/her own concrete approach for risk estimation, as depicted in the next section, adapted to his/her organisation and its context.

First, Section 5.1 describes the research method in order to define the ISSRM metrics. Then, Section 5.2 introduces the different concepts and methods used within this chapter. It presents the risk estimation, the Goal-Question-Metric (GQM) approach and the ROSI concept. Section 5.3 and Section 5.4 are the application of the two steps of the research method, respectively for what we call metrics elicitation and metrics validation. Finally, Section 5.5 presents the improvement of our domain model with the metrics. The paper ends with conclusion and future work in Section 5.6.

5.1   Research method

To achieve the objective of defining relevant ISSRM metrics, we propose a research method based on a combination of approaches (Figure 5.1). The outcome of this research method is the introduction of ISSRM metrics as attributes to the ISSRM conceptual model, coming with their explanation .

The first approach, used during Step 1 of the research method, is the GQM paradigm [BCR94]. This approach is used for eliciting metrics in a top-down manner, from general objectives to achieve, to suited metrics to be used for achieving the objectives. Thus, the benefit of using GQM is that we focus on the main objectives of ISSRM to define the metrics. GQM is applied on the ISSRM domain. Therefore, the domain model presented in Section 4.4 is an input for this step. The application results in GQM models, leading to the set of ISSRM metrics. However, this elicitation work remains subjective and potentially incomplete.

The second approach, used as a validation[1]/improvement of the first step, and appearing in Step 2 of the research method, is based on a survey of ISSRM standards and methods. This approach is bottom-up, being an analysis of existing ISSRM sources to identify the metrics currently used. The sources are all those surveyed in Chapter 4 (cf. Section 4.2) that contain a process description and perform concept measurement. Sources dealing only with vocabulary are not considered here. We first gather and summarise the steps related to measurement. In general, this task is not only done by copying a set of sentences from the source document. It is sometimes necessary to rephrase and clarify what are the measured concepts, and what are the associated metrics, for having a relevant information. We thus obtain an overview of the underlying estimation process of each studied ISSRM source. The outcomes of this step, for each source, are a) the set of its metrics, b) an analysis table of the metrics c) some conclusions for the source with regards to our final set of metrics. The set of metrics identified for each source are presented as attributes of the ISSRM conceptual model, for clarity and comparison purpose. Then, we compare the metrics of the studied source to those defined through GQM. This comparison is summarised

---

[1]The term 'validation' may appear to be used improperly, because real validation generally implies direct empirical evidence. In our case, evidence is only gathered through the literature, which is assumed to reflect current practice.

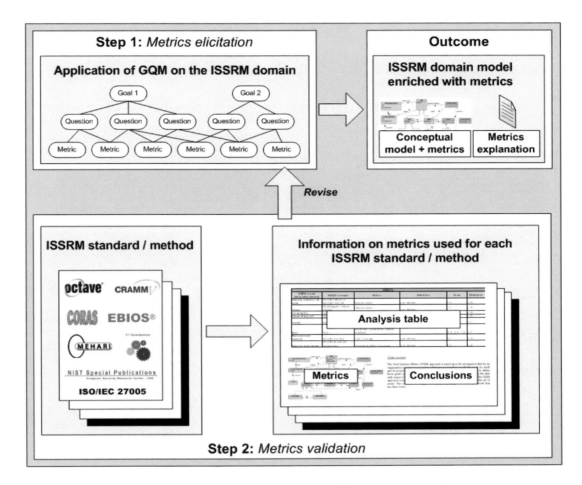

Figure 5.1: Research method for the ISSRM metrics elicitation

in an analysis table. This table recalls the measured concepts of the source and the associated metrics. They are aligned with the concepts of the ISSRM domain model and the metrics obtained during the GQM study. If a metric not identified with the GQM framework is found, it is necessary to evaluate its relevance. Sometimes, it can highlight a deficiency in the GQM study, and thus the GQM models are reviewed and improved considering this new issue, or a justification for the exclusion of the metric shall be given. Conclusions about the metrics of the source and their difference with regards to our metrics are finally provided. The tasks composing Step 2 of the research method are performed iteratively for every selected source of the literature.

Once the literature is completely surveyed, leading to the GQM models in their last version, the final set of metrics is introduced in the ISSRM domain model as attributes of the classes. Some complementary explanations are also provided, proposing definitions for each metric, and an example of their use is proposed.

5.2 Theory

In this section, we introduce some theoretical concepts and methods used in this chapter. First, risk estimation is presented, showing the different categories of risk estimation in ISSRM. Second, the GQM approach, used in Step 1 of the research method, is introduced. Finally, the ROSI notion is explained, in the aim of identifying the underlying objectives to be used for the application of GQM on the ISSRM domain.

5.2.1 Introduction to risk estimation

As discussed in Section 2.1, risk analysis consists in identifying and estimating the different risk components. Regarding risk estimation, various approaches exist [ISO08, AS/04]. The same approaches are adopted for measuring the asset- and risk treatment-related concepts. They can be classified in the following categories: qualitative, quantitative, or a combination of both, commonly called semi-quantitative estimation:

- **Qualitative risk estimation**
  Qualitative risk estimation approaches are currently the most widespread in the industry [ENI06, DCS04b, CLU07b, AD01b]. They propose a scale of levels for qualitatively describing the concepts to measure. These scales are *ordinal* scales [FP97]. An advantage of qualitative estimation is its ease of understanding by the staff involved in the estimation task, while a disadvantage is the dependence on the subjective choice of the scale [ISO08]. Examples of qualitative scales, for a financial cost or an unavailability length, are shown in Table 5.1.

Table 5.1: Examples of qualitative scales

Level	Financial cost	Unavailability length
1	Low	Short
2	Moderate	Moderate
3	Important	Long
4	Very important	Very long

- **Quantitative risk estimation**
  Quantitative risk management approaches propose to 'precisely' measure each concept of ISSRM. By 'precisely', we mean through *ratio* or *absolute* scales[2] in terms of the scales provided in [FP97]. The quality of estimation depends on the accuracy and completeness of the numerical measures and the validity of the used models [ISO08]. For example, a financial cost will be estimated in terms of € [Ins03] or an unavailability length will be reported in hours, as depicted in Table 5.2. Most often, historical incident data of an organisation or of a sector, like provided by the CERT[3], is used to provide quantitative indications. Naturally, an advantage of such an approach is its accuracy, but its cost and the lack of useful data are the main disadvantages [ISO08].

- **Semi-quantitative risk estimation**
  In semi-quantitative estimations, *ordinal* scales are also given to estimate concepts, but based this time on quantitative values. In other words, a quantitative

---

[2]No examples of *interval* scales have been found for the ISSRM domain, but they may theoretically be relevant quantitative scales.
[3]http://www.cert.org/cert/

Table 5.2: Examples of quantitative scales

Financial cost	Unavailability length
Amount of money in €	Length in hours

scale is reduced to a discrete scale, to become an *ordinal* scale [FP97]. The objective is naturally to produce in a cost-effective manner more precise results than those obtained by qualitative approaches. However, the estimation remains naturally less accurate than quantitative estimation. A particular care should be given to the definition of the scales, to keep relevance in the equivalent levels and to obtain useful information about the relative criticality of the studied concepts. Examples of semi-quantitative scales are proposed in Table 5.3.

Table 5.3: Examples of semi-quantitative scales

Level	Financial cost	Unavailability length
1	Loss < 1000$	Unavailability > 1 week
2	1000$ < Loss < 5000$	1 day < Unavailability < 1 week
3	5000$ < Loss < 10000$	1 day < Unavailability < 1 hour
4	Loss > 10000$	Unavailability < 1 hour

In a given method, existing or defined by an user, the different approaches can be mixed, depending on the concepts analysed and the objective to be reached. For example, qualitative estimation could be first used to obtain a coarse grained estimation of risks, and later, a quantitative estimation could provide further information on major identified risks. Finally, it is interesting to note that some approaches focus on concept identification, whereas they provide very few guidelines for risk estimation all along their process [Bun05c, AD01b]. These approaches are more directing towards reaching a 'reasonable' security level and a complete identification, understanding, and coverage of risks.

Regarding the preceding approaches, it is also important to distinguish the scope of the metrics we identify. In our context, a metric indicates the magnitude of a concept, according to a given dimension (security, cost, etc.), as appears in the definition proposed in [ISO05a]. A metric should thus be differentiated from what we call indicators, which in our context, are "variables that can be set to a prescribed state based on the results of a process or the occurrence of a specified condition" [ISO05a]. The main difference between a metric and an indicator is that the first one is ordered and the second one not. Indicators are based on *nominal* scales [FP97], proposing a non-ordered classification scheme. An indicator is something that gives information about a particular situation, but does not estimate the magnitude of a concept (e.g., Is the motivation of an attacker based on the financial interest or on the challenging aspect? Is the attack method accidental or intentional?). In our context, indicators generally help to estimate the different metrics.

5.2.2 The GQM approach

GQM's basic idea is deriving metrics from measurement questions and goals. The GQM method was originated by V.Basili and D.Weis, as a result of both practical experience and academic research [SB99]. By now, it is widely used in a number of contexts, like in the aeronautics or telephony industry [BCR94, Kil01].

In the GQM approach, measurement is defined in a top-down fashion [BCR94]. GQM is based upon the assumption that, for an organisation to measure in an efficient way, it must specify the goals for itself and its projects first, then it must trace those goals to the data intended to operationalise them. Finally, it must provide a framework for interpreting the data with respect to the stated goals [BCR94]. The result of the application of the GQM approach is the definition of the measurement system targeting a particular set of issues. The outcome is a GQM model that has three levels:

1. Conceptual level, called GOAL level: A goal is defined for an object (like a product, a process or a resource).

2. Operational level, called QUESTION level: A set of questions is used to characterize the way the assessment/achievement of a specific goal is going to be performed.

3. Quantitative level, called METRIC level: A set of data is associated with every question in order to answer it in a quantitative way.

Therefore, a GQM model is a hierarchical structure (Figure 5.2) starting with a goal. The goal is refined into several questions. Each question is then refined into metrics. The same metric can be used in order to answer different questions. More information about GQM can be found in [BCR94, GC87].

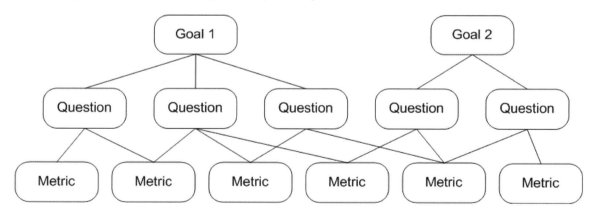

Figure 5.2: Example of GQM model (extracted from [BCR94])

5.2.3 The ROSI concept

The main outcome of the ISSRM process, and one of the main motivations, is to obtain the best ROSI [ISA06, SGF02]. CLUSIF proposes a state of the art around the notion of ROSI [CLU04b]. There is no clear consensus about the definition of ROSI, but two proposals are the most used. The first one relates security costs to the expected benefits [CLU04b, SAS05]:

$$ROSI = \frac{Expected\ Returns - Cost\ of\ Investments}{Cost\ of\ Investments} \qquad (1)$$

The second proposal is focused on incidents and calculates the ROSI with the help of the notion of ALE (Annual Loss Expectancy) [CLU04b, Mic04]. ALE expresses the monetary loss that can be expected for an asset due to security incidents (designated by i in the following equation) over a one year period:

$$ALE = \sum Costs_i * Frequency_i$$

$$ROSI = ALE1 - ALE2 - CS \qquad (2)$$

With:

     ALE1 = ALE before security solutions
     ALE 2 = ALE after security solutions
     CS = Cost of Security solutions

These two definitions differ on two points:

(a) Definition (2) fixes the time period for the calculatin of ROSI to 1 year, while definition (1) can be used on any period of time, to be defined by the user.

(b) Definition (1) involves *expected returns* while definition (2) involves the *loss expectancy* before and after security solutions.

Therefore, if we want to compare both definitions, we first need to fix the time period. We propose to bind definition (1) to a 1 year period, to be compliant with definition (2). Second, *expected returns* of definition (1) may be defined, over a given time period, in terms of a difference of loss. The expected returns are in fact the loss expectancy before security solution minus the loss expectancy after security solution. Over a 1 year period, definition (1) is in fact equivalent to:

$$ROSI = \frac{ALE1 - ALE2 - Cost\ of\ Investments}{Cost\ of\ Investments} \qquad (1')$$

As a conclusion, both definitions are proportional, differentiating by a coefficient $\frac{1}{Cost\ of\ Investments}$ (or $\frac{1}{Cost\ of\ Security\ solutions}$).

5.3 Application of the GQM framework on the ISSRM domain

As discussed in Section 5.2.3, whichever definition of ROSI is chosen, to reach the best ROSI (which is the highest value of ROSI) means to:

1. Maximise the difference between the loss expectancy before security solution and the loss expectancy after security solution;

2. Minimise the cost of investment.

Coming back to the ISSRM domain, the difference between the loss expectancies is related to the *risk* reduction while the cost of investment is related to the *risk treatment* cost (including the concepts of risk treatment, security requirement and control). This assumption thus provides two objectives for the GQM study, which are respectively the two roots of the GQM models (Figure 5.3 and 5.4):

1. Maximise the risk reduction

2. Minimise the risk treatment cost

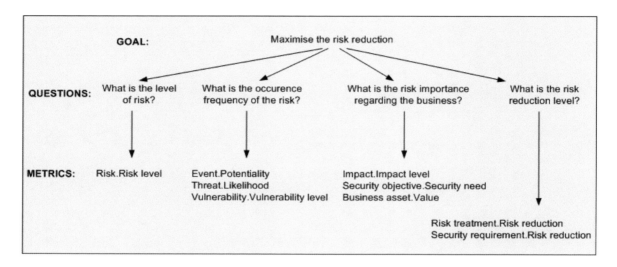

Figure 5.3: GQM model for the first goal

With regards to the concepts of the ISSRM domain model, to maximise the risk reduction involves first knowing *what is the level of risk*, depending on its *occurrence frequency* and its *importance regarding the business*. Second, it is necessary to know *what is the risk reduction level*. From these questions and based on the set of ISSRM concepts (Figure 4.4), related metrics are proposed. All of the elicited metrics are represented in the GQM model (Figure 5.3), at the metric level, with the following notation: "Class of the ISSRM model.Metric". The first metric is the *Risk level* and is naturally associated with the concept of risk. Occurrence frequency of risk is depicted in the causal part of risk in the domain model. It is summarised in the *Potentiality* metric of the event concept, depending on the *Likelihood* of threat and *Vulnerability level* of vulnerability. The risk importance is depicted in the consequence part of risk, represented by the concept of impact. The *Impact level* is the metric measuring the importance of impact. The risk importance is also related to the intrinsic *Value* of business assets. To correctly describe the risk importance, a new concept, motivated by the need of a metric, is introduced in the domain model. This concept is "Security objective". It expresses the application of a security criterion on a business asset. For example, the confidentiality of technical plans or the integrity of the structure calculation process are security objectives. This concept is needed because, to completely describe the risk importance, it is necessary to estimate the *Security need* associated to each security objective. This metric is a key indicator to estimate the real impact on the organisation and thus the risk importance regarding the business. Finally, regarding risk reduction, *Risk reduction level* shall be estimated for each risk treatment and each security requirement. The control concept cannot be estimated in terms of risk reduction. The explanation is obvious when illustrated with an example. Let us consider that the security requirement "Perform network filtering" is implemented by the controls "Firewall" (the IT element) and "Perform firewall maintenance". It is not possible to allocate a risk reduction level to the control "Perform firewall maintenance" taken alone. The risk reduction estimation is only viable on risk treatment and security requirement.

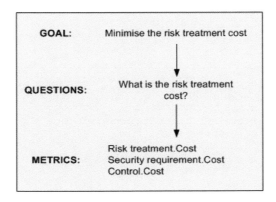

Figure 5.4: GQM model for the second goal

The second goal of minimising the risk treatment[4] cost involves less concepts and thus less questions. Only one related question is necessary: *what is the risk treatment cost?* Regarding the associated metrics, we know from the domain model that three risk treatment-related concepts are involved. A *Cost* metric is thus proposed for each of them to know their respective cost (Fig. 5.4).

It is necessary to note that, for clarity purpose, the GQM models presented in Figure 5.3 and 5.4 are those obtained after the last iteration of Step 2 (Figure 5.1). They thus represent the final set of metrics. Further explanations about each metric is provided in Section 5.5.

5.4 Survey of ISSRM methods for metrics validation

The sources surveyed for the metrics validation are all ISSRM sources containing a process description. RM standards [ISO02b, AS/04], security standards [ISO04b, Com06a] and RE security frameworks [Fir03, HLMN08] are therefore not studied in this part,

---

[4]Here, it is necessary to distinguish the elicited concept of *Risk treatment*, depicting the choice among one of the four risk treatment proposals (Section 4.4), and the risk treatment in its general sense, as it should be understood in this question, covering the entire set of risk treatment-related concepts of the ISSRM domain model.

because mainly focused on the terminological and conceptual aspects of ISSRM. Instead, we retain security RM standards [ISO08, SGF02, Bun05c] and security RM methods [DCS04b, CLU07b, AD01b, Ins03, VML+07]. Study of each such source results first in the metric-related elements gathered in the source. Then, (1) the metric analysis table, (2) the ISSRM domain model enriched with the metrics proposed following the source, and (3) some conclusions regarding its compliance with the GQM study (Section 5.3) are provided.

5.4.1 Security RM standards

The three security RM standards studied are: ISO/IEC 27005 [ISO08], NIST 800-30 [SGF02] and the IT Grundschutz [Bun05c]. We first present the artefacts produced for ISO/IEC 27005. For the other two standards, only the metric analysis tables and the conclusions are presented. Their respective metric-related steps and the enriched ISSRM domain model are provided in Appendix D.

ISO/IEC 27005

As depicted in the research method (Section 5.1), we first gather all metrics used throughout the standard [ISO08]. The steps of the standard involving concept measurement are described below. The following conventions are used: *metrics* are in italic and **associated concepts** in bold. The page number of the standard, providing information about the metric, is mentioned for traceability purpose.

- Assign *values* to the **assets** under review. [ISO08, p. 15]

- Express the *business impact value* for the **consequence**. [ISO08, p. 15]

- Assess the *likelihood* of the incident scenarios, or **event**. [ISO08, p. 15]

- Take into account *how often* the **threats** *occur*. [ISO08, p. 15]

- Take into account *how easily* the **vulnerabilities** may be *exploited*. [ISO08, p. 15]

- Estimate *how effectively* **controls** reduce vulnerabilities. [ISO08, p. 16]

- Estimate the *level* of **risk**, which is a combination of the likelihood of an incident and its consequence. [ISO08, p. 16]

The various metrics used are analysed in a table. The two first columns are for the concepts of the ISSRM domain model and the concepts of the studied approach. This alignment is a reminder of the one of Table B.1 in Appendix B. The concepts are ordered by category, respectively standing in the asset-, risk- and risk treatment-related categories. The categories are delimited by a double line in the table. The two following columns depict the associated metric(s) of the studied approach, as called in the approach, and the associated metric(s) of the ISSRM domain model. Next, a "Definition" column indicates how this metric is defined or calculated. For example, if a level has only to be chosen by the user in a scale, this column indicates "User defined" for this metric. At the opposite, if the metric depends, to be calculated, on other metrics or on some tools (matrix, software tools), this is mentioned in this column. Finally, the last column is the "Unit" column. If the metric is quantitative, its unit is displayed (e.g., €, hours, etc.). Otherwise, the proposed scale is reported.

The only asset-related concept measured in ISO/IEC 27005 is the concept of asset (in general) (Table 5.4). The related metric is the *value* of assets. Primary asset and supporting asset, being specialisations of asset in general, are also measured with this metric. Then, the *business impact value* associated to each asset is estimated, based on the *value* of the asset. Risk estimation is based on the successive considerations of threat and vulnerability, leading to event *likelihood*. Combining it with the *business impact value*, it is possible to estimate the *risk level*. Finally, controls from ISO/IEC 27005, which can be aligned with both security requirement and control from our domain model, are estimated according to their *effectiveness*, mainly in reducing vulnerabilities. The standard, as opposed to most of the methods, only provides a general guideline to ISSRM. As a consequence, it is generally up to the user to define if the concepts are qualitatively or quantitatively estimated (cf. "Unit" and "Definition" column).

Table 5.4: Metrics analysis table for ISO/IEC 27005

ISO/IEC 27005 [ISO08]					
ISSRM concept	**ISO/IEC 27005 concept**	**ISO/IEC 27005 metric**	**ISSRM metric**	**Definition**	**Unit**
Asset	Asset	Value	/	User defined	User defined
Business asset	Primary asset	Value	Value	User defined	User defined
IS asset	Supporting asset	Value	/	User defined	User defined
Risk	Risk	Risk level	Risk level	f(Event,Consequence)	User defined
Event	Event	Likelihood	Potentiality	f(Threat,Vulnerability)	User defined
Impact	Consequence	Business impact value	Impact level	f(Asset)	User defined
Threat	Threat	Frequency of occurrence	Likelihood	User defined	User defined
Vulnerability	Vulnerability	Easiness of exploitation	Vulnerability level	User defined	User defined
Security requirement Control	Control	Effectiveness	Risk reduction	User defined	User defined

In ISO/IEC 27005, as said above, the value of asset in general is estimated for asset-related concepts. In the GQM study (and after the complete review of the ISSRM sources), the focus is rather put on the value of business assets, which is more relevant. IS assets being only the support of business assets, it is worth to consider the value of only business assets. Moreover, in IS security, the value of IS assets (e.g., the replacement cost of a computer) is generally considered as negligible compared to the value of the processed information at the business level (e.g., the client information, the estimates, etc.). Finally, it is necessary to consider the value of business assets for estimating the security objectives and assess the significance of risks, as depicted in the ISSRM domain model (cf. Figure 4.4). IS assets are not involved in this process. For risk-related concepts, the metrics are very close to those proposed in Section 5.3. Risk, event, consequence, threat and vulnerability of ISO/IEC 27005 have all an associated metric. Moreover, ISO/IEC 27005 proposes additional characteristics for threat source (equivalent to threat agent in the ISSRM model). For example, it is possible to define the motivation, the capabilities and the resources available of a threat source for a deliberate threat, or some factors that could influence the threat source in the case the threat is accidental. However, such characteristics are not included in the metric analysis table, because they are indicators helping to define frequency of occurrence and the risk level in general, rather than metrics themselves (cf. Section 5.2.1. For the risk-treatment related concepts, the effectiveness of controls is estimated, which has the same objective as risk reduction of security requirements in the ISSRM domain model. The concept of risk treatment is not estimated in terms of effectiveness. Finally, the cost dimension is not needed to be measured in ISO/IEC 27005.

Figure 5.5 summarises the metrics proposal of ISO/IEC 27005 from the point of view of the ISSRM domain model. The reader should note the introduction of the *Security objective* class, compared to the preceding domain model of Figure 4.4.

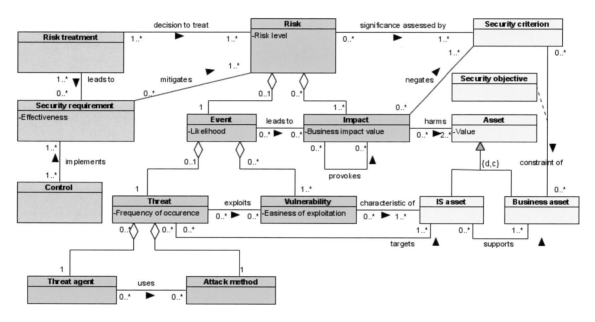

Figure 5.5: ISSRM domain model enriched with the metrics proposed by ISO/IEC 27005

NIST 800-30

Estimation in NIST 800-30 focuses on the concept of risk (Table 5.5). First, the user defines the *likelihood* of the threat and then the *magnitude* of impact. Based on these two estimations, the *risk level* is defined with the help of a matrix. NIST 800-30 proposes three-level qualitative scales for each metric: High, Medium, Low.

The metrics proposed by NIST 800-30 (or semantically-equivalent metrics) have all already been identified with the GQM approach.

The IT-Grundschutz

For this standard, we study the third part entitled "*Risk analysis based on IT-Grundschutz*" [Bun05c]. Although the name of the document mentions "risk analysis", the scope of the standard is RM, going from asset identification to control selection, as described in Section 2.1.

Table 5.5: Metrics analysis table for NIST 800-30

NIST 800-30 [SGF02]					
ISSRM concept	**NIST 800-30 concept**	**NIST 800-30 metric**	**ISSRM metric**	**Definition**	**Unit**
Risk	Risk	Risk level	Risk level	Defined with a risk-level matrix	High, Medium, Low
Event	Threat (vulnerability exercised by a given threat-source)	Likelihood	Potentiality	User defined	High, Medium, Low
Impact	Impact	Magnitude	Impact level	User defined	High, Medium, Low

The part of the IT-Grundschutz dealing with risk analysis, like the part called "Methodology", is mainly devoted to binary checks of adequate protection provided by (implemented or envisaged) security measures. The concepts are not valued qualitatively[5] or quantitatively. The only exception is the security requirement concept, which is estimated at the beginning of the process on the scale normal/high/very high, in the aim of identifying the assets that need a higher level of security (Table 5.6).

When applying GQM, we also propose to estimate the security need of security objectives, which are equivalent to the security requirements in the IT-Grundschutz.

Table 5.6: Metrics analysis table for the IT-Grundschutz

The IT-Grundschutz [Bun05c]					
ISSRM concept	**IT-Grundschutz concept**	**IT-Grundschutz metric**	**ISSRM metric**	**Definition**	**Unit**
Security objective	Security requirement	Security requirement level	Security need	User defined	Normal, High, Very high

5.4.2 Security RM methods

There are five security RM methods studied: EBIOS [DCS04b], MEHARI [CLU07b], OCTAVE [AD01b], CRAMM [Ins03] and CORAS [VML+07]. As for security RM standards, first we present all artefacts produced for EBIOS. The metric analysis table and the conclusions are then presented for the other methods, their measurement-related steps and their enriched ISSRM domain model being proposed in Appendix D.

EBIOS

The measurement-related steps of the EBIOS method are:

- Define *security needs* of **essential elements** with **security criteria** constraining them. [DCS04b, p. 24]

- Define *attack potential* of relevant **threat agents** combined with **attack methods**. [DCS04b, p. 26]

---

[5]The binary check can in a sense be seen as a special case of qualitative estimation. However it is not standing in 'traditional' qualitative estimation, like the other presented standards and methods.

- Define the *level* of **vulnerabilities** associated to selected threat agents. [DCS04b, p. 28]

- Define the **threat** *opportunity* based on the level of associated vulnerabilities or directly. [DCS04b, p. 29]

- Define the **impacts** of the risks equal to the maximum of the *security needs concerned.* [DCS04b, p. 31]

- Define the risk **level**, composed by the *opportunity*, the *attack potential* and the maximum of the *security needs concerned.* [DCS04b, p. 31]

- Define risk *coverage* by selected **security objectives**. [DCS04b, p. 34]

- Define security objectives *coverage* by selected **security requirements**. [DCS04b, p. 40]

Table 5.7 summarises the different concepts measured and their associated metrics. EBIOS starts by asking the user to value the *security needs* of essential elements for each security criterion. Then, the risk level is defined incrementally. First, the *attack potential* is defined , characterising a threat agent using an attack method. Second, the *opportunity* of the threats is estimated, based on the *vulnerabilities level*. Third, the impact is defined, being equivalent to the maximum of elicited *security needs* for the assets concerned by the impact. The level of risk is defined as the set of the three previous metrics. As for ISO/IEC 27005 [ISO08], EBIOS proposes to identify some characteristics of threat agents and attack methods, like motivation or type. Regarding risk-treatment related concepts, security objectives are estimated in terms of their *risk coverage*. Then, security requirements are estimated in terms of their *security objective coverage*. The various concepts in EBIOS are estimated by qualitative values. Table 5.7 recapitulates these scales, which the method recommends to adapt depending on the context.

Table 5.7: Metrics analysis table for EBIOS

EBIOS [DCS04b]					
ISSRM concept	**EBIOS concept**	**EBIOS metric**	**ISSRM metric**	**Definition**	**Unit**
Security objective	Security criterion on Essential element	Security need	Security need	User defined	0-4
Risk	Risk	{Security needs concerned ; Opportunity ; Attack potential}	Risk level	/	{0-4 ; 0-4 ; 1-3}
Event	Threat	Opportunity	Potentiality	f(Vulnerability level)	0-4
Impact	Impact	Security needs concerned	Impact level	max(Security needs) for each Business asset	0-4
Threat	Threat agent and Attack method	Attack potential	Likelihood	User defined	1-3
Vulnerability	Vulnerability	Vulnerability level	Vulnerability level	User defined	0-4
Security requirement	Security objective	(risk) Coverage	/	User defined	0-2
Security requirement	Security (functional) requirement	(security objective) Coverage	/	User defined	0-2

The set of metrics proposed by EBIOS is close to the one defined in the GQM study. At the level of asset- and risk-related concepts, we do not notice any important difference compared to the metrics of the GQM models. Only some minor differences are observed. For example, the risk metric is decomposed into three metrics (security needs concerned, opportunity and attack potential) instead of a single element (risk level). Another example is that the value of the business assets is not estimated in the aim of defining the security needs. Security needs are directly defined by the user. The main difference resides at the level of risk treatment-related concepts. EBIOS proposes a metric for assessing the coverage of risk by security objectives and another one for the coverage of security objectives by security requirements. This can be explained by the main objective of the EBIOS method, which rather than reaching the best ROSI, is to cover the identified risks completely. These two metrics do not represent first class metrics regarding our objectives and are therefore not included in our set of metrics represented in the GQM models. However, they remain relevant and potentially implementable, mainly as additional information showing that no risk has been forgotten. Moreover, these two metrics can help in the implementation of the risk reduction, because they indicate the current state of considered risk (treated or not) at any time. Figure 5.6 summarises the metrics proposal of EBIOS from the viewpoint of the ISSRM domain model.

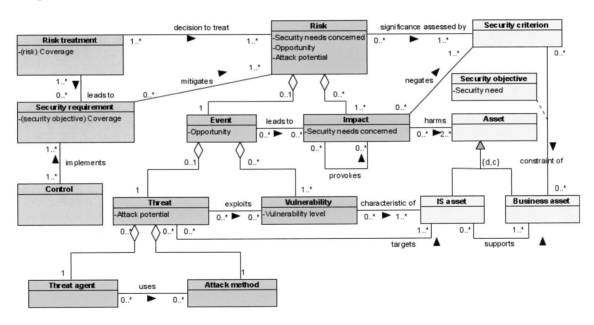

Figure 5.6: ISSRM domain model enriched with the metrics proposed by EBIOS

MEHARI

First, MEHARI defines the *classification value* of each asset for each classification criterion on a proposed scale from 1 to 4 (Table 5.8). The second step is the estimation, based on various criteria, of the *quality* of each implemented security service. This quality level helps for the determination of the (so called) *seriousness* of the risk and its components. Based on this quality level, the user of the method estimates various factors playing a role in the risk measurement. First, factors related to the cause of the risk are estimated. The factors (so called) are *natural exposure to risk*, *effectiveness of dissuasive measures* and *effectiveness of preventive measures*. Then, with the help of these factors, the *potentiality* of the cause of the risk is estimated. Second, factors related to the consequence of the risk are estimated. They include the so called *effectiveness of protective or confinement measures*, *effectiveness of palliative measures*, *effectiveness of recuperative measures*. They are used as a mitigator of the estimated *intrinsic impact* (i.e. impact without any measure) to determine the real *impact*. Finally, the seriousness of the risk is deduced based on the potentiality metric of the cause and on the impact metric of the consequence.

Table 5.8: Metrics analysis table for MEHARI

MEHARI [CLU07b]					
ISSRM concept	**MEHARI concept**	**MEHARI metric**	**ISSRM metric**	**Definition**	**Unit**
Security objective	Classification criterion on Asset	Classification value	Security need	User defined	1-4
Risk	Risk	Seriousness	Risk level	Seriousness = f(Potentiality, Impact) defined with tables	Tolerable risk, Inadmissible risk, Unsupportable risk
Event	Cause	Potentiality	Potentiality	Potentiality=f(Natural exposure to risk, Effectiveness of dissuasive measures, Effectiveness of preventive measures) defined directly or with tables	1-4
Impact	Consequence	Intrinsic impact	Impact level	Intrinsic impact=classification value	1-4
Impact	Consequence	Impact	Impact level	Impact=f(Intrinsic impact, Effectiveness of protective or confinement measures, Effectiveness of palliative measures, Effectiveness of recuperative measures) defined directly or with tables	1-4
Security requirement	Security service	Quality	/	Questionnaire or user defined with guidelines, f(efficiency, robustness, permanency)	1-4
Security requirement	Security measure	Effectiveness of dissuasive measures	Risk reduction	f(quality security service) with tool or user defined	1-4
Security requirement	Security measure	Effectiveness of preventive measures	Risk reduction	f(quality security service) with tool or user defined	1-4
Security requirement	Security measure	Effectiveness of protective or confinement measures	Risk reduction	f(quality security service) with tool or user defined	1-4
Security requirement	Security measure	Effectiveness of palliative measures	Risk reduction	f(quality security service) with tool or user defined	1-4
Security requirement	Security measure	Effectiveness of recuperative measures	Risk reduction	f(quality security service) with tool or user defined	1-4
/	/	Natural exposure to risk	/	f(quality security service) with tool or user defined	1-4

As already seen in other ISSRM standards and methods like [DCS04b, Bun05c], at the asset-related concepts level, the security need is directly estimated. It is the only asset-related concept estimated. For risk-related concepts, our set of metrics does not take into account such precise factors mitigating the risk level. MEHARI is designed to assess a running IS. In this case, defining risk mitigating factors coming from already implemented security measures is suited. In our case, our set of metrics should be usable for existing IS assessment, but also for IS in development. We, thus, do not propose to use pre-defined mitigating factors. Instead, the risk reduction metric used once a risk treatment and/or a security requirement is defined plays the role of risk mitigator. First, it is more generic, so the user can determine himself how he will use this metric. Second, in the case of IS assessment based on our ISSRM model, the risk reduction metrics can be used in the same way as the mitigating factors of MEHARI. It is also necessary to note that the metric of natural exposure to risk is not associated to any concept of the ISSRM domain. It is indeed related to the context of the organisation defined during the first step of the ISSRM process (Figure 2.1). Quality of security services has also no direct semantically equivalent concept, but regarding the set of metrics of Figure 5.3, it is directly dependent on the total risk reduction of each security requirement.

OCTAVE

Like the IT-Grundschutz [Bun05c], OCTAVE is poor in terms of estimation (Table 5.9). The method proposes to estimate the impact of the risk on a qualitative scale. This estimation provides information supporting risk ranking and countermeasures prioritisation.

As already mentioned, the impact level is taken into account in the GQM set of metrics.

Table 5.9: Metrics analysis table for OCTAVE

OCTAVE [AD01b]					
ISSRM concept	OCTAVE concept	OCTAVE metric	ISSRM metric	Definition	Unit
Impact	Impact	Impact level	Impact level	User defined	High, Medium, Low

CRAMM

CRAMM is one of the few methods suggesting quantitative estimation (Table 5.10). For example, the *severity* of impacts is estimated on a scale from 1 to 10, but their *cost* in financial figures. Then, the *value* of assets is determined based on both previous metrics. For threat and vulnerability, CRAMM proposes a qualitative estimation based on pre-defined scales. The *measure of risk* is further defined with the help of a matrix combining *asset value*, *threat level* and *vulnerability level*. Based on the different risks levels obtained, the method proposes suited countermeasures, each having its own *security level*. Their *priority* is finally assessed with the help of various factors, determining the theoretical implementation rank of each countermeasure. Some of them are the *cost* of the countermeasure and its *effectiveness*.

Compared to the set of metrics elicited with GQM in Section 5.3, the metrics of CRAMM are all covered by equivalent metrics, except for security level, effectiveness and priority, that are associated to the security requirement concept. For the two

Table 5.10: Metrics analysis table for CRAMM

CRAMM [Ins03]					
ISSRM concept	**CRAMM concept**	**CRAMM metric**	**ISSRM metric**	**Definition**	**Unit**
IS asset	Asset	Value	Value	f(Severity, Cost)	1-10; $
Risk	Risk	Measure of risk	Risk level	Measure of risk=f(Threat level, Vulnerability level, Asset value) using risk matrix	1-7
Impact	Impact	Severity	Impact level	User defined	1-10
Impact	Impact	Cost	Impact level	User defined (only for Unavailability and Physical Destruction impacts)	$
Threat	Threat	Threat level	Likelihood	User directly defined or with the help of a questionnaire	Very Low, Low, Medium, High, Very High
Vulnerability	Vulnerability	Vulnerability level	Vulnerability level	User directly defined or with the help of a questionnaire	Low, Medium, High
Security requirement Control	Countermeasures	Security level	/	Provided in the countermeasure library	1-7
Security requirement Control	Countermeasures	Priority	/	Priority=f(cost, effectiveness, various characteristics)	*Rank*
Security requirement Control	Countermeasures	Cost	Cost	Provided by tool	Low, Medium, High
Security requirement Control	Countermeasures	Effectiveness	/	Provided by tool	Low, Medium, High

first, they are close to, and redundant with, the risk reduction. Instead of measuring an intrinsic effectiveness leading to a security level, we estimate the risk reduction level that is more explicit considering our objective of maximising risk reduction. Regarding the priority of security requirement, it is not mandatory regarding the ROSI optimisation. However, it is sometimes interesting, like for defining a risk treatment plan [ISO05b], to schedule the control implementation.

CORAS

Table 5.11: Metrics analysis table for CORAS

CORAS [VML+07]					
ISSRM concept	**CORAS concept**	**CORAS metric**	**ISSRM metric**	**Definition**	**Unit**
Asset	Asset	Asset value	Value	User defined	Very low, Low, Medium, High, Very high
Risk	Risk	Likelihood	Potentiality	User defined	Rare, Unlikely, Possible, Likely, Certain
Risk	Risk	Consequence	Impact level	User defined	Insignifiant, Minor, Moderate, Major, Catastrophic
Risk	Risk	Risk level	Risk level	Defined with tables	Low, Moderate, Major, Extreme
Security requirement	Treatment	Risk reduction	Risk reduction	User defined	{Low, Mod., Maj., Ext.} => {Low, Mod., Maj., Ext.}
Security requirement	Treatment	Cost	Cost	User defined	Low, Medium, High

The first concept estimated in CORAS is the asset one through the *asset value* (Table 5.11). It is estimated on a qualitative scale having five levels. *Risk level* is then defined, based on its *likelihood* and *consequence* estimation (qualitative scale with five levels too). Finally, for treatments, their *risk reduction* (showing the final risk level compared to the initial risk level, e.g., a major risk becomes moderate) and their *cost* are estimated.

Compared to our set of metrics, the set of CORAS is included and well suited, mainly at the level of risk treatment-related concepts, where it also considers both the risk reduction and the cost of security requirements. No metric not having a semantically equivalent one in our set of metrics (presented in the GQM models of Section 5.3) is identified.

5.5 Enrichment of the ISSRM domain model with metrics

Elicitation (Section 5.3) and validation (Section 5.4) of the metrics result in the enrichment of the ISSRM domain model, by completing it with the ISSRM metrics. The metrics are reported in the domain model under the form of class attributes, as already done for each studied standard and method in the preceding section. The resulting ISSRM domain model is presented in Figure 5.7.

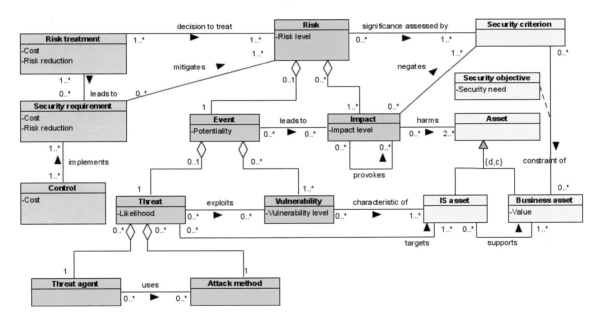

Figure 5.7: ISSRM domain model enriched with metrics

The first modification of the ISSRM domain model is the introduction of a new concept, necessary to the metric of *security need*. This concept is security objective and it represents the application of a security criterion on a business asset. For example, the confidentiality of the technical plans or the integrity of the structure calculation process are security objectives of the running example. The *security need* metric expresses the importance level of the security objective concept. It is also interesting to determine the *value* of business assets. Only business assets are estimated in terms of *value*. First, business assets are involved to define and estimate security objectives and to assess the significance of risks (Figure 4.4). IS assets are only the support of business assets and are not involved in this process. Moreover, the value of IS asset (e.g., the replacement value of a computer) is generally considered as negligible compared to the value of the information supported (e.g., the client information, the estimates, etc.). Finally, the same IS asset may support different business assets, having different *values* and different associated *security needs*. For example, a server can support two different processes, or store both public and private information. The *value* of business assets is used as input to estimate the *security need* of each business asset, e.g., in terms of confidentiality, integrity and availability. An asset with a great value may generally have a greater security need than an asset with a low value in the business of the organisation. For example, new technical plans are estimated to have a greater value than the file of clients of the organisation. Both need to be confidential. As a consequence, the security objective "confidentiality of new technical plans" has a greater security need than "confidentiality of the file of clients".

Example: The process of technical plans design has been identified as a business asset. Its value is considered as very high, regarding the context of @rchimed. Now the security need of this asset is estimated for each selected security criterion. On a scale from 1 to 4, its confidentiality is estimated as 4, its integrity as 2 and its availability as 2. Not to disclose confidential plans to competitors is seen as major, compared respectively to the integrity of plans and their availability, that can be both recovered in our context. However, although they are less important, they are also to be considered.

For risk-related concepts, risk is estimated by its level. The *risk level* depends on the event *potentiality* and the *impact level*, these two concepts composing the one of risk. Event is composed of threat and vulnerability. Their respective levels are estimated through *likelihood* and *vulnerability level*. It is necessary to note that threat agent and attack method do not have their own metric representing their level. Only their composition is estimated and this assumption has been confirmed during metrics validation. Some characteristics of threat agents and attack methods can be identified independently, like the motivation and the competence of the threat agent or the kind of attack method (natural, human, etc.), as seen, for example, in ISO/IEC 27005 [ISO08] and EBIOS [DCS04b]. However, they can be used as indicators to well estimate the risk-related concepts and mainly the *likelihood* of a threat.

Example: A thief can penetrate the organisation's building, in the aim to steal a copy of some technical plans. Regarding the context (motivation of plans theft, exposition of the building, etc.), the likelihood of such a threat is estimated as 2 on a scale going from 1 to 3, i.e., this threat can happen sometimes[6]. A set of vulnerabilities is highlighted, regarding this threat, like the lack of physical access control. The total vulnerability level is estimated at 2 on a scale from 0 to 3, i.e. the vulnerability is high because no effective measure is in place. Based on these two levels, the potentiality of the event is estimated at 3 on a scale from 0 to 5. The impact coming from this event, directly related to the security objective of confidentiality of technical plans, has a level of 4. Finally the risk level is estimated at 12, based on the potentiality of the event and the impact level.

In risk treatment-related concepts, risk treatment and security requirements are estimated in terms of *risk reduction* performed and in terms of *cost* incurred. As

---

[6]Every level of the qualitative scales are not described here, the objective of this example being only to show an instance of each metric on our running example. The reader wanting to see a complete description of what can be concrete scales shall refer to Chapter 7 about an experiment report.

discussed in Section 5.3, controls can be only estimated in terms of *cost* (cost of buying a firewall, cost of maintaining it by a security officer, etc.). The *risk reduction* of some controls taken alone has no sense. For example, the *risk reduction* of the security officer maintaining the firewall can not be estimated alone, without considering the global effectiveness of the firewall (described at the security requirement level by, e.g., "Perform network filtering"). To come back to the *risk reduction* metric, it applies obviously for the risk reduction treatment but also to the other risk treatment decisions, except for risk avoidance (Section 2.1). First, if the risk is transferred, a residual risk, that is the *risk level* remaining after its treatment, can remain. This leads to a *risk reduction* level of the risk transfer treatment and of the associated requirements. For risk acceptance, the risk reduction is equal to 0, the risk being accepted as is. Finally, for risk avoidance, the risk is withdrawn (except maybe for traceability purpose) and so the *risk reduction* metric can no more apply. It is necessary to note that the *risk reduction* and *cost* metrics are not directly derived one from the others. One can think that the *cost* of a risk treatment is the total *cost* of the related security requirements, and analogously that the *cost* of a security requirement is equal to the total *cost* of the related controls. However, as seen in the domain model, a security requirement can be used in several risk treatments. For example, a security requirement like "Access to information by users shall be restricted according to the access control policy" can be used to reduce a risk involving a threat agent external to the company and a risk involving an employee of the company. The same applies for controls, that can be used to implement several security requirements. For example, a firewall can provide data filtering and access control capabilities, and thus implement several security requirements. Defining such a function, relating the *cost* of risk treatment to the *cost* of security requirements, and the *cost* of security requirements to the *cost* of controls, is not the topic of this chapter. Each user defining his/her own set of concrete metric, will define his/her function relating the different risk treatment-related metrics. For example, if the *cost* is estimated quantitatively, the *cost* of a security requirement composed of two controls could be the sum of the *cost* of the two controls. At the opposite, if the *cost* is estimated on the qualitative scale low/medium/high, and if the two controls have a medium *cost*, the security requirement *cost* could be medium. The same reasoning applies for the *risk reduction* metric.

Example: The decision of reducing the risk by some controls is chosen. The security requirement "Secure areas shall be protected by appropriate entry controls to ensure that only authorized personnel are allowed access" is selected and implemented through doors equipped with detectors, each employee having his own access badge. The total cost of the controls implemented and so of the security requirement is 8000$. The risk treatment needing only this requirement, the total risk treatment cost is also of 8000$. Regarding the risk reduction, for both the security requirement and the risk treatment, it has the level of 8, because the new risk level, reviewed considering the new vulnerability level defined now to 0, is 4.

5.6   Conclusion of the ISSRM metric elicitation

The objective of this chapter is to identify and define a set of metrics for the ISSRM domain, with a systematic and scientific approach. The research method we defined provides this capability through the combination of two complementary approaches. First, the GQM approach is used to elicit the different metrics through a focus on the objectives of the ISSRM domain, i.e. reaching the best ROSI. Then, a review of the metrics proposed in the literature helps to be exhaustive in our metric elicitation, with regards to what is currently used in security RM standards and methods.

It is necessary to note that this set of metrics is proposed at an abstract level. The metrics can be implemented differently within a method (qualitatively, quantitatively, etc.), or through several metrics, depending on the aim of the method. For example, the *likelihood* metric of a threat can be implemented through several attributes of the threat class, the first one being the statistic probability of occurrence of natural threats (in %) and the second one being based on a qualitative level evaluation of human threats. Before implementing these metrics in a method or a tool, it is necessary to think about the best way of using them, depending on the objective and the granularity level wanted. Therefore, this set of metrics has to be considered with an implementation variability.

Although the elicited metrics are validated through literature analysis, their testing in a real case would provide a concrete instantiation and validation of their relevance. Chapter 7 is about the feedback of their use in an organisation in the frame of an ISO/IEC 27001 certification, where ISSRM is at the core of the standard. A concrete instantiation of these metrics is proposed and a feedback is given with regards to their use.

5.7   Chapter summary

In this chapter, the ISSRM domain model was completed by the metrics used in ISSRM, in order to reach the best ROSI. They were represented through attributes of the conceptual model and defined through a glossary.

A research method was first presented, in order to define the metrics. Then, a section dedicated to the theory of the different concepts and techniques used in this chapter was proposed. It presented an introduction of the risk estimation, an overview of the GQM method and a definition of the ROSI concept. The research method relied on two steps, which were then performed through the rest of the chapter. The first one was the application of the GQM method on the ISSRM domain model. This method produced as output the set of metrics needed to perform ISSRM and reach the best ROSI. The second step of the research method was the validation of the GQM study performed during the first step. This validation relied on a survey of the literature, focussed on the standards and methods allowing concept measurement. For each approach, its ISSRM metrics were identified. The GQM study was thus reviewed iteratively, based on the results obtained for each approach surveyed. Finally, the domain model was enriched by the final set of metrics, defined through the application of the research method. Some conclusions ended this chapter.

After defining the ISSRM domain model and its metrics, the objective is now to compare it with the existing security-oriented modelling languages. The topic of the next chapter is the assessment of the support of each security-oriented modelling languages, with regards to the concepts of the ISSRM domain model.

Chapter 6

Assessment of ISSRM Support by Security-oriented Modelling Languages

T he aim of this section is to confront security-oriented modelling languages of Section 3.2 with the ISSRM domain model. Those languages are Misuse cases [SO05], Abuse case [MF99], Mal-activity diagrams [Sin07], Abuse frames [LNI+03b, LNIJ04, LNI+03a], KAOS extended to security (KeS) [vL04], the Tropos Goal-Risk framework [AG06] and Secure Tropos [MG09, MGMP02, GMZ05]. Our objective is to improve them to support the ISSRM activities, as depicted in Section 2.1. The research question of this chapter is thus: *what is the ISSRM support provided by security-oriented modelling languages and how it can be improved?* The main expected results of this chapter are:

- the validation of the claim that the studied languages overlook RM,

- the assessment of the coverage that each modelling language has with respect to ISSRM concepts;

- the identification of the improvements (extensions/revisions) to be made to the languages to make them suitable for ISSRM.

Although we acknowledge that security and risk are crosscutting concerns that should also be dealt with at all stages of IS development, we recall that our scope is limited to ISSRM during early RE (Section 1.2). Hence, we are not considering languages such as UMLsec [Jö2] or SecureUML [LBD02], which are languages used later in the lifecycle, after the scope of the future system has been clarified. Moreover, in the frame of this thesis, we only give details about the evaluation of KeS, Misuse cases and Secure-Tropos. The complete assessment of Abuse case, Abuse frames, Mal-activity diagrams and Tropos Goal-Risk framework remains future work. Furthermore, Secure Tropos is the only language for which we provide improvements.

Section 6.1 explains the research method applied for language assessment. It is used from Section 6.2 to 6.4, to report the assessment of Misuse cases, KeS and Secure Tropos. Section 6.5 summarises the results and discussions of the assessment of languages. Then, a Risk-aware Secure Tropos is presented in Section 6.6. Finally, conclusions of this chapter are given in Section 6.7.

6.1 Research method

The outcome of a language assessment is the concept alignment between the security-oriented modelling language and the ISSRM domain model, showing the concept coverage of ISSRM by the language (Figure 6.1). Our approach is based on the definition of the language, composed of the language meta-model and the textual documentation of the language in the literature. The ISSRM domain model is used as a reference for the language comparison.

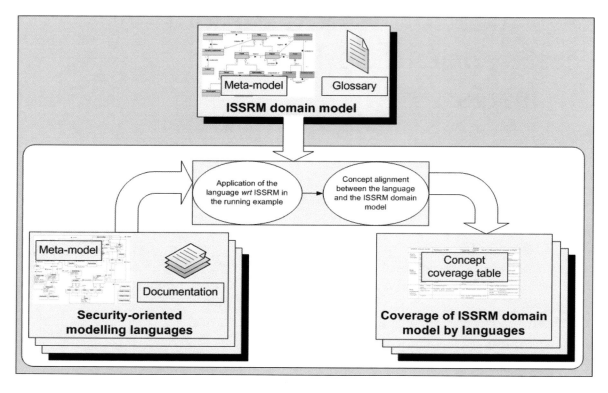

Figure 6.1: Research method applied for the assessment of ISSRM support by security modelling languages

For each language, we use the running example to explain the alignment of the language with regards to the ISSRM domain model. The running example is initially used to illustrate the use of the language for addressing the security risks, during early IS development. It follows the ISSRM steps presented in Section 2.1. We then consider how the concepts of the language are used to address ISSRM. The alignment is performed by focusing on concepts definition and relationships between them. This step is performed incrementally, by iterative analysis of the textual document(s) and the meta-model. The artefact produced is a table, highlighting the lack in each existing modelling languages to support ISSRM. In this table, for each ISSRM concept, we gather the *synonyms* found in the literature of the language. Then, we identify what is the *modelling construct* (coming from the meta-model of the security-oriented language) used for representing this concept. Finally, the last column illustrates the constructs with some *examples* extracted from the running example.

The reader should note that this alignment does not represent an equivalence between the language concept and the ISSRM concept. We highlight only the support provided by the language to model ISSRM. At the opposite, no information is given about how a concept of a language is mapped/represented in the ISSRM domain model. For example, Section 6.2 shows that, in Misuse cases, an *actor* can be used to represent an ISSRM *threat agent*. It does not mean that the concept of *actor* is strictly equivalent to the concept of *threat agent*: *actors* can also represent regular agents performing a task in the organisation, like an engineer or a drawer in the running example.

6.2 Assessment of ISSRM support by Misuse cases

The assessment of ISSRM support by Misuse cases is done by analysing the Misuse cases meta-model [SO05] and textual explanations provided in the associated literature [SO00, SO01, SOB02, SFO03, SO05]. First, an illustration of the use of Misuse cases for supporting the ISSRM steps is proposed. Then, the constructs of the language are semantically aligned with the ISSRM domain model. Finally, a discussion is provided with regards to this alignment.

6.2.1 Modelling ISSRM with Misuse cases

In this section, we illustrate with the running example how Misuse cases can be used for security RM. Our application follows the steps of the ISSRM process described in Section 2.1. We adapt the example of Section 3.2.2 and exploit the concepts of Misuses case, which are presented in the same section.

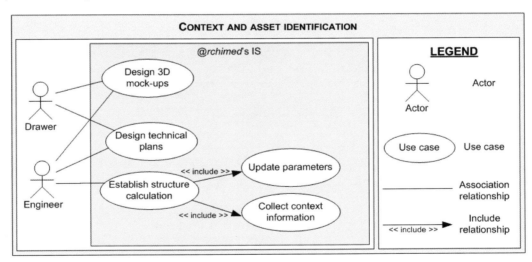

Figure 6.2: Asset modelling in Misuse cases

- ***Context and asset identification.*** In Figure 6.2, a use case diagram for the @rchimed's IS is presented. We focus on the actors `Drawer` and `Engineer`, who communicate with `@rchimed's IS`. `Engineer` is involved in `Establish structure calculation` and both actors in `Design 3D mock-ups` and `Design technical plans`. `Establish structure calculation` includes two use cases: `Update parameters` and `Collect context information`.

- **Determination of security objectives.** Determination of security objectives is not supported by Misuse cases, because no suited construct is proposed. In our example, we concentrate on the integrity of structure calculation, meaning that once the structure calculation is done, it cannot be changed by unauthorised people.

- **Risk analysis and assessment.** In Figure 6.3, we identify misuse cases, which involve the misuser `Crook`. The `Crook` threatens the integrity of `Establish structure calculation` with the misuse case `Steal login information`. This misuse case includes another misuse case, which describes certain steps in more details: `Use social engineering`. In Figure 6.4, we illustrate the misuse case `Steal login information` with an extensive template.

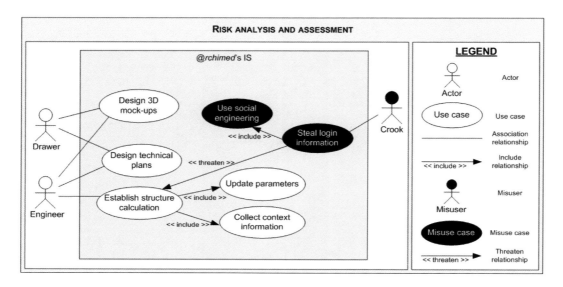

Figure 6.3: Risk modelling in Misuse cases

- **Risk treatment.** Misuse cases do not suggest any risk treatment. Following the general ISSRM process, we apply risk reduction by introducing security use cases.

- **Security requirements definition.** The use case `Perform awareness training` (cf. Figure 6.5) is the security use case, which mitigates the identified misuse case `Use social engineering`. It is part of the use case `Establish a security training plan` initiated by the `Security officer`. The template for `Steal login information` (cf. Figure 6.4) gives more details about this security use case.

- **Control selection and implementation.** Misuse cases do not suggest any technique to select and implement controls. Thus, one needs to resort to other means to select between alternative controls.

Name:	Steal login information
Summary:	A crook steals some login information allowing him to access to internal applications
Basic path:	**bp1**: Crook calls an employee by phone
	bp2: Crook introduces as someone else
	bp3: Crook uses social engineering techniques for asking login information
	bp4: Employee discloses his personal login information
	bp5: Crook logs into the system
Mitigation points:	**mp1**: Employees are aware of security and know the social engineering techniques
Extension points:	**ext1**: Includes misuse case "Use social engineering"
Trigger:	Always true, this can happen at any time
Assumption:	**as1**: No fingerprint logon is used
Preconditions:	**pc1**: The crook is able to find employees phone numbers, either because they are publicly available, or because an accomplice can provide them to him
Worst case threat:	Someone unauthorised modifies structure calculation
Mitigation guarantee:	The employees never disclose their personal login information (see mp1)
Related business rules:	Only authorised people should be able to connect to internal applications
Misuser profile:	Skilled. Knowledge of social engineering techniques.
Stakeholder and risks:	**Engineer**: Structure calculations modified, leading to waste of time by establishing the calculations again.
	Client: Loss of reputation and danger for human life if not detected.
Scope:	Entire business
Abstraction level:	Misuser goal
Precision level:	Focussed

Figure 6.4: Example of the misuse cases template

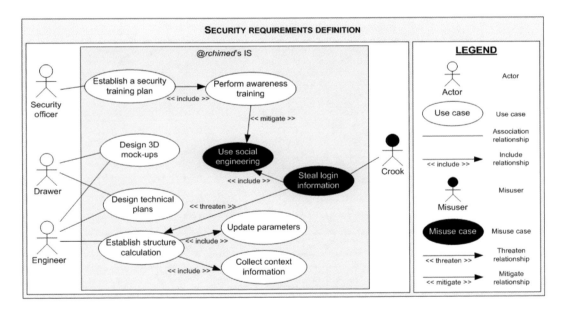

Figure 6.5: Security requirements modelling in Misuse cases

6.2.2   Alignment of Misuse cases with ISSRM domain model

In this section, we analyse how Misuse cases constructs are interpreted with respect to the ISSRM concepts. Figure 6.6 suggests an alignment between the ISSRM domain model and Misuse cases. Both Misuse cases diagram and Misuse cases template are analysed.

ISSRM domain model		Misuse cases			
		Synonyms	Misuse case diagram	Elements of the example	Misuse case template
Asset-related concepts	Asset	Vulnerable asset, critical asset, materials, information, (virtual) location, (computerised) activities, knowledge and skills of workers	Actor and use case	-	-
	Business asset	Business use case		Design technical plans, Establish structure calculation	Related business rules
	IS asset	-		Update parameters, Collect context information	-
	Security criteria	Security goal, type of security breach	-	-	-
Risk-related concepts	Risk	Risk of various threats	-	-	Stakeholders and risks
	Impact	Cost of the damage, cost of potential losses	-	-	Worst case threat
	Event	-	-	-	-
	Threat	Security threat	Misuser and misuse case	Crook and Steal login information	-
	Vulnerability	-	-	-	Assumption, precondition, trigger
	Threat agent	-	Misuser	Crook	Misuser profile
	Attack method	Action sequence, sequence of both action and interaction, step	Misuse case	Steal login information, Use social engineering	Basic path, alternative path, extension points
Risk treatment-related concepts	Risk treatment	-	-	-	-
	Security requirements	Security use case, security requirement, countermeasure	Use case	Perform awareness training	Mitigation points
	Control	-	-	-	-

Figure 6.6: Concept alignment between Misuse cases and the ISSRM domain model

Asset-related concepts

Some of the most important assets in the organisation are identified as the knowledge and the skills of the workers; however, they are only vulnerable indirectly through the misuse of other more tangible assets [SFO03]. According to [SO05], a *use case* "achieves something of value for the system owner". This corresponds to the ISSRM notion of asset. The process guidelines for misuse cases modelling recommend "to concentrate on the normal actors and the main use cases requested by these" [SO01] and to identify the "critical assets in the system" [SO05]. Here, the notion of critical assets includes materials, information, locations, activities, knowledge and skills of workers [SFO03], virtual locations, and computerised activities [SO05]. Thus, in Figure 6.2, we consider *use cases* as ISSRM assets. The combination of *use cases* using relationships (*extend*, *includes*, and *generalise*) forms new assets. We consider the relationships as the part of the assets, too.

The literature provides various definitions for a use case:

- a means to understand and describe business processes, where they are called business use cases [BDG05],

- a means of focusing discussion about requirements of the system to be built. Here *use cases* are eventually transformed into lists of typical functional requirements

[BDG05] , and

- a part of the functional requirements of the system to be build [BDG05].

The first definition suggests to consider *business use cases* as ISSRM business assets (e.g., `Design 3D mock-ups`, `Design technical plans` in Figure 6.2), whereas the second and the third definitions suggest to consider *use cases* as IS assets. However, the Misuse cases literature does not precisely distinguish *business use cases* from ordinary *use cases*.

In the literature, we also find confusion seeking a correspondence for the notion of ISSRM security criteria. In [SFO03], Sindre *et al.* speak about a security goal, which is specified "in terms of (1) who are the potential misusers, (2) the type of security breaches the asset is vulnerable to and (3) the security level necessary for that type of breach". Here, "the security types are violations of" [SFO03] system integrity, availability and confidentiality, and is identified using security taxonomies. Elsewhere [SO05], the notion of security goal is different: "for each asset preferably aided by a standard typology of security goals" [SO05]. In both cases, no specific graphical construct is suggested, so security criteria has to be specified using other modelling means.

Risk-related concepts

The risk is "the estimated likelihood of occurrence and cost of the damage if the threat occurs" [SFO03]. This definition corresponds to the definition of risk in the ISSRM domain model in terms of involved concepts (this definition just put more emphasis on the level of risk than of the components of risk). The notion of impact in Misuse cases appears as the cost of the damage. It is claimed that relationships *includes, extend,* and *generalises*, "identified between misuse cases can aid risk analysis" [SO05]. This means that *misuse cases* can be defined at different level of abstraction. If a *misuse case* is defined at a high level, it might refer to a risk. However, the literature does not give any example. Thus, risk remains a concept without a specific graphical notation.

"The security threats identified can be described as misuse cases and misusers" [SO05]. This statement corresponds to the definition of the ISSRM threat, which is composed of a threat agent and an attack method. Thus, we identify correspondences between the *misuser*, who is the "actor that initiates misuse case" [SO05] (e.g., `Crook` in Figure 6.3), and ISSRM threat agent. Also we align the *misuse case*, which is "a sequence of actions [...] interacting with misuser and causing harm to stakeholder" [SO05] (e.g., `Steal login information`, `Use social engineering` in Figure 6.3) and the ISSRM attack method. Finally, the *threatens* relationship, which indicates how a "use case is exploited or hindered by a misuse case" [SO05], can be seen as the 'target' relationship between threat and IS asset.

Risk treatment-related concepts

Sindre *et al.* recommend "for each identified threat and taking its risk into account, [to] determine requirements to mitigate the threat" [SFO03]. This means that "appropriate security requirements must be determined and specified" [SFO03] and that "the use case is a countermeasure against a misuse case" [SO05]. Further, "security requirements defined are specified [...] as independent security use cases" [SO05] and the *security use case* must eventually have a *mitigate* relationship to a *misuse case*. This concludes that *security use cases* (e.g., `Perform awareness training` in Figure 6.5) correspond to the ISSRM security requirements.

The misuse cases *mitigates* link corresponds to the ISSRM mitigates relationship. However here, the relationship is used at a lower level indicating how the threat (the *misuse case*) is mitigated by the means of the *security use cases*. Misuse cases do not indicate anything that would correspond to the ISSRM notions of risk treatment or control.

6.2.3   Alignment of Misuse cases template and ISSRM

Use case diagrams have to be understood only as a table of content for the textual templates to be filled for each of the *use case*. Although we dedicated most of the discussion to the Misuse cases diagrams, in this subsection we will also consider how the entries of the Misuse cases template correspond to the concepts of the ISSRM domain model. The "extensive template" for Misuse cases is presented in [SO01, SO05] and an example is given in Figure 6.4.

The analysis of the extensive template [SO05] indicates only one asset-related entry, called *Related business rules* as a kind of ISSRM business asset. The extensive template concentrates on risk-related concepts. For instance, ISSRM risk is addressed by the entry *Stakeholders and risks*; ISSRM vulnerability is specified by the entries *Trigger*, *Assumption*, and *Precondition*; ISSRM impact is described by the *Worst case threat*; ISSRM attack method by the entries *Basic path*, *Alternative path*, and *Extension points*. Finally, in the entry *Misuser profile*, it is possible to give details about the *misuser*.

The Misuse cases template depends on the level of detail of the studied *misuse case*. For example, if a misuse case is specified at a high level of granularity (e.g., `Steal login information` in Figure 6.3), the *precondition* would correspond to ISSRM vulnerability. But if a misuse case is defined at a lower level of detail (e.g., `Use social engineering` in Figure 6.3) the *precondition* will define a state of the system (state where the misuse case begins). In this case, the *precondition* will not have a correspondence in the ISSRM domain model. Similar issues arise with other entries of the template.

A *Mitigation points* entry links a *misuse case* with *security use cases*. This means correspondence between *mitigation points* and ISSRM security requirements. Other details of the risk treatment can be specified in the templates of the security use cases.

6.2.4   Discussion

Figure 6.6 gives a clear view of the coverage of Misuse cases with respect to the ISSRM domain model. Some improvements can be suggested to Misuse cases (both graphical diagrams and textual template) if used for ISSRM:

- Misuse cases do not distinguish some constructs that represent different concepts of the ISSRM domain model. For example, IS assets, business assets and security requirements are represented using the same visual construct for a use case. A tag to the *use case* label could be introduced to differentiate the concepts. For example, in Figure 6.2, the *use case* label [BS] – `Obtain available dates` would indicate a business asset; [IS] – `Store available date` would indicate an IS asset; in Figure 6.5 [SR] – `Perform cryptographic procedures` would mean a security requirement. However this might not completely solve the problem. For example, in Figure 6.2, the *use case* `Establish structure calculation` might be understood as a business asset (the engineer establishes the structure calculation) and as an IS asset (he uses the software to do it).

- For some concepts (e.g., security criteria, risk, and impact), Misuse cases do not provide modelling constructs. For instance ISSRM risk is not precisely defined. In [SOB02, SO05], risk is said to be represented using the *generalisation/specialisation*, but we did not find sufficient information on this. The only place where *risk* is specified is the entry of the textual template called *Stakeholders and risks*. Misuse cases do not cover all concepts of the ISSRM domain model. For example, when using misuse cases diagrams one needs to decide how to model security criteria, risk, impact, vulnerability, risk treatment decisions, and controls. Some of these concepts can be defined in the misuse cases template: for example impact in the entry *Worst case threat*, vulnerability in the entries *Trigger*, *Assumption*, and *Precondition*. Other concepts can be defined by extending the misuse cases template with additional entries. However, extending template gives a different level of granularity, thus the misuse cases model might become complex.

- We also observe partial coverage of some concepts. For example, Misuse cases allow modelling of assets such as workers who have skills and knowledge about the business, using the *actor* constructs. However the language excludes modelling of the threats to the actors.

6.3 Assessment of ISSRM support by KAOS extended to security

The assessment of ISSRM support by KeS is done by analysing the KAOS metamodel [MHO06] and textual explanations provided in the associated literature. Several papers are dedicated to KAOS and its concepts [vL03, Let01]. The concepts specific to KeS are described in [vL04]. The following sections present the use of KeS on the running example for supporting the ISSRM process, and, then, the alignment with the ISSRM domain model and related discussions are provided.

6.3.1 Modelling ISSRM with KAOS extended to security

In this section, the example proposed in Section 3.2.1 is adapted to illustrate ISSRM, following the steps described in Section 2.1. A summary of KeS concepts is also proposed in Section 3.2.1.

- ***Context and asset identification.*** This step is done through the definition of goals and their refinement in the KAOS goal model, as depicted in Figure

6.7. The main goal studied in the exemple is `Achieve[BuildingValidated]`, which is refined in: the domain property `ParametersAreReliable` (which is part of the context) and the subgoals `PerformStructureCalculation` and `Avoid-[StructureCalculationModifiedByCrook]`. More details about the IS are given in the operation model. The goal `PerformStructureCalculation` is associated to the agent **Engineer** and the operations `EnterBuildingInformation`, `Launch-Calculation`, and `SelectContextParameters`. Finally, the objects used within the operations are defined, like `DatabaseOfParameters`.

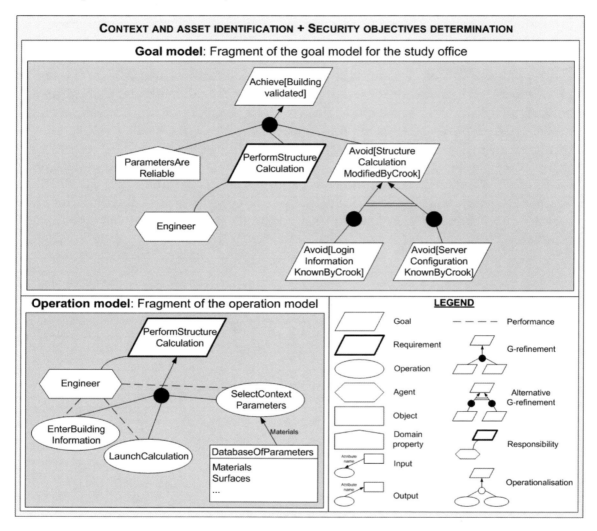

Figure 6.7: Asset and security objective modelling in KeS

- **Determination of security objectives.** As seen in Figure 6.7, the determination of security objectives is done in the same model and generally in the same time as the elicitation of other goals. `Avoid[StructureCalculation-ModifiedByCrook]` is an example of security objective, meaning that the integrity of structure calculation should be preserved. This security objective can be reached through two alternative goals: `Avoid[LoginInformationKnownBy-Crook]` and `Avoid[ServerConfigurationKnownByCrook]`.

- **Risk analysis and assessment.** Risk analysis is done by building an anti-model, like in Figure 6.8. In our example, the anti-goal analysed is `Achieve-[LoginInformationKnownByCrook]`. This anti-goal is refined in subgoals (e.g., `Achieve[LoginKnownByCrook]`, `Achieve[PasswordKnownByCrook]`, `Achieve[-PasswordLearntByTheUser]`) until reching anti-requirements (e.g., `Achieve[-UseSocialEngineeringToFindThePassword]`) assigned to anti-agent (`Attacker` in Figure 6.8). Vulnerabilities are also identified in anti-model, like `Employees-NotSecurityAware`. In the operation model, the operations performed to satisfy the goal `Achieve[UseSocialEngineeringToFindThePassword]`) are defined.

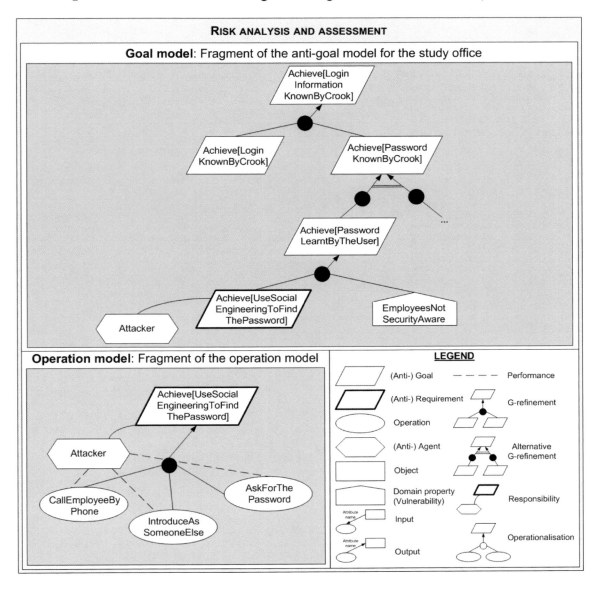

Figure 6.8: Risk modelling in KeS

- **Risk treatment.** In KeS, risk treatment is defined through the countermeasure chosen for handling the anti-model, and its associated vulnerabilities and anti-goals. In our example, the countermeasure chosen is `Vulnerability avoidance`, in order to avoid that employees are not security aware.

- **Security requirements definition.** New security goals are emerging from this countermeasure. A new goal model is thus built, with additional security goal(s), requirement(s) and/or expectation(s). In Figure 6.9, a new requirement called `PerformAwarenessTraining` is added to the goal model presented in Figure 6.7. This requirement is assigned to the `Security officer` agent.

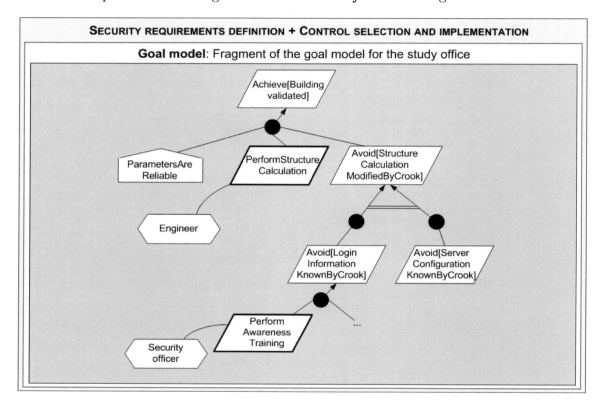

Figure 6.9: Security requirements and control modelling in KeS

- **Control selection and implementation.** The update of the goal model, which might include the refinement and the operationnalisation of the new added goals, constitutes the new system-to-be, as in Figure 6.9.

6.3.2   Alignment of KAOS extended to security with ISSRM domain model

In Figure 6.10, we present how KeS covers the ISSRM domain model. We illustrate the mapping with examples from Figure 6.7 to 6.9.

Asset-related concepts

KeS is mainly focused on the security of the system-to-be, but it does not make a separation between the IS and business aspects. Thus, we align all three ISSRM concepts concerning assets with the KAOS *goal, requirement* and *expectation* (Figure 6.10). Moreover, their operationalisation in *operation* and *object* are also assets. In KAOS, states of the system-to-be are described using *object attributes*. The purpose

ISSRM domain model		KAOS extended to security		
		Synonyms	Language concept (modelling construct)	Elements of the example
Asset-related concepts	Asset	Asset	Goal, requirement, expectation, operation, object	Achieve[BuildingValidated], PerformStructureCalculation, DatabaseOfParameters
	Business asset			
	IS asset			
	Security criteria	Security goal	Goal, object attribute	Avoid[StructureCalculationModifiedByCrook]
Risk-related concepts	Risk	-	-	-
	Impact	-	-	-
	Event	Malicious obstacle, anti-goal, goal-anchored, a goal negation, anti-requirement, anti-expectation, threat	Goal, requirement, expectation (in anti-model)	Achieve[LoginKnownByCrook], Achieve[PasswordKnownByCrook]
	Threat			
	Vulnerability	Vulnerability, domain property	Domain property	EmployeesNotSecurityAware
	Threat agent	Attacker, malicious agent, anti-agent	Agent	Attacker
	Attack method	Potential capabilities of the attacker	Operationalisation + domain and required conditions + operations	(Operationalisation of) Achieve[UseSocialEngineeringToFindThePassword]
Risk treatment-related concepts	Risk treatment	Countermeasures	-	Vulnerability avoidance
	Security requirements	Security goal, security requirement, security expectation	Goal, requirement, expectation	PerformAwarenessTraining
	Control	-	New model implementing security components	-

Figure 6.10: Concept alignment between KAOS extended to security and the ISSRM domain model

of the *security goals* is to protect system states against unauthorised access. In terms of KAOS, this means that the *security goals* should define confidentiality, privacy, integrity, and availability *goal*, and *object attributes*, which are concerned by potential risk events and threats [vL04]. Thus, we align both *(security) goals* and *object attributes* concerned by anti-goal with ISSRM security criteria.

Risk-related concepts

In Figure 6.10, we align together ISSRM event and threat with KAOS *anti-goal* (also called *malicious obstacle* or *threat*). *Anti-goals* can be identified at various abstraction levels, so they might need to be refined until they become *anti-requirements* or *anti-expectations* (assigned to an *anti-agent*). At higher abstraction levels, an *anti-goal* might be considered as the event, which, according to the ISSRM domain model, is a combination of a threat and one or more vulnerabilities. At lower abstraction (realisation) levels, an *anti-goal* (*anti-requirement* or *anti-expectation*) is a threat, which is a potential attack or incident to assets. The language concepts for *anti-goal, anti-requirement* and *anti-expectation* remains respectively *goal, requirement* and *expectation*. In Figure 6.10, we align ISSRM vulnerability and the KAOS *domain property*. The KAOS *domain property* is a hypothesis about the domain that holds independently of the system-to-be. In correspondence, ISSRM vulnerability is defined as a characteristic of assets. Following the ISSRM domain model, a threat is composed of a threat agent and an attack method. A threat agent can potentially cause harm to the assets. In KAOS, an *anti-agent* (e.g., `Attacker`) monitors or controls *objects* and their *attributes*, and is thereby capable to threaten the system-to-be. In Figure 6.10, we align ISSRM threat agent and KAOS *anti-agent*. The ISSRM attack method characterises the means by which a threat agent carries out the attack. In KAOS an *anti-agent* performs *operations* that satisfy an *anti-goal*. *Operations* change the state of the system-to-be using input/output relationships over the *objects* and their *attributes*. This means that by performing *operations*, the *anti-agent* breaks the security criteria (related to *object attributes*). We align ISSRM attack method with the KAOS constructs used to operationalise the *anti-goal*, namely *operationalisation, domain and required conditions* and *operation*. KAOS does not address two risk-related concepts from the ISSRM domain model: risk and impact.

Risk treatment-related concepts

ISSRM risk treatment corresponds to the *countermeasures* [vL04, vLL00] that are elaborated after identification of the *anti-goals*. Countermeasures are not KAOS modelling concepts, but rather modelling idioms or "patterns" adopted by modellers. In KAOS, the countermeasures usually result in new *security goals*, which need to be further refined into realisable *security requirements* and *expectations*. In Figure 6.10, we align ISSRM security requirements and the KAOS *security goals* (*requirements* and *expectations*). The refinement and operationalisation of the new *security goals*, their concerned *objects* and *attributes*, and their assignment to *agents*, lead to new system-to-be components realising the necessary security means. With respect to the ISSRM domain model, these new system components correspond to controls.

6.3.3   Discussion

The alignment of KeS with the ISSRM domain model highlights some limitations. The coverage of KeS is not perfect and some improvements can be proposed:

- We were not able to find sufficient empirical evidences that would provide to us a complete model of a secured system (neither security RM of IS) modelled with KeS. The works we succeeded to identify on the KAOS extensions to security include [vL04, vLBLJ03]. However they only illustrate the major security modelling principles. The models presented in these works are limited and do not provide much modelling details. As the conclusion, Figure 6.10 lists only the primitive language constructs and their correspondences to the ISSRM domain model. However, we must note that one also can identify construct combinations in order to model some aspects of the security RM as the modelling patterns. The models presented in Figures 6.7 and 6.8 are adapted from [vL04]. This model suggests few simple modelling patterns to address security RM concerns. For example, we can observe that a threat (e.g., `Achieve[UseSocialEngineering-ToFindThePassword]`) will be presented as (anti) *requirement* or *expectation* and always will be assigned to (anti) *agent* (e.g., `Attacker`). This combination of constructs leads to a simple pattern combining together ISSRM *threat, threat agent* and *attack method* and shown in Figure 6.11. Here, the `operationalisation` relationship combines (at least) two `operations` corresponding to the `attack method`.

Similarly, in Figure 6.12 we can also observe the pattern for risk *event*. It is a combination of the (anti) *goal* (e.g., `Achieve[PasswordLearntByTheUser]`), at least one (anti) *requirement* or *expectation* (e.g., `Achieve[UseSocialEngineeringTo-FindThePassword]`) and *domain property* (e.g., `EmployeesNotSecurityAware`). The pattern is shown in Figure 6.12.

- Similar constructs of KeS are used to support different ISSRM concepts. For example, a *goal* can be used to model (business or IS) asset, security criteria, event, threat or security requirement. We can determine that a *goal* is a threat or an event whether it is part of an anti-model. However, for the other cases, no way to distinguish one ISSRM concept to the other is provided. As for Misuse cases, a solution could be to introduce labels in front of the construct label: e.g., `[BS]` – *business assets*, `[IS]` – *IS assets*, `[SR]` – *security requirements*. Another proposal could be to determine a new concrete syntax for these concepts.

- KAOS does not address two concepts from the ISSRM domain model: risk and impact. This can be partly explained by the fact that KAOS was not specifically designed to consider the business context of an IS. However, these concepts might be derived from the implicit description of the modelled problem. For example, in Figure 6.8, we present a risk event as the goal `Achieve[PasswordKnownBy-Crook]`. Achievement of this goal might lead to the impact called `Structure calculation modified by crook`. Further this might form a chain of impacts, like `Construction mistake`, `Loss of reputation`, and so on. The impact might be characterised both by introducing additional goals and by defining *concerns* relationships between the goal/anti-goal and object/anti-object models. However, this requires further theoretical and empirical investigation. Similar argumentation can also be provided about other ISSRM concepts, like *risk*.

- Finally, some KeS constructs only provide partial coverage of ISSRM concept. For example, the countermeasures proposed by KeS only partially cover the ISSRM risk treatment. For example, *agent substitution* is used in KeS to replace a vulnerable agent assigned to a threatened goal by a less vulnerable one for the threatening anti-goal. However, it only partially covers the risk treatment of risk transfer, because the vulnerability is not always on an agent when choosing the risk transfer treatment.

6.4 Assessment of ISSRM support by Secure Tropos

In this section, we illustrate how we can use the Secure Tropos approach to analyse security risks and how to derive suited countermeasures from these risks. We summarise the discussion on alignment in Figure 6.17. This alignment is based on the Secure Tropos literature [MG07a, MGM02, MJF06, MGM03b, Mou04, GMZ07, MG09, MG04, MGMP02, MGM03a, MGM05], sometimes presenting (part of) the Secure Tropos meta-model [SPM05].

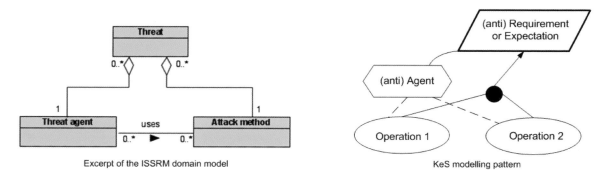

Figure 6.11: KeS pattern for ISSRM threat

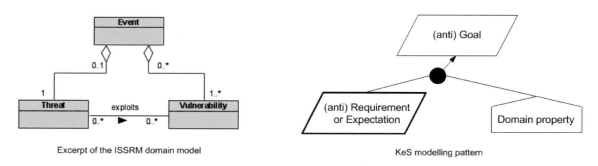

Figure 6.12: KeS pattern for ISSRM event

6.4.1 Modelling ISSRM with Secure Tropos

In this section, the example proposed in Section 3.2.5 is adapted to illustrate ISSRM, following the steps described in Section 2.1. A summary of Secure Tropos concepts is also proposed in Section 3.2.5.

- *Context and asset identification.* Figure 6.13 shows an actor model, representing the actors playing a role in the estimate definition, and the associated dependencies between actors. In our example, the actors are `Study office`, `Sales department` and `Client`. The dependencies are of two kinds: resource dependency (`Estimates`, `3D mock-ups` and `Technical plans`) and goal dependendy (`Manage projects` and `Calculate structure`), but can also be softgoal or plan dependency. More information about the dependencies is provided in the goal model, making clear how the actors reason about goals to be fulfilled, plans to be performed and available resources. It completes the actor model with the reasoning that each actor makes about its internal goals, plans and resources. In Figure 6.13, the goal model of the `Study office` shows that, for satisfying the goal `Calculate structure`, two different means (i.e. plans) are possible: `By hand` or `By tool`. Plans and resources necessary to perform the structure calculation with a tool are also defined. The calculation through a tool helps to obtain documents of quality, as shown by the positive contribution between the plan `By tool` and the softgoal `Documents of quality`.

- *Determination of security objectives.* The ISSRM security objectives are expressed in Figure 6.14 through security constraints, restricting some depen-

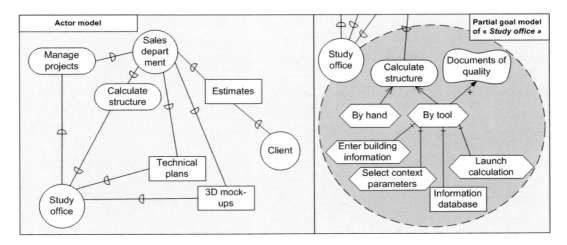

Figure 6.13: Asset modelling in Secure Tropos

dencies. For example, the `Sales department` should `Keep estimates private` and the `Study office` should `Keep integrity of calculation`. The latter is related with a constraint link (link with "restricts" label) to the plan `By tool` in the security-enhanced goal model (as explained in Section 3.2.5, by adding security constraints, the goal model becomes a security-enhanced goal model). This security constraint also helps to obtain `Documents of quality`.

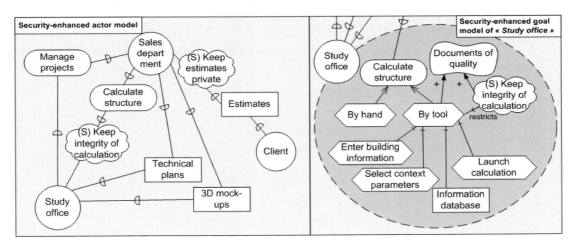

Figure 6.14: Security objective modelling in Secure Tropos

- ***Risk analysis and assessment.*** Figure 6.15 focuses on a possible risk event. A Secure Tropos threat to the softgoal `Documents of quality` is identified in the attack diagram of Figure 6.15. The attack diagram is an adaptation of a security reference diagram we introduce, including elements of a security-enhanced goal model. The threat is about `Authentication attack`, aiming for an attacker to authenticate to the tool. This diagram is completed by a security attack scenario. It shows that the goal of the `Attacker` is to know the login information of a user of the tool. To achieve his goal, he uses social engineering. His belief is that the employees are not security aware, that constitutes a vulnerability in this context.

His attack targets the resource **Information database** of the **Study office**. In Figure 6.15, the security attack scenario can be seen as the refinement of the security event identified in the attack diagram.

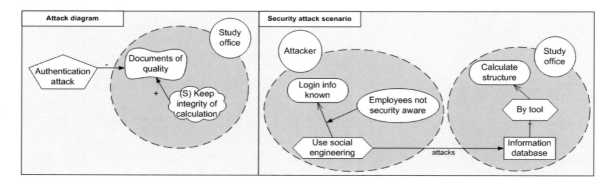

Figure 6.15: Risk modelling in Secure Tropos

- **Risk treatment.** In our example, the risk treatment chosen is to reduce the risk by adding some secure goals/plans/resources. Naturally, other decisions are possible, like avoiding the risk by modifying the security-enhanded actor and/or goal models, or adding another actor, as third party, to share the risk.

- **Security requirements definition.** The risk treatment chosen leads to modification of the security-enhanced goal model of Figure 6.14. A secure goal **Make users security aware** is added, satisfied by the secure plan **Perform awareness training**. This plan has a positive contribution to the security constraint **Keep integrity of calculation**, as depicted in Figure 6.16.

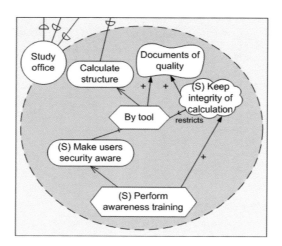

Figure 6.16: Security requirements and control modelling in Secure Tropos

- **Control selection and implementation.** Softgoals can be used to reason on the differences between control alternatives. This step takes place after controls are defined, that usually happens during the design phase.

6.4.2 Alignment of Secure Tropos with ISSRM domain model

To analyse how Secure Tropos can help to solve ISSRM problems at the early stages of IS development, we have surveyed the existing Secure Tropos literature in order to understand its major principles and concepts. Next, we have applied Secure Tropos in the running example. This application strongly follows the process proposed in Section 2.1 and the concepts suggested by the ISSRM domain model. We result in the semantic alignment between ISSRM and Secure Tropos as illustrated in Figure 6.17. This table shows how (and if) Secure Tropos can be aligned with the principles of ISSRM.

ISSRM domain model		Secure Tropos		
		Synonyms	Language concept (modelling construct)	Elements of the example
Asset-related concepts	Asset	-	Actor, goal, plan, resource, softgoal	-
	Business asset	-		Study office, Manage projects, Calculate structure, Estimates, Documents of quality
	IS asset	-		Enter building information, Select context parameters, Information database
	Security criteria	Security feature, protection property	Security constraint, softgoal	Keep estimates private, Keep integrity of calculation
Risk-related concepts	Risk	-	-	-
	Impact	-	Contribution between threat and softgoal	Contribution between Authentication attack and Documents of quality
	Event	-	Threat	Authentication attack
	Threat	-	Goal, plan	Login info known
	Vulnerability	-	Belief	Employees not security aware
	Threat agent	Attacker	Actor	Attacker
	Attack method	-	Plan	Use social engineering
Risk treatment-related concepts	Risk treatment	-	-	Risk reduction
	Security requirements	Secure goal, secure plan, secure resource, protection objective, security requirement	Actor, goal, softgoal, plan, resource, security constraint	Make users security aware, Perform awareness training
	Control	-	New model implementing security components	-

Figure 6.17: Concept alignment between Secure Tropos and the ISSRM domain model

Asset-related concepts

In Secure Tropos, we identify that the *actor, goal, resource* and *plan* constructs (and appropriate relationships among them) are used to model both business and IS assets. For instance, on the one hand, the actors **Study Office** and **Sales department**, the goals **Manage projects** and **Calculate structures** (cf. Figure 6.13) describe the process necessary for the organisation to achieve its objectives. On the other hand, the resources **Technical plans** and **3D mock-ups** characterise the valuable information.

All the mentioned examples are identified as business assets with respect to the ISSRM domain model.

The business processes and information management are mainly supported by the IS of the `Study office`. In more details (cf. Figure 6.13), the support for the business asset `Calculate structure` is performed through the plans `By hand` or `By tool`. `By tool` is itself refined by the plans `Enter building information`, `Select context parameters`, `Launch calculation` and by the resource `Information database`. The concepts which describe how a component or part of the IS is necessary in supporting business assets are called IS assets.

The ISSRM security criteria are properties or constraints on business assets characterising their security needs. In Secure Tropos, *softgoals* can help to identify higher level security criteria, like confidentiality, integrity and availability. Depending on the context, it might be necessary to refine them or to specify more precise security criteria, like we do by using the *security constraints* `Keep estimates private` and `Keep integrity of calculation` (cf. Figure 6.14).

Risk-related concepts

Risk is described by the event of the risk, corresponding to the `Authentication attack` in Figure 6.15. The potentional negative consequence of the risk, identified by a negative contribution link between the `Authentication attack` and the softgoal `Documents of quality` is called impact of the risk. Here, the impact negates the security criteria `Keep integrity of calculation`.

In Figure 6.15, the goal `Login info known` corresponds to the threat describing the potential attack targeting the IS asset `Information database`. The threat is triggered by the threat agent `Attacker` who knows about the lack in security awareness for employees, as identified by the *belief* in Figure 6.15. To break into the `Study office` system, the `Attacker` carries an attack method consisting of the plan `Use social engineering`.

Note that in Figure 6.17, *belief* only partially corresponds to ISSRM vulnerability. Firstly, the fact that the actor (who has the role of the attacker) thinks he knows, might be true. In this case, the *belief* will correspond to vulnerability in the sense of the ISSRM. However, facts known by the attacker might be wrong: in this case there is no corresponding concept in the ISSRM. Finally, *belief* does not represent vulnerabilities which exist in the system, but is not known by the attacker. We will come back to the discussion about *belief* in Section 6.6, where we suggest to use vulnerability points to address the ISSRM concept of vulnerability.

Risk treatment-related concepts

In our case, we apply risk reduction decision. This leads to a modification of the IS design, reducing the identified risk. New security requirements (cf. Figure 6.16) are identified as the goal `Make users security aware` and the plan `Perform awareness training`. We illustrate the countermeasure only using the Secure Tropos *goal* and *plan* constructs, however we must note that, depending on the selected risk treatment decision, the combination of *actor*, *goal*, *softgoal*, *resource*, *plan*, and *security constraint* might result in different security control systems. A new model implementing the necessary security components is the output of this phase.

6.4.3 Discussion

Our alignment of Secure Tropos constructs with the concepts of the ISSRM domain model has shown several limitations of Secure Tropos, to investigate security RM at the early stages (requirements) of the IS development. At the same time, it suggests a number of possible improvements for Secure Tropos, in the context of security RM:

- Analysis showed that Secure Tropos has to provide guidelines as to when and how to use each construct, in order to avoid misinterpretations of the ISSRM concepts. For example, as shown in Figure 6.17, the *plan* construct can be used to model business assets, IS assets, threats and security requirements. One possible solution in this situation might be introduction of labels in front of the construct label (e.g., [BS] – *business assets*, [IS] – *IS assets*, [Th] – *threat*, and [SR] – *security requirements*). Another solution is to design a discriminating concrete syntax, which would allow to separate these concerns. Finally, decomposition of the model into separate diagrams, where separate concerns (business assets, IS assets, attack scenario and security requirements) would be modelled, should be considered. The latter two aspects we develop in Section 6.6.

- We have also noticed that Secure Tropos could be improved with additional constructs to better cover the concepts of ISSRM. Figure 6.17 indicates that several concepts such as risk, risk treatment, and control are not in the Secure Tropos approach. Thus, one needs either to define graphical constructs to address these concepts, or to provide methodological guidelines how these concepts might be addressed in the model.

- Finally, the semantics of individual modelling constructs should be adapted so that they adequately represent ISSRM concepts. For example, as discussed previously, the *belief* construct only partially covers vulnerability. A possible improvement, on the one hand, is to suggest the modelling construct which would adequately support modelling of system vulnerabilities. On the other hand, recently in [EY07], Elahi and Yu have introduced *vulnerable points*. We will investigate the latter option in Section 6.6.

6.5 Summary of language comparison

Our provisional general remarks about security-oriented languages, after their alignment with the ISSRM domain model, are the following. Misuse cases [SO05] and Abuse Cases [MF99] are mainly focused on eliciting *threat agents* and their *attack methods*. The main difference between the two is that Misuse cases integrate regular Use Cases with threatening Use Cases, whereas Abuse Cases only focus on the latter. KeS already integrates some core ISSRM concepts like *threat* or *vulnerability*. KAOS was initially designed to cope with safety-critical software systems [vLL00]. However, the approach is not risk-driven and the concept of *risk* does not appear. Secure-Tropos

[MG09, MGMP02, GMZ05] features three complementary kinds of models: classical Secure-Tropos models, attack diagrams (adaptation of security reference diagrams) and security attack scenarios [MMM+08]. None of those three kinds of models addresses security with a risk-driven approach, and some core components of the concept of risk are missing (e.g., *risk, impact*). Table 6.1 summarises the ISSRM support by these security-oriented languages.

Table 6.1: Survey of ISSRM support by security-oriented languages

	Misuse cases	Misuse cases template	Secure Tropos	KeS
Asset	Actor and Use case	-	Actor, Goal, Softgoal, Plan, Ressource	Goal, Requirement, Expectation, Operation, object
Business asset		Related business rules		
IS asset		-		
Security criterion	-	-	Security constraint, Softgoal	Goal, Object attributes
Risk	-	Stakeholders and risks	-	-
Impact	-	Worst case threat	Contribution between threat and softgoal	-
Event	-	-	Threat	Goal, Requirement, Expectation (in anti-model)
Threat	Misuser and Misuse case	-	Goal, Plan	
Vulnerability	-	Assumption, Precondition	- [1]	Domain property
Threat agent	Misuser	Misuser profile	Actor	Agent
Attack method	Misuse Case	Basic path, Alternative path, Extension points	Plan, relationship attack	Operationalisation + Domain and required conditions + Operations
Risk treatment	-	-	-	-
Security requirement	Use case	Mitigation point	Actor, Goal, Softgoal, Plan, Ressource, Security constraint	Goal, Requirement, Expectation
Control	New model implementing security components	-	New model implementing security components	New model implementing security components

Our assessment provides a path for improving each proposed language with ISSRM concepts, as we already started to discuss for selected languages (Section 6.2 to 6.4). The main ways of improvement are:

- to be able to distinguish the ISSRM concept represented, when several concepts are supported by the same modelling construct;

- to complete the coverage of the language for the ISSRM concepts not supported;

- to extend or precise the language when some ISSRM concepts are only partially covered.

Although we did not completely study the other security-oriented modelling languages, we surveyed them and provided some preliminary conclusions. The coverage of Abuse Frames [LNI+03b, LNIJ04, LNI+03a] is close to KAOS', apart from the concepts related to *risk treatment*. Abuse Frames are indeed focused on detailing the

---

[1]According to the definition found in Tropos literature [BGG+04], *Belief* can partially be compliant with vulnerability modelling. However we did not observe any example of its use.

security problem domain rather than investigating possible designs. Mal-activity diagrams [Sin07] are focused on detailing a threat scenario, by precisely describing the behaviors of the involved actors, including naturally malicious ones. Finally, the Tropos Goal-Risk framework [AG06] deals with RM at a general level, without taking into account security-specific concepts. A complete analysis of those languages will provide more precise results.

6.6 A Risk-aware Secure Tropos

The purpose of this section is to develop syntactic, semantic and methodological extensions to Secure Tropos, that would support modelling of security risks and their countermeasures. First, we suggest extensions to the concrete syntax and show how they are addressed in the abstract syntax. Next, we define methodological guidelines. Finally, we discuss the extensions with respect to the ISSRM domain model.

6.6.1 Concrete syntax extension

In Section 6.4 (Figure 6.17), we have separated the concrete syntax of Secure Tropos according to three construct categories: asset-related concepts, risk-related concepts, and risk treatment-related concepts. In addition to the ISSRM constructs aligned in Figure 6.4, here in Figures 6.18, 6.19, 6.20 and 6.21, we consider how ISSRM relationships (e.g., *supports, constraint of, exploits, targets, mitigates,* and others) can be expressed with Secure Tropos. We also make a link between Secure Tropos concrete and abstract syntax, which is considered in Section 6.6.2.

Asset-related concepts.

The ISSRM *assets* (cf. Fig. 6.18) are modelled using *actor, hardgoal, plan, resource, softgoal* constructs and their compositions constructed using *dependency, means-ends, contribution,* and *decomposition* relations. Moreover, ISSRM *supports* relationship, between IS and business assets, is expressed using the different Secure Tropos relationships.

The ISSRM *security criterion* is represented through *softgoal* and/or *security constraint. Softgoal* represents generally high-level *security criteria* and *security constraint* their refinement. Note that in Secure Tropos, one *security constraint* can be decomposed to others, thus, forming a *security constraint* hierarchy.

The ISSRM relationship *constraint of* is addressed both implicitly and explicitly in Secure Tropos. Firstly, in the Secure Tropos security-enhanced actor model, we can observe an implicit restriction of the dependum (*hardgoal, task* or *resource*) in the *dependency* relationship. This means that *security constraint* is imposed to the depender or/and dependee *actor.* Secondly, in the security-enhanced goal model, the ISSRM *constraint of* relationship is presented explicitly by the *restricts* relationship. It shows the actual goal, plan or resource restricted by the *security constraint.*

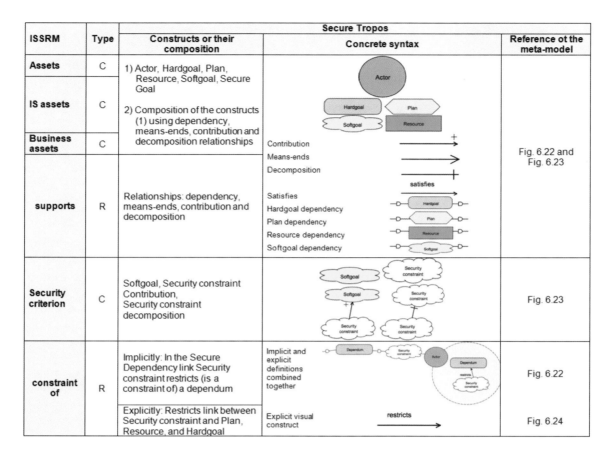

ISSRM	Type	Constructs or their composition	Secure Tropos		Reference ot the meta-model
			Concrete syntax		
Assets	C	1) Actor, Hardgoal, Plan, Resource, Softgoal, Secure Goal			Fig. 6.22 and Fig. 6.23
IS assets	C	2) Composition of the constructs (1) using dependency, means-ends, contribution and decomposition relationships			
Business assets	C				
supports	R	Relationships: dependency, means-ends, contribution and decomposition			
Security criterion	C	Softgoal, Security constraint Contribution, Security constraint decomposition			Fig. 6.23
constraint of	R	Implicitly: In the Secure Dependency link Security constraint restricts (is a constraint of) a dependum	Implicit and explicit definitions combined together		Fig. 6.22
		Explicitly: Restricts link between Security constraint and Plan, Resource, and Hardgoal	Explicit visual construct		Fig. 6.24

Figure 6.18: Asset-related concepts (C – concept, R – relationships)

Risk-related concepts.

As presented in Figure 6.17, standard Secure Tropos constructs can be used to model risk-related concerns. However, there exists a high degree to misinterpret the presented information. Thus, we recommend to differentiate concrete syntax of these Secure Tropos concepts. In [LYM03] and [EY07], black shadows are used to represent malicious language constructs. Elsewhere, in [SO05], malicious information is modelled using contrasting construct colours (e.g., white *vs.* black). For Secure Tropos, we suggest to use more solid (darker) colours applied for the construct background (cf. Figure 6.19). We represent *threat agent* as an *actor*, *attack method* as a *plan*, *threat* as a *hardgoal* and/or *plan*. As proposed in Section 6.4.3, *vulnerability point* is introduced to represent a vulnerability. This extension coming from [EY07] is more aligned with *vulnerability* of ISSRM than the existing *Belief*. Secure Tropos *attacks* relationship represents the *targets* relationship of ISSRM. In order to be compliant with ISSRM, we also introduce the *exploits* relationship, which defines a link between a *plan* (ISSRM *threat*) and an *asset* with a *vulnerability point*.

After defining how we can represent *threat agent*, *attack method*, and *vulnerability*, we can combine these concepts to represent the *event* of the risk (cf. Figure 6.20). To generalise this representation, one can use the Secure Tropos *threat* constructs. The former representation of the risk *event* is used in the *security attack scenario*, in

| ISSRM | Type | Secure Tropos | | Reference to the meta-model |
		Constructs or their composition	Concrete syntax	
Threat agent	C	Agent		Fig. 6.25. Fig. 6.22 and Fig. 6.23 are also relevant
Attack method	C	Plan		Fig. 6.25 Fig. 6.23 is also relevant
uses	R	Agent executes Plan	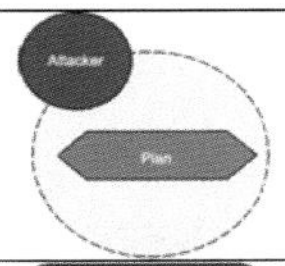	Fig. 6.23
Threat	C	Goal, Plan	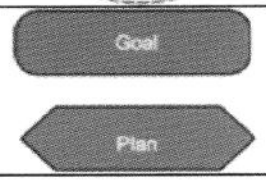	
Vulnerability	C	Vulnerability is not modelled, but vulnerability points can be identified by the attributes of the assets (presented as Hardgoal, Plan, Resourse)		
exploits	R	Exploits	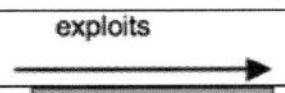 exploits	Fig. 6.25
characteristic of	R	An attribute of the vulnerable asset (presented as Hardgoal, Plan, Resourse)		
targets	R	Attacks	attacks	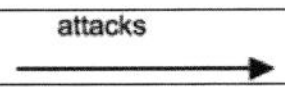

Figure 6.19: Risk-related concepts - I (C – concept, R – relationships)

order to represent details of the event. The latter representation is used in the *attack diagram*, to identify risks to assets. Here, a *risk* is understood as the combination of the risk *event* (represented as the Secure Tropos *threat*) and *impact* (represented using the *impacts* relationship).

| ISSRM | Type | Secure Tropos | | Reference to the meta-model |
		Constructs or their composition	Concrete syntax	
Event	C	1) Composition of an agent, goal, plan, targets, exploits, and vulnerability point 2) Threat	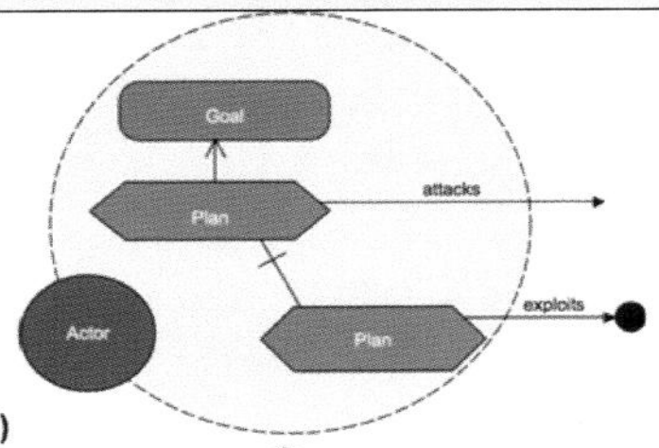 	Fig. 6.25 Fig. 6.24
Impact	C	Impacts	 impacts	Fig. 6.24
leads to	R			
harms	R			
negates	R			
provokes	R	—	—	—
Risk	C	Composition of a Threat and Impacts relatioship	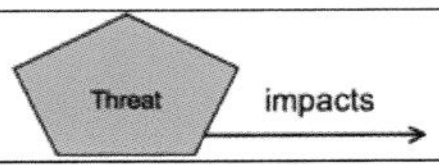	Fig. 6.24
significance assessed by	R	—	—	—

Figure 6.20: Risk-related concepts - II (C – concept, R – relationships)

Risk treatment-related concepts.

For the necessity of differentiating ISSRM concepts, we also need to update the visual syntax of risk treatment-related concepts. Constructs, like *actor, hardgoal, plan, softgoal*, and *security constraint* (and/or their combinations), which represent *security requirements* and/or *controls*, need to carry a dotted background pattern (cf. Figure 6.21). Security requirement mitigates the identified risk. To represent this, we introduce *mitigates* relationship, defining a link between constructs representing the ISSRM *security requirement* concept and the *threat* (as the ISSRM *event* of the risk).

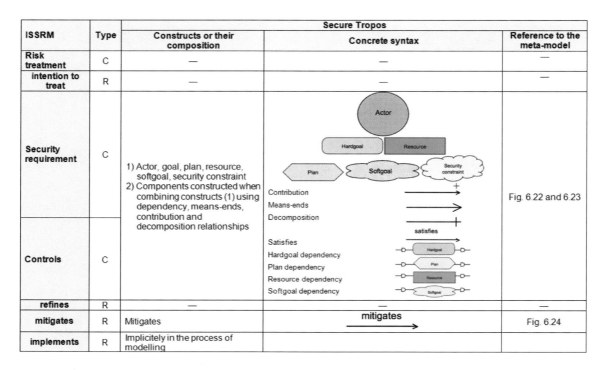

Figure 6.21: Risk treatment-related concepts (C – concept, R – relationships)

6.6.2 Abstract syntax extension

In Section 6.4, we have not presented abstract syntax of Secure Tropos due to the need of the simple introduction of the language itself. However, to illustrate how the proposed syntactic Secure Tropos extensions are used, we need to present abstract syntax elements and the rules how they can be combined together.

The abstract syntax of Secure Tropos consists of two meta-models: SEAM (Security-Enhanced Actor Model) and SEGM (Security-Enhanced Goal Model). Due to the need of reducing presentation complexity, in addition to these two meta-models, we will discuss abstract relationships of the *security constraint* and *security attack scenarios* separately.

Security-Enhanced Actor Model

Figure 6.22 presents the SEAM abstract syntax. The major element is an `Actor` who might be a *depender* or *dependee* in a `Dependency` relationship [BGG+04, Yu97]. A `Security Constraint` is imposed to an `Actor`, that represents a restriction on the `Hardgoal(s)`, `Plan(s)` and/or `Resource(s)` on an `Actor` related to security issues [MG07a]. A `Security Constraint` enhances the language by defining the notion of `Secure Dependency`.

A `Secure Dependency` introduces one or more `Security Constraint(s)` that must be fulfilled for the dependency to be valid [MG07a]. We distinguish among three types of secure dependencies: *dependee secure dependency*, *depender secure dependency*, and *double secure dependency*. Different `Secure Dependency` types are defined using `Depender` and `Dependee` attributes of `Security Constraint`.

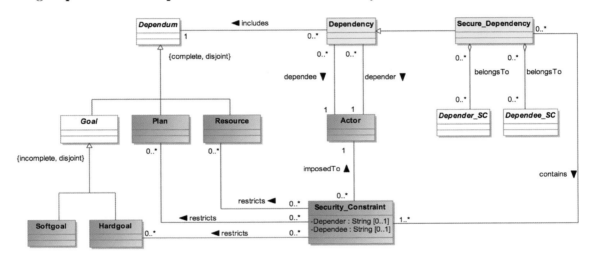

Figure 6.22: SEAM abstract syntax

Security-Enhanced Goal Model

Figure 6.23 presents the SEGM abstract syntax. Again, the major element of this meta-model is an `Actor` who *executes* `Plans`, *uses* `Resources`, and *has* `Goals`. `Plans` can be and/or `decomposed` to other `Plans`, `Resources`, or `Hardgoals`. `Hardgoals` (and *Secure goals*) are achieved through and/or `Means-ends` relationship by satisfying other `Hardgoals`, executing `Plans` or making `Resources` available. In order to *satisfice* `Softgoals`, a sufficient degree `contribution` should be defined with other `Softgoals`, `Security constraints`, `Plans`, `Resources` or `Hardgoals`.

Security constraint and Threat

As already illustrated in the SEAM meta-model, `Security constraint` is *imposed* to `Actor`. It `Restricts` (cf. Figure 6.24) execution of `Plans`, availability of `Resources` and achievement of `Hardgoals` held by this `Actor`. One analyses `Security Constraints` using a number of modelling techniques, such as *security constraint decomposition*; *security constraint delegation* and *security constraint assignment* [Mou04]. A *secure*

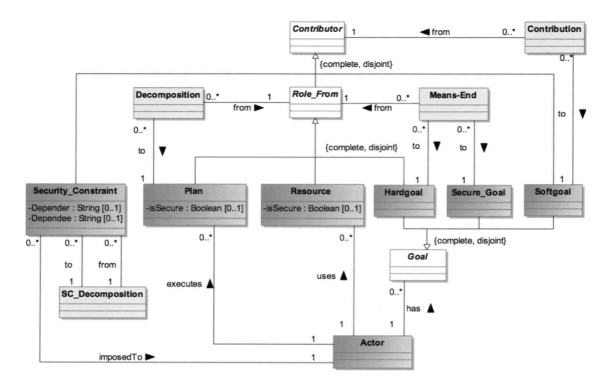

Figure 6.23: SEGM abstract syntax

goal represents the strategic interest of an `Actor` with respect to security. *Secure goals* are mainly introduced to contribute to the satisfaction of `Security Constraints` by defining `Satisfies` relationship (cf. Figure 6.24). A *secure plan* is defined as a `Plan` (by managing `isSecure` attribute) that represents a particular way for satisfying a *secure goal*. On the other hand, a *secure resource* is defined as an entity that is security critical for the system under development.

A proper definition of how `Security constraint` is satisfied, is needed to illustrate how it can `mitigate` a `Threat`. `Threats` are mitigated to lower the `Impact` to `Plans`, `Resources` and `Hardgoals`.

As discussed above, `Security Constraint` is one of the major elements which defines security concerns in the model; thus, it requires a special attention (cf. Figure 6.24). `Security Constraint` has a number of relationships with other concepts of the language. `Security Constraint` can `Restrict Plan`, `Resource` and `Hardgoal`. The visual representation for `Restrict` is used in the SEGM model, however its implicit meaning is contained already in the SEAM model because `Security Constraint` places restrictions on the `Secure Dependency` fulfillment.

Security attack scenarios

Figure 6.25 presents the abstract syntax of Secure Tropos used when defining the *security attack scenarios*. Here we have to note that, in *security attack scenarios*, two conceptually different sets of constructs are used: asset- and risk-related constructs to address the corresponding ISSRM concepts. Thus, they both obey the same syntax rules (presented in Figure 6.22 and 6.23) when combined within this conceptual

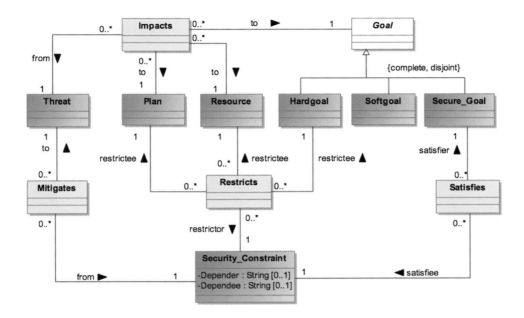

Figure 6.24: Abstract syntax of Security constraint and Threat

boundary. The difficulty arise when one wants to show relationship between them both.

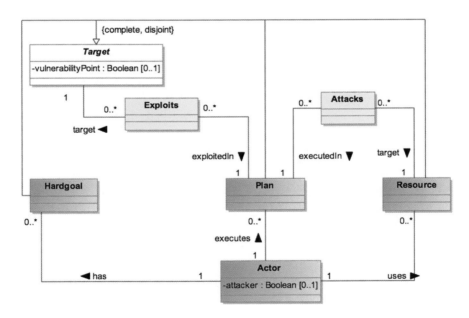

Figure 6.25: Abstract syntax of Security attack scenario

We need to distinguish system actors (*assets*) from malicious actors (*attackers*). First, we introduce an attribute `attacker` to the class `Actor`, as shown in Figure 6.25. Next, we define an integrity constraint, saying that `Actor A` who executes a `Plan` *exploiting/attacking* other elements in the diagram, and `Actor B` who holds *exploited/attacked* elements, are different. Finally, for actor **A**, we set an attribute `attacker` *true*, meaning a malicious actor (graphical representation is provided in Figure 6.19). Actor **B**'s attribute is set as false, meaning that this actor represents attacked assets (graphical representation in Figure 6.18).

Two relationships are defined between elements held by these two actors. A `Plan` executed by an *attacker* `Exploits` a target (`Hardgoal`, `Resource`, or `Plan`). `Exploits` relationship points to the vulnerability point (cf. attribute `vulnerabilityPoint`) of the target. The `Attacks` relationship shows a link between a `Plan` executed by a *malicious actor* and the `Resource` used by an attacked actor.

In the next subsection, we will provide methodological guidelines for the Risk-aware Secure Tropos application. We will use the running example, and improve the illustration provided in Section 6.4.

6.6.3   Application of Risk-aware Secure Tropos

The objective of this section is to demonstrate how concrete and abstract syntax extensions are used in an example. Here, we will use the running example again and incrementally provide guidelines for modelling with Risk-aware Secure Tropos.

Language application includes three major stages. The first stage covers the two first steps of the ISSRM process, presented in Section 2.1: *Context and asset identification* and *Determination of security objectives*. The second stage comprises *Risk analysis and assessment*. Finally, the third stage corresponds to *Security requirements definition*, coming from *Risk treatment* decisions, and leading to new controls.

Stage 1. Asset identification and determination of security objectives.

At this stage, concrete syntax of Secure Tropos does not differ from the standard one presented in [MGM02, MGMP02, MPM03, MG04, MJF06] and used in Section 6.4. However, as we discussed in Section 6.4.3, here we need to make a separation between two ISSRM concepts, namely *business assets* and *IS assets*. We do this separation by constructing two diagrams: one presenting business assets (Figure 6.26), another introducing IS assets (Figure 6.27). In the first diagram shown in Figure 6.26, there is no information about how the IS supports different processes or information (i.e. how it supports the business assets). Here, we represent only goals (e.g., `Calculate structure`), plans and resources (e.g., `Technical plans`) related to business artefacts and activities.

Following the steps of the ISSRM process (Figure 2.1), we need to define security objectives. In Secure Tropos, it is possible to identify general security objectives using softgoals (e.g., `Documents of quality` in Figure 6.26) and then to refine them using security criteria expressed with security constraints (e.g., `Keep integrity of calculation` and `Keep estimates private`). This strategy is a 'top-down' security objectives identification. However, in Secure Tropos, after defining actor model, it is more natural to define implicit security objectives as the secure dependencies. Then, identified security constraints (e.g., `Keep integrity of calculation`) are examined with respect to security objectives of higher level (e.g., `Documents of quality`) for the system. This strategy we name as 'bottom-up'.

Then, the IS assets are represented in a diagram, shown in Figure 6.27. Here, the main objective is to discover what *plans* have to be performed, *resources* should be available, and *goals* need to be fulfilled, in order to *support business assets*. For example, in Figure 6.27, *plans* (e.g., By hand, By tool) are introduced in order to fulfil the goal Calculate structure.

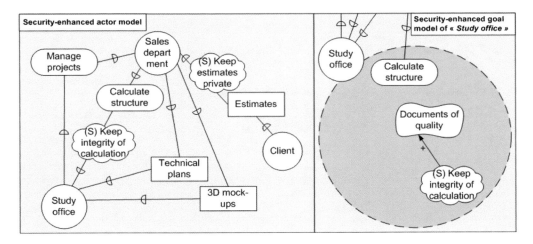

Figure 6.26: Modelling of business assets

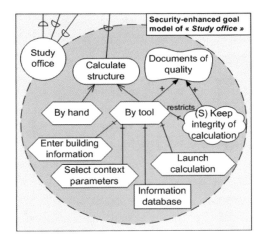

Figure 6.27: Modelling of IS assets

Stage 2. Risk analysis and assessment.

At the second stage, we introduce possible risks. We start by determining the security events. Figure 6.28 focuses on a possible *event* of the risk to which the IS could be exposed, called Authentication attack. It describes a situation where a *threat agent* passes himself off as a trusted actor by stealing an identity, and damages the data in the Information database. The Authentication attack impacts Documents of quality. The traceability between Documents of quality and Calculate structure shows the *harm* at the business level (Figure 6.26). However, in this situation Documents of quality can be interpreted twofold. Firstly, it can represent an *asset*, which is important to an organisation. Then, the impacts link represents a *harm* the risk makes.

Secondly, `Documents of quality` could be considered as a *security criterion*, which needs to be respected. In this case, *impact* defines *negation* of the security criterion.

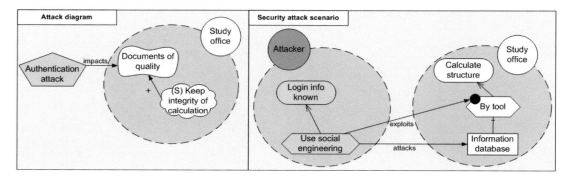

Figure 6.28: Identification of an authentication attack

After identifying the possible risk, we need to refine it in terms of *threat, vulnerability, threat agent* and *attack method*. This is done in the security attack scenario in Figure 6.28. Here, an `Attacker` has a *threat* (`Login info known`) to an IS asset `Information database`, which supports business asset `Calculate structure`. `Attacker` *attacks* `Information database` through exploiting the vulnerability identified in fulfilling the goal `By tool`. Thus, the *exploits* link shows a relationship between an *attack method* (`Use social engineering`) and a *vulnerable IS asset* (`By tool`).

Stage 3. Security requirements definition.

In order to mitigate the identified risk about an `Authentication attack`, in our example, we have chosen a *risk reduction* decision. This means we have to design goals and plans that mitigate the risk. In this example, we add the secure goal `Make users security aware` and the secure plan `Perform awareness training`. Note that new goals and plans have a dotted background pattern, thus, identifying that they represent security requirements in this diagram. In this situation, the `Keep integrity of calculation` also becomes a security requirement mitigating the risk.

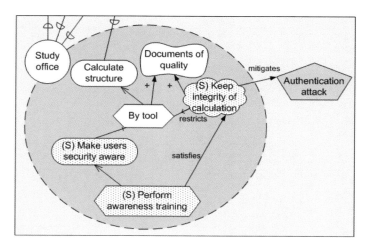

Figure 6.29: Risk treatment and security requirements definition

As discussed in Section 2.1, the ISSRM process is iterative. After definition of security requirements, one needs to test the system again against new possible risk events. For example, modeller can now identify `Internal threat`. This means that the modeller will need to analyse new vulnerabilities and define new countermeasure related to an intentional bad information during security trainings. The first iteration activity is to assume new security requirements become controls, and are, therefore, part of IS. This means that goal `Make users security aware` and plan `Perform awareness training` become IS assets, so removing their pattern in the diagram. A risk analysis and assessment can be performed again.

6.6.4   Theoretical evaluation

We will evaluate our proposal according to the principle of semiotic clarity [OHS05, Moo08]. According to this principle, there should be a one-to-one correspondence between a visual language construct and its referent concept. Otherwise we need to speak about language *redundancy, overload, incompleteness* (*deficit*), and *under-definition* (*excess*) problems.

Redundancy

Redundancy means that two language constructs have the same or overlapping semantics. Redundancy problems with respect to ISSRM were identified in Secure Tropos and discussed in Section 6.4.3. Firstly, in Risk-aware Secure Tropos, we have decreased redundancy level by introducing different visual constructs to model asset-, risk-, and risk treatment-related concepts. Secondly, it might seen that, within the conceptual groups, there is still a high degree of redundancy. For example, an ISSRM *asset* can be expressed using almost all concepts of Risk-aware Secure Tropos (e.g., `Actor`, `Hardgoal`, `Softgoal`, `Plan`, `Resource`). However, we do not see it as a limitation, but rather the opposite. When following the ISSRM *asset* definition, we need to have means to express information (by `Resource`), process (by `Plan`) and different organisational objectives (by different types of a `Goal`). Similar needs can be observed within other two conceptual groups.

An ISSRM *security criterion* can be represented either by `Softgoal` or by `Security constraint`. This correspondence is not used for the same modelling purpose. We represent abstract *security criterion* (e.g., confidentiality, integrity, and availability) using *Softgoals* and more concrete *security criterion* using *Security constraints*.

As mentioned previously, the concept of *event* is represented by `Threat` in the *atack diagram* and by a set of constructs (e.g., `goals`, `plans`, `actors`, etc.) in the *security attack scenario*. Hopefully, this separation of concepts to different levels of abstraction gives better model analysis possibilities, and facilitates the user to catch the information provided in the diagrams [Moo02]. However, this needs to be validated in empirical settings.

Overload

An overload exists if the same language construct has several meanings. In our proposal, there is a link `impacts`, which is used to represent *impacts negates* and *impact harms* concepts of the ISSRM domain model. We allow this overload, first, because it keeps the language relatively simple, without too many modelling constructs. Second, the semantical difference is captured in the label of the impacted construct (`Goal`, `Plan`, `Resource` or `Softgoal`), as we have discussed in Section 6.6.3.

Incompleteness

Incompleteness (or deficit) appears when a language does not convey information on a certain phenomenon. With respect to the incompleteness, first, we need to discuss concepts, which, although present in the ISSRM domain model, are skipped in the Risk-aware Secure Tropos. These are *Risk treatment* (and relationships *decision to treat* and *leads to*), relationships *provokes* and *refines*.

We do not define visual construct for *Risk treatment* (also relationships *decision to treat* and *leads to*), because this concept does not present any modification done to the modelled IS. This concept stands as a rationale and indicates modeller's mental decision. Nevertheless, it needs to be recorded in the system specification, additionally to the created IS model, using other means.

In Risk-aware Secure Tropos, we do not define the single concept of *Risk*. We represent it as combination of a `Threat` and `Impacts` relationship. This means that the ISSRM relationship *significance assessed by* is not explicitly represented by a link. However, we can implicitly identify this relationship by analysing links between *security criteria* (expressed using `Softgoals` or `Security constraints`) and the concerned *risk* (expressed by the `Threat` and `Impacts`).

Due to the overlapping semantics of the `Impacts` relationship, we can only implicitly define *provokes* relationship. This is done through multiple use of the `impacts` link. However, language does not allow modelling which impact has provoked which impact. This information needs to be captured using other means.

Some concepts addressed in Risk-aware Secure Tropos are considered differently than how they are defined in the ISSRM domain model. For example, the ISSRM *threat* consists of a *threat agent* and an *attack method*. Following principles of Tropos, we define that attack agent (`Actor`) holds *threat* and *attack method* (expressed using `Hardgoals` and `Plans`).

Further, the ISSRM *event* consists of *threat* and *vulnerability*. In case of Risk-aware Secure Tropos, we define *event* either as a `Threat` or as a combination of an `Actor`, `Goal`, `Plan`, `Vulnerability point`, `Targets` and `Exploits`. In this situation, we are not able to identify the precise vulnerability *per se* (only the point where it exists). This means that exact vulnerability needs to be specified using other means.

Under-definition

Under-definition (or excess) arises when a language construct has no semantics. In our proposal, we do not observe any under-definition problem.

Secure Tropos

Our proposal has few limitations with respect to Secure Tropos, from which it was derived. In this work, we have stressed that our purpose is to develop a security risk management approach specifically used during the early stages of IS development. This means that we do not consider Secure Tropos extensions to security, which are defined at the late stages of system development. For example, we do not take into account actor *capability* analysis [MGM04, MG07b], or how Secure Tropos models can be used in the system design stages [MJF06]. We understand that these extensions are important for the later modelling stages, however, with respect to Risk-aware Secure Tropos, they require additional investigation.

6.7 Conclusion

This section provides conclusions for the different sections of this chapter.

6.7.1 Research method

The objective of this chapter is to assess the ISSRM support of security-oriented modelling languages. Following the research method we have proposed, we analyse Misuse cases, KeS and Secure Tropos. We show which construct of these languages could be used to support one (or several) ISSRM concept(s), and give some explanations for these assumptions. Our research method did not propose any quantitative assessment of the matches/mismatches between the ISSRM concepts and the language concepts, like, e.g., no match / marginal / partial / total. Such a quantitative estimation has deemed to be too risky in our context. The results we might obtain would not have been reproducible. The quantitative level of match might be indeed different regarding the people involved. Moreover, such an experimentation would have been difficult to set up, mainly regarding our time frame.

6.7.2 Assessment of ISSRM support by security-oriented languages

As a contribution, we highlight the coverage level of ISSRM concepts by security-oriented languages. In most cases, the proposed modelling languages have not been originally designed with security in mind. Such aspects have been incrementally introduced and have enriched existing languages, because of the growing importance of security. As a consequence, such languages have progressively included security risk concepts without a real systematic language design approach. Moreover, most languages are dedicated to specific phases of the system design lifecycle. Therefore, depending on the considered focus, some languages put more emphasis on RM required at the business level (*security goals*, *business assets*, *security requirements*) like Secure-Tropos, while others, more oriented towards late requirements and design, cover concepts like IS asset, vulnerabilities and controls in their scope, like KAOS.

6.7.3 Summary of language comparison

Table 6.1 shows what is missing in terms of concepts for the three completely studied languages to fully support the ISSRM domain. The main observation concerning the coverage table is that currently no perfect match with respect to ISSRM is provided by any existing RE modelling language. Although the languages actually include some risk concepts, their approaches are not complete regarding ISSRM. The coverage table helps to choose the most suitable language, considering the modelling scope of the analyst and the needed concepts and associated activities. For example, Misuse cases appear adequate for eliciting threat agents and attack methods, whereas Secure-Tropos will be more suitable for identifying assets and associated security constraints of an organisation.

This table can also facilitate interoperability between security-modelling languages. Since some languages are better suited to support some risk-related activities than others, they can be used in a complementary manner during the IS development. The coverage table provides a reference for linking and mapping different languages at the ISSRM conceptual level. Moreover, someone already familiar and happy with a language would not be satisfied if he must change this language for another to be able to perform ISSRM at the RE level.

6.7.4   A Risk-aware Secure Tropos

Finally, based on the suggestions for improvement made during the assessment of the language, we have extended both language syntax and semantics, in order to comply with the ISSRM. This has resulted in the Risk-aware Secure Tropos. In addition to the language itself, we have defined methodological guidelines for the application of the language, illustrated through the running example.

The results are discussed in a theoretical evaluation through semiotic clarity. It is generally a difficult task to define an effective modelling language, producing "good" diagrams in the sense that they help to communicate effectively [Moo06b]. A trade-off should be found between extending a language and improving its expressive power, and keeping it simple. Risk-aware Secure Tropos should thus be evaluated through additional criteria. Some modelling practices, like using views, decomposition (use small models and link them with one another) or concept abstraction (use one construct to represent several concepts and thus omit unimportant details), should be assessed [Moo06b]. This discussion should be completed by an experiment in a real environment. Such an experiment would provide the clues of the effectiveness of this extension to support ISSRM and highlight its weaknesses.

6.8   Chapter summary

In this chapter, security-oriented languages were compared to the ISSRM domain model. The objective was to assess their coverage level for ISSRM concepts.

First, a research method was proposed. This research method describes how we proceeded to compare a language with respect to the ISSRM domain model. The languages analysed were Misuse cases, KeS and Secure-Tropos. Then, a summary of language comparison and ways of improvement for a better coverage level was proposed, and some preliminary remarks were suggested for Abuse cases, Abuse frames, Mal-activity diagrams and Tropos Goal-Risk framework, based on our current knowledge of these languages.

The identified ways of improvement were then particularly examined for Secure Tropos. We proposed a concrete and abstract syntax extension of Secure Tropos. This extension was applied on the running example. Finally, an evaluation of this extension was performed based on the principle of semiotic clarity. The chapter ends by some conclusions.

Part III

Applications

Chapter 7

Evaluation

T his chapter reports on an experimentation of the domain model and its associated metrics on a Luxemburger SME, in the context of an ISO/IEC 27001 certification [ISO05b]. More and more companies are interested in the ISO/IEC 27001 certification in Europe and particularly in Luxembourg. It is also becoming a source of interest for the security research community. Consequently, it is deemed a valuable application case to experiment some artefacts produced in this thesis, since the set up of an ISO/IEC 27001 compliant ISMS relies on a security risk management approach. The research question addressed in the reported experiment can be formulated as: *Are the ISSRM domain model and its associated metrics a sufficient guideline for ISSRM activities in the frame of an ISO/IEC 27001 certification?*

The ISO/IEC 27001 certification is considered as complex and difficult to set up, mainly for SMEs, which generally have a low budget and very few human resources to allocate to such a project. Helping the SMEs to reach the certification is an objective of the CRP Henri Tudor, in its role of assistance to SMEs. The Codasystem company, in the aim to obtain the certification, accepted to be the target of an experimentation of some research results developed at the CRP Henri Tudor, for supporting SMEs in their certification process. The experimentation started in June 2006 and ended in May 2008. The collaboration between our team and Codasystem is evaluated at about 100 man-days of CRP resources. The total documentation produced is over 300 pages. In this context, the ISSRM domain model and its associated metrics were experimented. This chapter reports on this experimentation and evaluates some of our research results. The complete study cannot be shown. For confidentiality reasons, only excerpts are provided for illustration purposes.

Section 7.1 presents the Codasystem company. The experiment being based on an ISO/IEC 27001 certification, an introduction to the certification appears in Section 7.2. Section 7.3 explains how the ISSRM domain model was a key driver for our experiment. Then, Section 7.4 reports on the experiment with the ISSRM metrics, defined in Chapter 5. Section 7.5 discusses about the metrics used, their implementation and the differences with the metrics proposed in Chapter 5. Section 7.6 lists the threats to validity. Finally, Section 7.7 draws conclusions from our experimentation.

7.1   The Codasystem company

Codasystem is a SME in Luxembourg offering innovative security services based on new IT technologies. The value proposition associated to their services is based on the management of the authenticity of digital documents. It is further detailed in Section 7.1.1 and relies on an authenticity process presented in Section 7.1.2. The security of its IS is a main issue, considering its business.

7.1.1   Context and proposed product

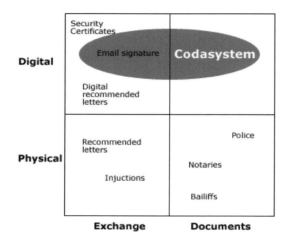

Figure 7.1: Proposed product (as appears in [Cod])

Digitalisation of documents and communications brought considerable advantages: speed, ease of use, ease of communication, forwarding, improved editing and archiving, gain of physical space, increase in search speed and ease of exchange of large amounts of information. However, it also comes with quantity of risks: information access to unauthorised individuals (aggravated by ease of transfers), content alteration (photo editing, creation of fakes, etc.), uncertainty of provenance (hoaxes, misinformation, etc.), viruses, etc.

The product of Codasystem addresses the need for a reliable, secure and easy to use system, capable of circumventing these risks both on electronic documents and exchanges (Figure 7.1). Currently solutions available on the market are focused on securing exchanges (authentication, email signatures, cryptography, as depicted in the left part of Figure 7.1). No solution exists that could provide undisputable proof in court for both the electronic document and its exchange exists.

Codasystem offers the first integrated solution for the creation of digital proofs and their secure distribution. The solution of Codasystem has been examined by a law firm expert in digitalisation and legal property, and has received an approval regarding its legal value. The technology of Codasystem is patented in France and extended worldwide.

7.1.2 Technology

The process guaranteeing the authenticity of a document (called "the authenticity process") consists in the following steps, illustrated in Figure 7.2, and extracted from [Cod]:

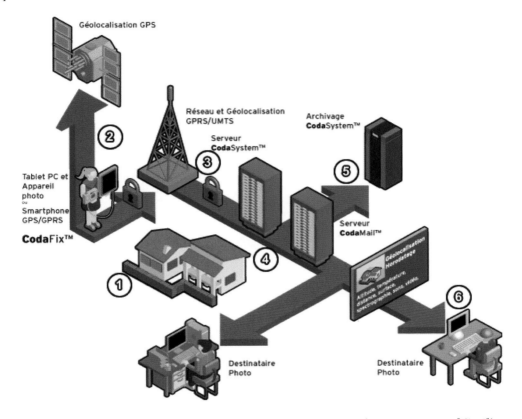

Figure 7.2: The authenticity process of Codasystem (as appears in [Cod])

Step 1

- A place, an object, a document, an event requires control.

- With a Tablet PC and a digital camera, or a smartphone device, a digital picture is taken on the spot.

- It can also be a digital audio recording or a short video recording.

Step 2

- The picture created is immediately tattooed (using steganographic[1] techniques) with the environmental information captured at the precise instant the picture was taken.

- The information captured can be : the author, the localisation (using GPS), time and date (certified), altitude, temperature or any other kind of numerical information.

---

[1]Steganography is used to insert hidden information without cryptography

- Pictures taken can also be instantly included in a document dynamically created by a word processing software.

Step 3

- The recipients of the documents are then selected in the software (email addresses).

- The pictures and the report are encrypted and sent via GPRS, EDGE, UMTS, WIFI or home/office Internet connection to the servers of Codasystem.

Step 4

- The Codasystem server authentifies the author of the picture and of the email and verifies the integrity of the files generated.

- The server stores the files in the private storage area of the author.

- The server notifies the recipients of the arrival of the files (notification sent by email with url to see them).

Step 5

- The files stored on the server are then digitally archived in conformity with European norm on digital archiving (NF Z 42-013 [NF 01]).

Step 6

- The recipients receive the notification and access the documents via the url provided.

- If the recipients are declared users of the system, they can, in turn, sign and send these proofs via our certified mail platform (Codamail) to other recipients.

- The ultimate proof stays on the Codasystem servers.

The authenticity process and its implementation are regularly evaluated by security experts. The objective is to audit the service proposed by Codasystem. The process is currently considered as secure regarding the last evaluations. However, even if the presented process is secure, some security flaws can emerge from the global organisation of Codasystem. The objective of Codasystem to obtain the ISO/IEC 27001 certification is motivated by the improvement of its global security, instead of focussing on the technical aspects of their proposed services. Codasystem now wants to broaden the scope of security risk management to the whole of its organisation.

7.2   The ISO/IEC 27001 certification

The outcome of an ISO/IEC 27001 certification is the effective establishment and management of an ISMS (cf. Section 2.4.1). It is built around a PDCA (Plan-Do-Check-Act) cycle, which objective is a continual improvement of IS security.

For an organisation to be certified, it is necessary to be compliant with the set of normative requirements defined by the standard. Those are expressed from [ISO05b,

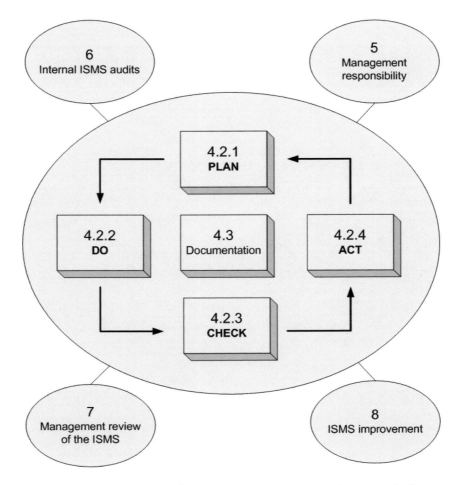

Figure 7.3: The ISO/IEC 27001 requirements in a nutshell

Section 4] to [ISO05b, Section 8] of the document. The other sections are considered to be informative, and hence not mandatory for the certification. The set of normative requirements can be summarised as represented in Figure 7.3. The figure presents the different parts of the standard, structured by section.

First of all, it is necessary to establish and manage the ISMS following the PDCA cycle, composed of four iterative steps (described from [ISO05b, Section 4.2.1] to [ISO05b, Section 4.2.4]). These four steps are supported by a specific documentation, whose requirements are explained in [ISO05b, Section 4.3]. The four steps and the documentation represent the core requirements that one should satisfy to be certified. Additionally, some requirements are especially developed in a dedicated section, because of their importance or complexity. The first one in this case is the management responsibility, explaining where it is necessary for the management to be specifically involved [ISO05b, Section 5]). A part is dedicated to the way to perform the internal ISMS audits, which are mandatory [ISO05b, Section 6]). Regular management reviews are necessary in the cycle. They also have a dedicated part [ISO05b, Section 7]). Finally, the normative requirements sections end with an explanation about how to perform the ISMS improvement [ISO05b, Section 8]).

Regarding the RM process, it is at the core of the standard. It first starts in the

'Plan' step, with a complete assessment and management of risks. In the 'Do', the risk treatment plan is applied and the selected measures are implemented. Then, in the 'Check' step, the risk assessment results and the efficiency of the RM process are evaluated. If some updates are necessary or if some ways of improvement are identified for either the risk assessment results or the RM process, the appropriate improvements are done in the 'Act' step.

7.3   Evaluation of the ISSRM domain model

The ISSRM domain model was used as a guideline to perform the different risk-related tasks and to explain the different concepts to the stakeholders. First, the domain model and its associated definitions were the central artefacts used during the trainings of the Codasystem team. Second, instantiating the different concepts of the domain model were used to produce all the risk-related artefacts required by the standard.

We chose to present the different tasks to perform and concepts to use with the help of the domain model, instead of using, as usual, documents (methods, standards, etc.) in natural language. No formal conlusion can be drawn from the efficiency of using our model instead of text for learning purpose. To compare both approaches, a dedicated experiment should be performed. However, the result we obtained is that the Codasystem team catched the domain quickly and without any problem. They considered our domain model easy to understand and helpful in gaining a general view of ISSRM. Moreover, they integrated the domain model in the training that has to be followed by each new employee.

As depicted in Figure 7.4, the instantiation of the meta-model led to different documents, that are the risk-related part of the whole ISMS documentation. Four different documents were built, following mainly the different tasks (Section 2.1) to perform. They concern:

1. *Business assets and the related security objectives*: we identified 6 business assets, leading to 18 security objectives in terms of confidentiality, integrity and availability.

2. *IS assets and their link to the business assets*: more than 100 IS assets were identified.

3. *Risk assessment and treatment decisions*: 78 risks were identified and treated.

4. *Statement of applicability, about the chosen security requirements and their concrete application, and risk treatment plan, about what still needs to be implemented and how, with respect to the statement of applicability*: 112 security requirements were selected and implemented.

As seen in Figure 7.4, every concept was part of a document (except *asset*, that is abstract). The validation that the instanciation of the meta-model is sufficient to cover the requirements of the standard in terms of risk-related tasks was provided by the auditors. Those had to check the documentation and highlight missing elements. However, they claimed that the documentation was complete with regards to the ISO/IEC 27001 requirements.

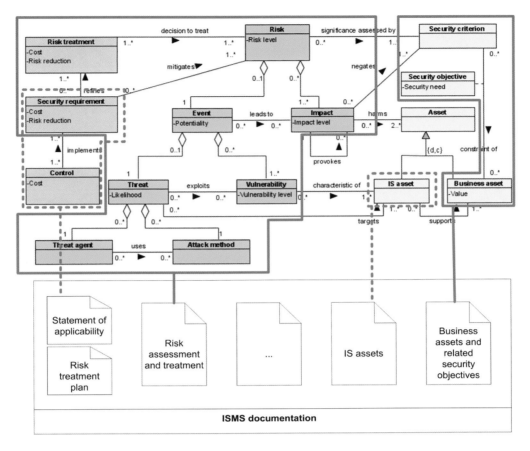

Figure 7.4: Mapping between the ISMS documentation and the ISSRM domain model

7.4 Evaluation of the ISSRM metrics

After checking the completeness of our domain model in terms of concepts to integrate in the risk-related tasks, we now focus on the ISSRM metrics. The following section is dedicated to the experimentation of the ISSRM metrics.

7.4.1 Process and approach

The process followed is mainly based on the ISO/IEC 27005 standard [ISO08], which provides guidelines for performing security risk management. This approach was chosen because it is the one specially developed to satisfy the requirements of the ISO/IEC 27001 standard. We complemented these guidelines with the knowledge bases and some methodological parts borrowed from the EBIOS method [DCS04b], like the security objective analysis, because they are well suited to satisfy the requirements of the standard. The key driver of our work was to be compliant with the ISO/IEC 27001 requirements.

As seen in Section 5.4.1, the ISO/IEC 27005 standard promotes the use of metrics. Yet, the user has to complete them and choose how they are defined and used. In our case, we tried to adapt and complete these metrics with regards to the ones we have identified in Section 5.5, to test their relevance in a concrete case. Our objective was therefore to validate that our set of metrics can be concretely instanciated, and that it satisfies the requirements related to estimation activities (i.e. estimation of each necessary concept). For each metric identified in Section 5.5, we proposed a concrete implementation, and discuss it now with regards to its application in our context and the requirements of the standard.

The presentation of the work done is performed following the steps identified in Section 2.1.

7.4.2 Context and asset identification

In this step the assets of Codasystem were identified. We started by defining what are the business assets of the organisation and then, based on the inventory of the IS assets, we mapped each IS asset to its related business asset(s). For identifying business assets, a process-oriented approach was chosen. We first modelled the Codasystem organisation under the form of processes, and then, each process represented an asset. The security-sensitive information was identified as input and/or output of the processes.

Each asset was then estimated in terms of its intrinsic value for the organisation, through the *business asset value* metric. A qualitative estimation was proposed based on Table 7.1. This table had three levels: normal, high and very high. The description column was filled with the help of Codasystem and mainly its management, who best knew what was of value for the company. A three-level scale was judged satisfactory by Codasystem. Situating an asset in one of the three categories was usually non subject to ambiguity. A business asset that concerned directly the authenticity process or had a great importance for the clients had a very high value. A high level concerned Codasystem's clients. Finally, an asset with normal value only concerned the internal functioning of Codasystem, that is, had no any direct relation with the clients. An asset considered to be of low value for the company was not retained as being of interest for the rest of the process. This explains why there was no 'Low' line in Table 7.1.

Table 7.1: Qualitative scale of value for the value of business assets

Business asset value	
Value	Description
Very high	Asset concerning the authenticity process or with great importance regarding the clients
High	Asset concerning the clients of Codasystem
Normal	Asset concerning the internal functioning of Codasystem

Example: The process of 'Photo taking', i.e. the first activity to perform in the whole authenticity process, is identified as a business asset of Codasystem. This process is described in terms of its tasks. Its inputs and outputs are also identified in order to highlight important information. They are not completely described here for confidentiality purpose. The value of this asset is naturally estimated to be very high, because it is part of the authenticity process.

7.4.3 Determination of security objectives

In this step, we cross-checked the business assets identified in the preceding step with the selected security criteria. With the Codasystem's management, we decided to select confidentiality, integrity and availability as the security criteria of interest regarding the business. They cover well the security issues of the company. Moreover, in ISO/IEC 27001 these are the main criteria to perform ISSRM.

For each of these criteria, a qualitative scale of four levels was defined (cf. Table 7.2), representing the level of *security need*. This scale was based on the results of the value estimation of business assets. Levels 1 to 3 were defined in accordance with the business asset value scale, aiming at aligning security objectives with business assets value. So, each business asset had at most (for a given criterion) the same level as the one obtained in the preceding step. Naturally, a business asset could even so have a lower level, for example when it was not concerned with the given criterion (e.g., a financial information with a very high value can need to be kept confidential, but can have no need of availability). The top level was level 3. For confidentiality, this meant the disclosure of information (external or internal to Codasystem) was restricted to the clients. For integrity, it was a modification of the authenticity of digital documents, which we saw was the top concern in the preceding step. Finally, for availability, it was a disruption with major effects on the clients. Level 2 was, for confidentiality, about the disclosure of information shared between Codasystem and its clients. It was one level below, because the Codasystem team was allowed to know this kind of information. For integrity, it was an acceptable modification of integrity (by 'acceptable' we meant that the integrity could be restored, e.g., through a backup). At last, for availability, it was a disruption with minor effect on the clients. Level 1 was, for confidentiality, about disclosure of information restricted to Codasystem (internal to the company) and hence not concerning the clients. For availability, it was about a disruption without any effect on the clients. For integrity, in agreement with the management, no relevant security need level was found, that was equivalent with this level of confidentiality or availability. This level was therefore not used for this criterion. That is neither a problem for the risk assessment, nor regarding the certification requirements. The lowest level was 0, used when the business asset had no security need for this criterion.

It is interesting to note that the description of each security need level was based on the potential impacts. This way of proceeding is common in several approaches, like the EBIOS method [DCS04b]. It aims at first focussing on impact when analysing risks. Therefore, it avoids to have a too long and complex set of risks to manage, because we ignore security events without relevant impacts. Each business asset was thus situated in this table in order to define the security objectives to consider and their associated security needs. We read the table in the the following way: "if the criterion X is not respected for the business asset Y, the impact would be [...]". So each business asset is associated with security criteria, defining security objectives with security needs.

Example: The process of 'Photo taking' has no need of confidentiality. This process covers the tasks performed on the device when taking the photo, until its transfer to the Codasystem production site. At this time, we consider that everyone in this context

Table 7.2: Qualitative scale of value for the security need metric

Security need levels			
	Confidentiality	**Integrity**	**Availability**
0	No need of confidentiality	No need of integrity	No need of availability
1	Disclosure of information restricted to Codasystem	/	Disruption internal to Codasystem without any effect on the clients
2	Disclosure of information restricted to Codasystem and its clients	Acceptable modification of integrity	Disruption with minor effect on the clients
3	Disclosure of information restricted to Codasystem's clients	Modification of the authenticity of digital documents	Disruption with major effect on the clients

knows the content of the photo (or can know, talking about people not taking the photo but around the actor taking the photo). However, the authenticity process starts by the tasks done by the device and the integrity is therefore maximum. A modification of integrity for this process leads to a modification of the authenticity of the document. The same applies for availability, on which a failure is considered for this business asset as having a major effect on the clients. Codasystem's clients have generally contractual requirements to respect that include time constraints. Not to be able to use its system can lead, for example, to financial penalties for the client. As a summary, the process of 'Photo taking' has respectively for the criteria of confidentiality, integrity and availability a security need of 0, 3 and 3.

7.4.4 Risk analysis and assessment

Once security needs of assets were defined for each security criterion, we analysed the risks. We first started by identifying the threats relevant to the IS. This task was done first by a brainstorming with some key actors of the company, like the security officer, and then complemented by an analysis of the available knowledge bases [DCS04b, ISO08] for completeness purposes.

The *likelihood of the threat* was estimated on a qualitative scale going from 1 to 3 (Table 7.3). As for business asset value, three levels were chosen in agreement with Codasystem. On this scale, it was possible for Codasystem to estimate threats in a non-ambiguous manner. The first level depicted threats that were unlikely regarding the statistics, the incurred cost or the necessary competence. These threats should happen rarely. The second level was a transitional level, including threats that could arrive sometimes but not very often, at the opposite of level 3. Finally, the third level was about threats that were very likely to happen, or easy to perform with no particular investment or competence necessary. Level 0 was not proposed because only the relevant threats, that might arrive at least rarely, were selected.

Threats were associated with some vulnerabilities that were exploited by the threat for the risk to take place effectively. Once again, the vulnerabilities were identified through a brainstorming with some key actors of the company and then complemented by an analysis of the available knowledge bases. EBIOS proposes, for example, for

Table 7.3: Qualitative scale of value for the likelihood metric

Likelihood of threat	
Level	Description
1	Unlikely regarding the statistics, the incurred cost or the necessary competence
2	Can happen occasionally
3	Very likely, easy to perform, no particular investment or competence necessary

each kind of threat, a list of vulnerabilities that are common and relevant regarding the threat. The vulnerabilities related to IS assets of Codasystem were taken into account.

A qualitative scale of four non-ambiguous levels was determined for *vulnerability level* estimation (Table 7.4). The first level corresponded to very low vulnerabilities, taking place when security measures were in place and efficient against the threat. This level was 0 because we considered the best was done regarding the state of the art of security measures, the threat concerned and the context. Level 1 corresponded to medium vulnerabilities. Some security measures were in place, but they were insufficient or not perfectly adapted to the situation. The next level appeared when vulnerabilities are high, and when no effective security measure was in place. However, at this level, some security measures were starting to be implemented or already implemented but not efficiently. The highest vulnerability level was 3, considered as very high vulnerabilities, with a lack of security measures, or some existing security measures that were obsolete or not applied. In our context, each vulnerability was not estimated independently. For each threat, a set of vulnerabilities was generally identified and then the global vulnerability level was estimated. This way of proceeding allows to have, for a given risk, only one likelihood and one vulnerability level, that facilitates the calculation of event potentiality. This point is further discussed in Section 7.5.

Table 7.4: Qualitative scale of value for the vulnerability level metric

Vulnerability level	
Level	Description
0	Very low, security measures in place and efficient against the threat
1	Medium, security measures insufficient or not adapted
2	High, no effective security measure in place
3	Very high, lack of security measure, obsolete or not applied

At this point, each element necessary to estimate the risk had been itself estimated: impacts in Section 7.4.3 through security needs determination, and threats and vulnerabilities in Section 7.4.4. We thus defined the following assumption for the concept of event: the potentiality of the event is calculated by summing the likelihood and the vulnerability level minus 1. Based on the examples already seen in the literature, the feedback received from other ISO/IEC 27001 implementers and our experience [Her], this equation produces some well-balanced risk levels, by better aligning the *impact level* with the *potentiality*. It is necessary to make such calculation assumptions for determining the *risk level*, and determining the *risk level* is mandatory for the certification. The ISO/IEC 27001 standard does not provide any constraint for this estimation. The same for ISO/IEC 27005 that only provides some examples for risk and event estimation. We are therefore free to define our own way of calculating the risk level.

Then, a risk matrix was produced (Table 7.5). This risk matrix indicated the risk level, based on the potentiality (equal to "likelihood + vulnerability level - 1") and the maximum impact level of the concerned impacts for the studied business asset. By 'concerned impact', we mean that each threat will not lead to impacts negating every security criteria for each asset. Some threats are particular to some kinds of security criteria. For example, a threat based on the 'Remote spying' attack method is only leading to impacts having effect on the confidentiality criterion [DCS04b]. This kind of threat cannot negate the integrity or the availability of assets, having not an active effect on the assets. Therefore, we defined the impact level of a risk as being the maximum of concerned security needs (Table 7.2). The risk level was calculated by multiplying the potentiality by the impact level. It was obtained by spotting the risk level in the risk matrix (Table 7.5).

Table 7.5: Risk matrix

Risk level							
Impact level \ Potentiality	0	1	2	3	4	5
1	0	1	2	3	4	5
2	0	2	4	**6**	**8**	**10**
3	0	3	**6**	**9**	**12**	**15**

As preliminary work for this step, we needed to define what was an intolerable risk and hence the acceptable level of risk. This is mandatory in ISO/IEC 27001. Each organisation has its own level of acceptable risk, depending on its objectives in terms of security. For example, one can determine that an unacceptable risk is a risk that can happen occasionally (likelihood=2), that has insufficient or not adapted security measures (vulnerability level=1) and that has an impact level of 3. In this case, the level of this unacceptable risk is 6 (Risk level=3x(2+1-1)=6) and each risk having a level below this one is considered as acceptable. This level has to be determined and formally approved by the management. Each risk having a level superior to the acceptable risk level has to be treated in the next step (represented in bold in Table 7.5).

Example[2]: 'Software malfunction' of the software provided by Codasystem and included in the device taking photos is a threat that can occur. Its likelihood is estimated at 2, because it can happen sometimes based on the experience of developers. Some vulnerabilities are identified that allow the threat to occur. 'Documentation not up-to-date', 'Deficiencies in software testing', 'Deficiencies in incident reports' are the

---

[2]This example and the associated levels of metrics are fictitious, and are not extracted from the real experimentation.

vulnerabilities highlighted that are related to the threat. The global vulnerability level is of 2 because no effective measures are in place for these vulnerabilities. Finally the impact level is 3, coming from the security need in terms of integrity and availability for 'Photo taking', that are both concerned by this threat. The level of risk is thus estimated to 9 according to the risk matrix. During risk evaluation, we compare this risk level with the risk acceptance level, that is of 6. This risk is therefore unacceptable and shall be treated.

7.4.5 Selection of risk treatment and security requirements

For each risk, it was now necessary to choose a suited risk treatment and associated security requirements. In our method based on ISO/IEC 27005, each risk having a level inferior to the risk acceptance level was systematically accepted. If the risk level was superior to the risk acceptance level, it was necessary to reduce, transfer or avoid the risk. In case of risk reduction, requirements (called 'controls' in ISO/IEC 27005, as seen in Section 4.3.3) were selected in the ISO/IEC 27002 standard [ISO05c], as recommended for the certification. However, it is possible to select requirements from other sources or define our own requirements if necessary. Requirements regarding the third parties were also recommended when some risks were transferred. With regards to the selection of these security requirements, the vulnerability level (called "New vulnerability level" in Table 7.6) was calculated, leading to a new risk level. Thus, the risk reduction of the chosen risk treatment was deduced, being the original risk level minus the new risk level. Table 7.6 recapitulates the risk assessment and treatment of our example.

Example: The risk treatment chosen is to reduce the risk with some security requirements. Three requirements are chosen to mitigate the three vulnerabilities found. First, the software developed shall be carefully documented for reducing the weakness of documentation that is not up-to-date. Second, test data shall be selected carefully. Moreover, test data shall be protected and controlled. This helps to mitigate the vulnerability of deficiencies in software testing. Finally information security events shall be reported through appropriate management channels and as quickly as possible. This last requirement covers the deficiencies in incident reports. These requirements lead to a new vulnerability level of 0, the security measures chosen being now efficient against the threat. Thus, the new risk level is 9, with respect to the risk matrix (Table 7.5). The risk reduction of the chosen treatment is 6.

7.4.6 Control selection and implementation

"Statement of applicability" and "Risk treatment plan" are two mandatory documents according to the standard requirements. The first one summarises the chosen security requirements and shows how they are currently implemented. The second one collects the controls that still need to be implemented, for completely fulfilling the chosen security requirements.

In the risk treatment plan, the costs of the controls were estimated. These costs are generally defined in terms of financial data or in man-day.

Table 7.6: Risk assessment and treatment table

Risk assessment and treatment				
Business asset		Photo taking		
Security need		C=0	I=3	A=3
Threat	**Likelihood**	Software malfunction		2
Vulnerability	**Vulnerability level**	Documentation not up-to-date	2	
		Deficiencies in software testing		
		Deficiencies in incident reports		
Risk level		9		
Risk treatment		Risk reduction		
Security requirement	**New vulnerability level**	The software developed shall be carefully documented	0	
		Test data shall be selected carefully, and protected and controlled		
		Information security events shall be reported through appropriate management channels as quickly as possible		
New risk level		3		
Risk reduction of the risk treatment		6		

Table 7.7: Risk treatment plan

Control selection and implementation					
Control	Start date	End date	Resource	Owner	Cost
Write documentation of existing developed software	01/04/09	31/06/09	John Doe	John Doe	10 man-days

Example: To fulfil the requirement of documenting carefully the developed software, a resource has been assigned to write documentation about the already developed software. The cost of this task is 10 man-days.

7.5 Discussion

From the feedback obtained through this experimentation, this section discusses some particularly interesting aspects. They are the methodological differences with the recommended ISO/IEC 27005 standard, the metrics definition and their implementation.

7.5.1 Methodological aspects

In the first step about context and asset identification, our method was slightly different from the one generally adopted when following ISO/IEC 27005. Instead of directly valuing the assets according to their impact value, as it is commonly done, we first valued the intrinsic value of the assets and then their security needs based on the potential impacts on the assets in terms of confidentiality, integrity and availability, as defined in Chapter 5. This method provided some benefits. It was first easier to explain this step of the process to the Codasystem team. This step of the process is indeed generally difficult to understand for the users seeking to estimate the assets. It also helped the users to limit their answers. Based on our experience, it was noticed that it is usually difficult for the stakeholders to precisely describe their security needs and to express all of them at the same level of granularity. The security need levels table was built thanks to the results of the asset estimation. For example, it was only there that we clearly defined that the most important assets (and so impacts) were those related directly to the clients and to the authenticity of digital documents.

7.5.2 Definition of the scales

With regards to our experience, we mainly used qualitative estimations. This choice was motivated by several arguments. First, qualitative scales are easier to define and use especially in SMEs. Qualitative estimation is suited for organisations that have few security incident in their history. This is the case for Codasystem, which is a young company. Moreover, the examples provided in ISO/IEC 27005 for performing ISSRM according to an ISO/IEC 27001 certification are mainly qualitative. Thus, such estimations are sufficient and suited in our context. The main difficulty regarding the set-up of the qualitative scales was to be precise and to avoid ambiguities as much as possible. This objective is considered to be reached, because the different people who used the estimation tables did not have any difficulty to use them and distinguish the different levels. It is however necessary to note that these scales were built incrementally, with refinements coming from comments of Codasystem's users.

7.5.3 Implementation of the metrics

Assets in general have to be estimated for the certification. So, although our set of metrics does not propose any metric for IS assets, it has been necessary to define a value for IS assets. Regarding the existing mapping between IS assets and business assets (*supports* link of the domain model in Figure 4.4), each IS asset inherits from the highest security needs (for each security criterion) of the business assets it supports. By applying this method, we got good results and improved the efficiency of the process. IS assets are usually numerous (about 100 in our case) and difficult to manage one by one. Focussing on business assets helps to concentrate on the main concerns of the organisation and give their right value to the IS assets regarding the business.

The threats and vulnerabilities were estimated in a classical manner with regards to the guidelines of the standard. The vulnerability level metric was not implemented, as suggested in the ISSRM domain model, by associating one level to each vulnerability. The vulnerability level was defined for the set of vulnerabilities exploited by the threat studied. The feedback coming from this implementation is that: either the ISSRM process could be improved by associating a vulnerability level to each vulnerability and thereby refine the risk analysis, or we should include the notion of *group of vulnerabilities* in the ISSRM domain model. In our context, defining a vulnerability level for each vulnerability was evaluated as too time-consuming. However, it is now identified as a way of improving our process.

The risk reduction was only calculated for the risk treatment chosen. Following our assumption of estimating the set of vulnerabilities and not each vulnerability separately, we estimated the risk reduction of the set of requirements refining the risk treatment, equal to the risk reduction of the risk treatment. It is difficult to precisely estimate the contribution of each security requirement with regards to the idenfitied vulnerabilities (cf. Section 5.5). One security requirement can mitigate several risks and one risk can be mitigated by several security requirements. However, to improve the risk reduction estimation, and refine the calculation of the ROSI of the security requirement, it is necessary to be able to estimate the contribution of each security requirement regarding the risks. Improving either the metric implementation, or the way of analysing the vulnerabilities and the security requirements, is considered as a possible improvement of the method. Another way to improve it could be to reformulate more precisely the different vulnerabilities and security requirements, to be able to define precisely the risk reduction of each security requirement. Moreover, this method implies to define new knowledge bases in support of the process. Within the 'Check' phase of the PDCA cycle, this represents a way of improving the efficiency of the RM process. Not having a precise estimation of the risk reduction of security requirements prevents a precise calculation of ROSI. Instead, the ROSI can only be calculated at the level of risk treatment.

Finally, the cost was not estimated for each security requirement and/or risk treatment. The cost was only estimated for the controls still in need of implementation, within the document called "Risk treatment plan". Thus, the ROSI was not formally calculated with the help of a metric. It was the role of the management to evaluate which security requirement (or set of security requirements) is cost-effective or not. Even so, we tried to implement the different cost metrics. It remained difficult to concretely implement them. The method used for the cost was the following: for each non-acceptable risk, its cost was roughly estimated. Then, the cost of the suggested security requirements (or of some other kind of risk treatment, e.g., risk transfer) was also estimated. Depending on both these costs, it was up to the management to accept this security solution to risk or a new risk treatment is chosen.

7.6 Threats to validity

The relevance of the evaluation results has to be confronted with the particularities of our experiment. We thus now discuss the threats to validity of the claim: the ISSRM domain model and its associated metrics are valid and useful to perform ISSRM activities.

7.6.1 Context of Codasystem

The business of Codasystem is to guarantee the authenticity of digital documents. This implies naturally to take into account many security aspects, like keeping these documents confidential or making sure the integrity is preserved. Despite the fact that the Codasystem team had no particular knowledges about ISSRM, their learning of the domain might have been facilitated by their security awareness.

Concerning the time spent on the certification, it is difficult to interpret the figures proposed in the introduction, and still more to use them, for example for comparison with other certification. First, the estimation done concerns only the time spent on site with the Codasystem team. It was not possible to estimate and trace our learning and preparation time, because it was completely mixed with other related research and standardisation activities. Second, the time spent was dependent of Codasystem's organisation. One of the major difficulty we had to face was the human resource changes. The team in charge of the certification changed actually two times during the experiment.

7.6.2 Certification specificities

Our evaluation was performed within the scope of an ISO/IEC 27001 certification. The domain model and the metrics were evaluated in this setting. Thereby, this evaluation corresponds to one application of the domain model and the metrics. A fixed conclusion on the validity and the usability of the domain model and the metrics can only be drawn based on several experiments. In a controlled experiment, we could compare in a controlled environment the efficiency and relevance of using the domain model and implementing the proposed metrics.

Moreover, our conclusions were mainly drawn based on the audit performed by the auditors. The audit was not performed on the whole ISMS, but on a sampling. Furthermore, the audit results were naturally subjective, because dependent of the experience, knowledge and culture of the auditors.

7.6.3 Experiment specificities

This experiment was led by our team and therefore by the creators of the domain model and the metrics. Naturally, our knowledge of these artefacts was already thorough and no time had to be spent on learning the concepts. This also means that the artefacts were clear to us and not subject to misinterpretation. However, this clarity cannot be generalized and this experiment cannot give information about the effectiveness of use of the domain model and the metrics by other people, without the guidance of their developers. Further evaluation is needed to answer this question.

7.7 Conclusion

The first conclusion we can draw from our evaluation is that our ISSRM approach was effective. Codasystem was certified and no nonconformity was related to the ISSRM process[3].

The metrics proposed in Chapter 5 were suited for performing ISSRM in the frame of an ISO/IEC 27001 certification. The auditors did not find any problem with regards to the related requirements of the standard. This experiment has thus shown that our set of metrics is sufficient for the risk-related activities of an ISO/IEC 27001 certification.

When comparing the metrics identified in Chapter 5 and the approach performed in our evaluation, the weakest point identified is related to the ROSI calculation. First,

---

[3]In our context, to be certified, the audit report should not mention any major nonconformity and not more than five minor ones. In our case, four minor nonconformities were found in the whole ISMS

vulnerabilities were estimated by group and hence risk reduction of security requirements follow the same approach. The risk reduction level was therefore only estimated
for each risk treatment. Moreover, the ROSI was not formally calculated. The risk
treatments and security requirements costs were roughly estimated and weakly documented (estimations of costs were depicted in the risk treatment plan, presenting the
cost of each requirement that still needed to be implemented). This is explained first
by the fact that the calculation of ROSI is not mandatory in the ISO/IEC 27001 standard. The main objective underlying the ISSRM process within the ISO/IEC 27001
standard is not to have the best ROSI[4], but to have the insurance that the organisation is aware of its risks and has risk governance. Second, it is necessary to note
that Codasystem already had a legacy in terms of security. Many security controls
were already implemented before starting the experiment. Some security requirements
selected after the risk assessment for mitigating some risks were thus already implemented, and hence did not need to be estimated in terms of implementation cost. In
the frame of an IS development, the ROSI calculation for each security requirement
has more sense. After our experiment, another remark on the complexity of the cost
metric implementation, is that it is difficult to compare qualitative metrics (risk reduction) with quantitative ones (cost of treatments). Finally, it is necessary to note
that in Codasystem (and, we guess, in most of companies seeking ISO/IEC 27001 certification) a global budget was allocated by the management to security. The initial
objective regarding the financial aspect was to respect this budget, rather than pur-
sue an optimal ROSI. A good and efficient estimation of costs and ROSI calculation
remains an open challenge. A new case study focused on ROSI calculation shall be
defined, to validate whether every metric of the ISSRM domain model is necessary
and adapted to ROSI calculation.

Finally, our approach was supported by tables and no dedicated software was developed to facilitate data gathering and the various estimations. To improve and
accelerate the process, a software tool would be useful.

7.8   Chapter summary

This chapter was about the experimentation of the ISSRM domain model and its
associated metrics. This experimentation was done in the frame of an ISO/IEC 27001
certification. We collaborated with the Codasystem SME to assist their team in the
implementation of their ISMS.

We first explained how the domain model was used as a training artefact for the
Codasystem team, and as a guideline for performing the different risk-related tasks.
The goal was to satisfy the requirements of the standard. Second, the set of metrics
defined in Chapter 5 was experimented. Throughout the RM process, we evaluated
whether instanciating the metrics we identified was sufficient or not to cover the requirements of the standard in terms of risk estimation. The results were positive, but
some possible improvements were nonetheless identified. We finally discussed about
the limitations of the work done and the threats to validity.

---

[4]Even if the RM process is especially used to balance the security risks and the costs involved in the
security

Part IV

Conclusion

Chapter 8

Conclusions and Future Work

N owadays, information security is not simply a technical problem any more. The management of security has become a key issue within organisations. The cost of a security solution is considered with as much attention as its effectiveness. Security risk management methods are methodological tools dealing with this concern. However, this research has observed that, first, despite structured processes, the (intermediate and final) products of those methods are generally informal. Second, those methods are usually designed to evaluate a posteriori existing IS, rather than supporting the IS development. Moreover, since each method uses its own terminology, it is difficult to combine them.

In this thesis, we have proposed a model-based approach for ISSRM, applicable since the early phases of IS development, but also applicable once the IS is designed. Our work focuses on the modelling support to such an approach, by proposing a domain model for ISSRM. We do not address the methodological aspects, nor the tool support. Our domain model helps improving the interoperability between the existing ISSRM approaches when combining them, as well as the different artefacts produced. The domain model is also used to compare the ISSRM support of existing security-oriented modelling languages. To meet these objectives, we have proposed three complementary contributions summarised in the next section. Then, limitations of the contributions and future work are described.

8.1 Research contributions

This section summarises the three contributions of this thesis. The first one is the definition of an ISSRM domain model. The second one is the definition of the ISSRM metrics and their integration in the domain model. Finally, the last contribution is the assessment of the ISSRM support of security-oriented modelling languages, and the improvement of Secure Tropos.

8.1.1 An ISSRM domain model

The first research question (addressed in Chapter 4) of this thesis is: *what are the concepts that should be present in a modelling language supporting ISSRM?* To answer it, a research method was defined. This research method is composed of two successive steps. Based on a survey of the literature, the first step was about an ISSRM concept alignment. Concepts related to ISSRM were gathered from the different sources in the literature. Then, the concepts of all sources were aligned, in order to find semantically equivalent concepts. Through iterative processing of the sources, the ISSRM domain model was built. This conceptual model takes the form of a UML class diagram, completed with definitions for each concept, provided in a glossary. Various kinds of validation of the domain model were done. First, a validation by experts: practitioners, scientists and standardisation experts reviewed the domain model. Second, the model was applied to assess a real IS, as part of an ISO/IEC 27001 certification.

The contributions related to this first research question are:

- *State of the art in ISSRM.* Chapter 2 provides an overview of the different approaches from the ISSRM domain, as input for the concept alignment. RM standards, security standards, security RM standards and security RM methods are surveyed and summarised. There are compared with respect to four criteria: are there i) security-oriented, ii) risk-based, iii) concentrating on RE, iv) model-based.

- *Semantic alignment of the ISSRM concepts and conceptual interoperability between the sources.* A conceptual study of the sources included in the state of the art was performed. It resulted in an alignment table, semantically analysing each concept. The table produced is a comparison framework, allowing to confront each new ISSRM source with those already studied, and assess its conceptual coverage with respect to the others. The table contributes to improve the interoperability between the various approaches. It highlights the equivalent concepts between two sources and thus suggests a path to shift from one method to the other, or to combine methods depending on one's specific needs.

- *Definition of an ISSRM domain model.* The domain of ISSRM is generally considered as difficult to catch, and the terminological difference between the sources is an additional gap. The ISSRM domain model proposes a unified terminology, represented under the form of a model, generally easier to understand than a method or a standard in pure natural language. It is built on ISSRM standards and methods, and its compliance with them is assured through the alignment table.

8.1.2 ISSRM metrics

To complete the domain model, the second research question (addressed in Chapter 5) is: *what are the metrics relevant to perform ISSRM and to reason about ROSI?* A new research method was defined and followed, in order to identify the ISSRM metrics. First, the GQM approach was applied on the ISSRM domain. It aims at defining metrics by focusing on the main objectives of ISSRM. This work was completed by an analysis of existing ISSRM sources, to identify the metrics currently used in practice. The resulting metrics were finally added to the domain model under the form of class attributes of the conceptual model. This set of metrics was experimented through their use in the risk assessment of a real IS, in the frame of an ISO/IEC 27001 certification.

The contributions related to this second research question are:

- *Metrics survey in the ISSRM literature.* Each ISSRM source that has a process description and that deals with measurement was surveyed. This work provides additional information for comparing and choosing a suited method, by making clear what are the concepts measured.

- *Definition of the metrics relevant for performing ISSRM and reasoning about ROSI.* The outcome of this contribution is the enrichment of the domain model with metrics suited for ISSRM. First, a generic measurement framework for performing ISSRM and reasoning about ROSI was proposed. This work can be used as input for any new ISSRM approach definition, like a method, a software tool, a modelling language, etc. Second, the conformity between the metrics highlighted in the literature and the metrics of the domain model was assured through the tables produced for each studied source. It thus becomes possible to link the results obtained by a method to the domain model, and, by analogy, to link an instance of the domain model to a given method. The interoperability between the domain model and sources of the literature is thus guaranteed. This work also contributes to the interoperability between methods.

- *An ISO/IEC 27001 compliant example of metrics instantiation.* The domain model with the metrics framework were deemed sufficient guidelines for performing risk-related tasks to obtain an ISO/IEC 27001 certification. This experiment also contributed to provide a concrete example of the proposed framework.

8.1.3 Assessment of ISSRM support by security-oriented modelling languages

Finally, our third research question (addressed in Chapter 6) is: *what is the ISSRM support provided by security-oriented modelling languages and how it can be improved?* A research method was designed, based on theoretical analysis of languages and their practical use on an example, to assess their support with regards to ISSRM. This research method was applied on three security-oriented modelling languages: Misuse cases, KAOS extended to security and Secure Tropos. For each of them, a table highlighting the constructs available for supporting the different ISSRM concepts was proposed, and improvements of the corresponding languages were suggested. For Secure Tropos, the work goes further and a syntactic and semantic extension was proposed to better support ISSRM. This extension was applied on an illustrative example.

The contributions related to this third research question are:

- *State of the art of security RE frameworks and security-oriented modelling languages.* Chapter 3 surveys security RE frameworks and security-oriented modelling languages, with a focus on concepts at stake. This literature is evaluated with respect to the same four criteria as for ISSRM standards and methods.

- *A method to assess how ISSRM is supported by existing modelling languages.* For reaching our objective of assessing the security-oriented modelling languages with regards to the ISSRM domain model, an assessment method was developed. This method can be further applied on each existing modelling language.

- *An assessment of Misuse cases, KAOS extended to security and Secure Tropos, and an improvement path for better supporting ISSRM.* First, guidelines for using these languages (as-is) for ISSRM were suggested, and illustrated through an example. Second, the conclusions drawn from the assessments helped to find ways of improving these languages to better support ISSRM.

- *An adaptation of Secure Tropos to better support ISSRM.* The outcome of this thesis is the proposal of a modelling support for ISSRM, applicable since the early phases of IS development. By proposing a Risk-aware Secure Tropos, we contribute to this objective.

8.2   Limitations

The work reported in this thesis has several limitations. The limitations we have noticed are:

- The application part of the thesis was about the evaluation of the domain model and its metrics in a real context. The conclusion drawn on this evaluation are limited, because no comparative analysis was performed to assess the efficiency of the domain model and the metrics. An experiment related to i) the efficiency of the use of the domain model, compared to the use of a method or standard in natural language, for learning purposes ii) the efficiency of the use of the domain model, compared to the use of a method or standard in natural language, as guidelines for risk assessment, would both increase the validation level of the contributions.

- The validation is also limited for the proposal of Risk-aware Secure Tropos. This extension was only illustrated on an example. Its use in a business case study or in a real environment would validate its usefulness and efficiency to support the different ISSRM steps. It would also highlight its limitations. Another limitation of the validation of Risk-aware Secure Tropos is that the example only assessed our work on an existing IS. Our contribution was not experimented during IS development.

- The ISSRM process depicted in Section 2.1 is one of our research assumption, used as an input for our research methods. However, it could be interesting to have the reverse approach: investigate the processes supporting the elicitation of models and introduce risk concepts. Such an approach would also validate the concepts of the domain model.

- The methodological part of how to use models to support ISSRM has just been started to be studied in Chapter 6. This represents a limitation with regards to the validation of the usability of a modelling support for ISSRM.

- In Chapter 5, we defined a set of metrics related to ISSRM. This set of metrics was compared to the ISSRM literature: the second part of the related research method was about an analysis of the literature and a comparison with the elicited metrics. However, it could be useful to compare these metrics with other security measurement frameworks, like [HGF+05]. This comparison could highlight strengths and weaknesses of ISSRM approaches with regards to other security approaches, and their differences at the metric level.

- Regarding the comparison of modelling languages, only conceptual support was taken into account. However, a comparison at the metric level is also necessary to fully assess a language, with respect to the domain model. For example, evaluation capabilities of Secure Tropos [CNYM00, CKM02] are not considered and should be analysed with regards to our estimation needs, to fully assess the language support. The same remark could be applied to each studied language.

- To support efficiently ISSRM through a model-based approach, a tool support is necessary. This part of the work has not been addressed.

8.3 Future work

The contributions and the limitations of our work point out some open issues for further research:

- *Validation of the domain model through further experimentation.* In order to further validate the domain model, an experiment should be designed for assessing its use, with regards to the use of a standard or a method, for learning ISSRM. This experiment could be developed, for example, as part of security master courses, or for security trainings in the frame of ISO/IEC 27001 certification.

- *Validation of Risk-aware Secure Tropos through further experimentation.* The extension proposed for Secure Tropos could be further validated through its experimentation i) in a real environment ii) during IS development.

- *Improvement of visual representations for models.* The work performed on modelling languages has shown some limitations, not only regarding ISSRM support, but also regarding the "cognitive effectiveness" [Moo06a] of their visual representations. Adapting security-oriented modelling languages to improve the support for ISSRM should naturally take this concern into account [Moo06b, Moo06a, Moo08].

- *Methodological analysis of ISSRM.* This thesis focuses on the conceptual aspects of ISSRM, and does not take into account the methodological part. The same kind of approach, based on a study of the literature, can be performed at the process level. Each ISSRM source could be analysed at the methodological level, and some method chunks [Rol07, MR05] (or method fragments [BSH98]) could be defined. The objective would be to identify the equivalent steps of each approach, and precisely specify the scope of the source, with respect to the whole ISSRM process. By combining these chunks (or fragments), one could define methods for different contexts (e.g., IS development or existing IS assessment, risk management or only risk assessment, etc.)

- *Traceability between the ISSRM steps.* After having proposed some methodological guidelines for performing ISSRM, it is necessary to guarantee the traceability between the different ISSRM steps. ISSRM is always seen as an iterative process, needing to be continuously monitored and reviewed [AS/04, ISO08] (cf. Section 2.1). Through the iterative use of the domain model and its instantiation through modelling languages, mechanisms should be defined in order to guarantee this traceability between the ISSRM steps.

- *Software tool support.* As depicted in the introduction (Section 1.5), this thesis focuses on the development of the modelling language part and does not address the tool support. To deal with issues like the complexity of models, the iterations in the activity of modelling, the need of traceability between models, etc., a software tool is needed, in order to manage the models.

- *Extending our focus from early requirements to RE in general.* One of our main assumptions is that it is necessary to deal with security since early stages of RE. We thus focus our work on early modelling approaches. By extending our approach to RE, we need to take into account other approaches such as UMLsec [Jö2], SecureUML [LBD02] or Mal-activity diagrams [Sin07]. The work on Secure Tropos could also be extended, in order to contain improvements not only for the RE stage of Secure Tropos, but also for the design stage.

- *The relation between trust and risk in a decision making process.* Usually, risk is not the only element involved in the decision process. For example, in a typical business environment, the client's trust in the supplier is of equal importance. A current running project aims at defining a trust model and integrate it with the ISSRM domain model [ADM+09]. Its definition could follow an approach analogous to the one followed for the ISSRM domain model definition.

- *A modelling support for argumentation.* The objective of the modelling language part is to represent the IS, taking into account identified risks. The reasoning behind risk decision is supported by the information available in these models, but it is not supported by the models themselves. To go further, a model-based argumentation of risk-related reasoning could be provided, for example with the Goal Structuring Notation (GSN) [SPW96].

8.4 Publications in relation to this thesis

Many aspects of this thesis have been published. The following list presents the most relevant publications ordered by type:

Book chapters

Eric Dubois, Nicolas Mayer, André Rifaut, and Vincent Rosener. *Enjeux de la sécurité multimédia (Traité IC2, série Informatique et systèmes d'information*, chapter Contributions méthodologiques pour l'amélioration de l'analyse des risques, pages 79-131. Hermes, 2006. [DMRR06]

Eric Dubois, Nicolas Mayer, and André Rifaut. *Social Modeling for Requirements Engineering*, chapter Improving Risk-based Security Analysis with *i** . Accepted for publication in MIT Press, 2009. [DMR09]

Journal papers

Nicolas Mayer, Eric Dubois, Patrick Heymans, and Raimundas Matulevičius. Défis de la sécurité de l'information – Support à la gestion des risques de sécurité par les modèles. In Colette Rolland, Oscar Pastor, and Jean-Louis Cavarero, editors, *Nouveaux challenges dans les systèmes d'information*, volume 13, pages 37-74. Hermes, March 2008. [MDHM08]

Conferences / Workshops

Baptiste Alcalde, Eric Dubois, Sjouke Mauw, Nicolas Mayer, and Saša Radomirović. Towards a Decision Model Based on Trust and Security Risk Management. In *Proceedings of the 7th Australasian conference on Information security (AISC '09)*. Australian Computer Society, Inc., 2009. [ADM$^+$09]

Nicolas Mayer, Eric Dubois, Raimundas Matulevičius, and Patrick Heymans. Towards a Measurement Framework for Security Risk Management. In *Modeling Security Workshop (MODSEC '08), in conjunction with the 11th International Conference on Model Driven Engineering Languages and Systems (MODELS '08)*. Toulouse, France, 2008. [MDMH08]

Raimundas Matulevičius, Nicolas Mayer, Haralambos Mouratidis, Eric Dubois, Patrick Heymans, and Nicolas Genon. Adapting Secure Tropos for Security Risk Management during Early Phases of the Information Systems Development. In *Proceedings of the 20th International Conference on Advanced Information Systems Engineering (CAiSE '08)*, pages 541-555. Springer-Verlag, 2008. [MMM$^+$08]

Raimundas Matulevičius, Nicolas Mayer, and Patrick Heymans. Alignment of Misuse Cases with Security Risk Management. In *Proceedings of the 4th Symposium on Requirements Engineering for Information Security (SREIS'08), in conjunction with the 3rd International Conference of Availability, Reliability and Security (ARES'08)*, pages 1397-1404. IEEE Computer Society, 2008. [MMH08]

Nicolas Mayer, Patrick Heymans, and Raimundas Matulevičius. Design of a Modelling Language for Information System Security Risk Management. In *Proceedings of the 1st International Conference on Research Challenges in Information Science (RCIS '07)*, pages 121-132. Ouarzazate, Morocco, 2007. [MHM07]

Nicolas Mayer, Eric Dubois, and André Rifaut. Requirements Engineering for Improving Business/IT Alignment in Security Risk Management Methods. In *Enterprise Interoperability II: New Challenges and Approaches, Proceedings of the Third International Conference on Interoperability for Enterprise Software and Applications (I-ESA'07)*, pages 15-26. Springer-Verlag, 2007. [MDR07]

Nicolas Mayer. Managing Security IT Risk: a Goal-Based Requirements Engineering Approach. In *RE'05 Doctoral Consortium, in conjunction with the 13th IEEE International Conference on Requirements Engineering (RE '05)*, 2005. [May05]

Nicolas Mayer, André Rifaut, and Eric Dubois. Towards a Risk-Based Security Requirements Engineering Framework. In *Proceedings of the 11th International Workshop on Requirements Engineering: Foundation for Software Quality (REFSQ '05)*, pages 83-97, 2005. [MRD05]

Bibliography

[ABG07]   Yudistira Asnar, Volha Bryl, and Paolo Giorgini. Using Risk Analysis to Evaluate Design Alternatives. In Lin Padgham and Franco Zambonelli, editors, *Agent-Oriented Software Engineering VII*, volume 4405 of *Lecture Notes in Computer Science*, pages 140–155. Springer, 2007.

[ACC⁺05]   Claudia P. Ayala, Carlos Cares, Juan Pablo Carvallo, Gemma Grau, Mariela Haya, Guadalupe Salazar, Xavier Franch, Enric Mayol, and Carme Quer. A Comparative Analysis of *i**-Based Agent-Oriented Modeling Languages. In William C. Chu, Natalia Juristo Juzgado, and W. Eric Wong, editors, *Proceedings of the 17th International Conference on Software Engineering and Knowledge Engineering (SEKE'2005)*, pages 43–50, 2005.

[AD01a]   Christopher J. Alberts and Audrey J. Dorofee. OCTAVE criteria, Version 2.0. Technical Report CMU/SEI-2001-TR-016, Carnegie Mellon University - Software Engineering Institute, Pittsburgh, Pennsylvania, 2001.

[AD01b]   Christopher J. Alberts and Audrey J. Dorofee. *OCTAVE Method Implementation Guide Version 2.0*. Carnegie Mellon University - Software Engineering Institute, Pittsburgh, Pennsylvania, 2001.

[ADM⁺09]   Baptiste Alcalde, Eric Dubois, Sjouke Mauw, Nicolas Mayer, and Saša Radomirović. Towards a Decision Model Based on Trust and Security Risk Management. In *Proceedings of the 7th Australasian conference on Information security (AISC '09)*. Australian Computer Society, Inc., 2009.

[AG06]   Y. Asnar and P. Giorgini. Modelling Risk and Identifying Countermeasure in Organizations. In *Proceedings of the 1st Interational Workshop on Critical Information Intrastructures Security (CRITIS '06)*, pages 55–66. Springer-Verlag, 2006.

[AGMS07]   Yudistira Asnar, Paolo Giorgini, Fabio Massacci, and Ayda Saidane. Secure and Dependable Patterns in Organizations: An Empirical Approach. In *Proceedings of the 15th IEEE International Conference on Requirements Engineering (RE '07)*, pages 287–292. IEEE Computer Society, 2007.

[AGMZ07]   Yudistira Asnar, Paolo Giorgini, Fabio Massacci, and Nicola Zannone. From Trust to Dependability through Risk Analysis. In *Proceedings of the 2nd International Conference on Availability, Reliability and Security (ARES '07)*, pages 19–26. IEEE Computer Society, 2007.

207

[Ale02]   Ian Alexander. Initial Industrial Experience of Misuse Cases in Trade-Off Analysis. In *Proceedings of the 10th IEEE International Conference on Requirements Engineering (RE '02)*, pages 61–68. IEEE Computer Society, 2002.

[AMSZ08]   Yudistira Asnar, Rocco Moretti, Maurizio Sebastianis, and Nicola Zannone. Risk as Dependability Metrics for the Evaluation of Business Solutions: A Model-driven Approach. In *Proceedings of the 3rd International Conference on Availability, Reliability and Security (ARES '08)*, pages 1240–1247. IEEE Computer Society, 2008.

[Ant97]   Annie I. Antón. *Goal Identification and Refinement in the Specification of Software-Based Information Systems*. PhD thesis, Georgia Institute of Technology, Atlanta, GA, June 1997.

[AS/04]   AS/NZS 4360. *Risk management*. SAI Global, 2004.

[Bas02]   Basel Committee on Banking Supervision. *International Convergence of Capital Measurement and Capital Standards. A Revised Framework*. Bank for International Settlements Press & Communications, CH-4002 Basel, Switzerland, 2002.

[BCR94]   Victor R. Basili, Gianluigi Caldiera, and H. Dieter Rombach. The Goal Question Metric Approach. In *Encyclopedia of Software Engineering*, pages 532–538. John Wiley & Sons, Inc., 1994.

[BDG05]   B. Bernardez, A. Duran, and M. Genero. Metrics for Use Cases: A Survey of Current Proposals. In M. Genero, M. Piattini, and C. Colero, editors, *Metrics for Software Conceptual Models*, pages 59–98. Imperial College Press, 2005.

[BGG⁺04]   P. Bresciani, P. Giorgini, F. Giunchiglia, J. Mylopoulos, and A. Perini. TROPOS: An Agent-Oriented Software Development Methodology. *Autonomous Agents and Multi-Agent Systems*, 8(3):203–236, May 2004.

[BGL05]   Lawrence D. Bodin, Lawrence A. Gordon, and Martin P. Loeb. Evaluating Information Security Investments Using the Analytic Hierarchy Process. *Communications of the ACM*, 48(2):78–83, 2005.

[BMO00]   Bernhard Bauer, Jörg P. Müller, and James Odell. Agent UML: A Formalism for Specifying Multiagent Software Systems. In Paolo Ciancarini and Michael Wooldridge, editors, *Proceedings of the 1st International Workshop on Agent-Oriented Software Engineering (AOSE '00)*, volume 1957 of *Lecture Notes in Computer Science*, pages 91–104. Springer, 2000.

[Boe91]   B.W. Boehm. Software Risk Management: Principles and Practices. *Software, IEEE*, 8(1):32–41, 1991.

[BSH98]   Sjaak Brinkkemper, Motoshi Saeki, and Frank Harmsen. Assembly Techniques for Method Engineering. In *Proceedings of the 10th International Conference on Advanced Information Systems Engineering (CAiSE '98)*, pages 381–400. Springer-Verlag, 1998.

[Bun05a] Bundesamt für Sicherheit in der Informationstechnik. BSI Standard 100-1: Information Security Management System (ISMS), December 2005.

[Bun05b] Bundesamt für Sicherheit in der Informationstechnik. BSI-Standard 100-2: IT-Grundschutz Methodology, December 2005.

[Bun05c] Bundesamt für Sicherheit in der Informationstechnik. BSI Standard 100-3: Risk analysis based on IT-Grundschutz, September 2005.

[Bun05d] Bundesamt für Sicherheit in der Informationstechnik. The IT-Grundschutz Catalogues, 2005.

[Car00] João Alvaro Carvalho. Information System? Which One Do you Mean? In *Proceedings of the IFIP TC8/WG8.1 International Conference on Information System Concepts: An Integrated Discipline Emerging (ISCO-4)*, pages 259–277, Deventer, The Netherlands, The Netherlands, 2000. Kluwer, B.V.

[CED03] CEDITI. A KAOS Tutorial, September 2003.

[CHR05] Karl Cox, Jon G. Hall, and Lucia Rapanotti. A Roadmap of Problem Frames Research. *Information & Software Technology*, 47(14):891–902, 2005.

[CILN02] Robert Crook, Darrel Ince, Luncheng Lin, and Bashar Nuseibeh. Security Requirements Engineering: When Anti-Requirements Hit the Fan. In *Proceedings of the 10th IEEE International Conference on Requirements Engineering (RE '02)*, pages 203–205. IEEE Computer Society, 2002.

[CKM02] J. Castro, M. Kolp, and J. Mylopoulos. Towards Requirements-Driven Information Systems Engineering: The TROPOS Project. *Information Systems*, 27:365–389, 2002.

[CLU98] CLUSIF. *MARION (Méthodologie d'Analyse des Risques Informatique et d'Optimation par Niveau)*. 1998.

[Clu04a] Club de la Sécurité des Systèmes d'Information de la région Rhône Alpes. Point sur les méthodes, 2004. http://www.clusir-rha.fr/.

[CLU04b] CLUSIF, Groupe de travail ROSI. Retour sur investissement en sécurité des systèmes d'information : quelques clés pour argumenter, 2004.

[CLU07a] CLUSIF. *MEHARI 2007: Concepts and Mechanisms*. France, 2007.

[CLU07b] CLUSIF. *MEHARI 2007 (MEthode Harmonisée d'Analyse du Risque Informatique)*. https://www.clusif.asso.fr/fr/production/mehari/, France, 2007.

[CNYM00] Lawrence Chung, Brian A. Nixon, Eric Yu, and John Mylopoulos. *Non-Functional Requirements in Software Engineering*. Kluwer Academic Publishers, Boston, October 2000.

[Coc01] A. Cockburn. *Writing Effective Use Cases*. Addison-Wesley, 2001.

[Cod] Codasystem. http://www.codasystem.com.

[Com05]   Common Criteria version 2.3. *Common Criteria for Information Technology Security Evaluation*. 2005.

[Com06a]   Common Criteria version 3.1. *Common Criteria for Information Technology Security Evaluation - Part 1: Introduction and general model*. 2006.

[Com06b]   Common Criteria version 3.1. *Common Criteria for Information Technology Security Evaluation - Part 2: Security functional components*. 2006.

[Com06c]   Common Criteria version 3.1. *Common Criteria for Information Technology Security Evaluation - Part 3: Security assurance components*. 2006.

[Com07]   Common Criteria version 3.1. *Common Methodology for Information Technology Security Evaluation - Evaluation methodology*. 2007.

[cra]   CRAMM website. http://www.cramm.com/.

[Dav03]   Alan M. Davis. The Art of Requirements Triage. *Computer*, 36(3):42–49, 2003.

[DCS04a]   DCSSI. *EBIOS - Etude de cas @rchimed*. France, July 2004.

[DCS04b]   DCSSI. *EBIOS - Expression of Needs and Identification of Security Objectives*. http://www.ssi.gouv.fr/en/confidence/ebiospresentation.html, France, 2004.

[DCS04c]   DCSSI. *Section 1 - Introduction*. EBIOS - Expression of Needs and Identification of Security Objectives, France, 2004.

[Dir89]   Direction des Constructions Navales. *MELISA (Méthode d'Evaluation de la Vulnérabilité Résiduelle des Systèmes d'Information)*. 1989.

[DMR09]   Eric Dubois, Nicolas Mayer, and André Rifaut. *Social Modeling for Requirements Engineering*, chapter Improving Risk-based Security Analysis with i^*. Accepted for publication in MIT Press, 2009.

[DMRR06]   Eric Dubois, Nicolas Mayer, André Rifaut, and Vincent Rosener. *Enjeux de la sécurité multimédia (Traité IC2, série Informatique et systèmes d'information*, chapter Contributions méthodologiques pour l'amélioration de l'analyse des risques, pages 79–131. Hermes, 2006.

[DS00]   Premkumar T. Devanbu and Stuart Stubblebine. Software Engineering for Security: a Roadmap. In *Proceedings of the 22nd International Conference on Software Engineering (ICSE '00), Future of Software Engineering Track*, pages 227–239. ACM, 2000.

[ENI06]   ENISA (European Network and Information Security Agency). Inventory of risk assessment and risk management methods, 2006.

[EY07]   Golnaz Elahi and Eric Yu. A Goal Oriented Approach for Modeling and Analyzing Security Trade-Offs. In Christine Parent, Klaus-Dieter Schewe, Veda C. Storey, and Bernhard Thalheim, editors, *Proceedings of the 26th International Conference on Conceptual Modelling (ER '07)*, volume 4801, pages 87–101. Springer-Verlag, 2007.

[FDF98]   William B. Frakes, Rubén Prieto Díaz, and Christopher J. Fox. DARE: Domain Analysis and Reuse Environment. *Annals of Software Engineering*, 5:125–141, 1998.

[FHL⁺98]   Eckhard D. Falkenberg, Wolfgang Hesse, Paul Lindgreen, Björn E. Nilsson, J. L. Han Oei, Colette Rolland, Ronald K. Stamper, Frans J. M. Van Assche, Alexander A. Verrijn-Stuart, and Klaus Voss. FRISCO - A Framework of Information System Concepts - The FRISCO Report. Technical report, IFIP WG 8.1 Task Group FRISCO, 1998.

[Fir03]   Donald G. Firesmith. Common Concepts Underlying Safety, Security, and Survivability Engineering. Technical Report CMU/SEI-2003-TN-033, Carnegie Mellon University - Software Engineering Institute, Pittsburgh, Pennsylvania, 2003.

[Fir04]   Donald G. Firesmith. A Taxonomy of Safety-Related Requirements. In *Proceedings of the 3rd International Workshop on Requirements for High Assurance Systems (RHAS '04)*, 2004.

[Fir05]   Donald G. Firesmith. A Taxonomy of Security-Related Requirements. In *Proceedings of the 4th International Workshop on Requirements for High Assurance Systems (RHAS '05)*, 2005.

[Fir07a]   Donald G. Firesmith. Engineering Safety - and Security-Related Requirements for Software-Intensive Systems. In *Proceedings of the 6th International IEEE Conference on Commercial-off-the-Shelf (COTS)-Based Software Systems (ICCBSS '07)*, page 9. IEEE Computer Society, 2007.

[Fir07b]   Donald G. Firesmith. Engineering Safety and Security Related Requirements for Software Intensive Systems. In *ICSE COMPANION '07: Companion to the proceedings of the 29th International Conference on Software Engineering*, page 169. IEEE Computer Society, 2007.

[FKG⁺02]   Rune Fredriksen, Monica Kristiansen, Bjørn Axel Gran, Ketil Stølen, Tom Arthur Opperud, and Theodosis Dimitrakos. The CORAS Framework for a Model-Based Risk Management Process. In *Proceedings of the 21st International Conference on Computer Safety, Reliability and Security (SAFECOMP '02)*, pages 94–105. Springer-Verlag, 2002.

[FMPT01]   Ariel Fuxman, John Mylopoulos, Marco Pistore, and Paolo Traverso. Model Checking Early Requirements Specifications in Tropos. In *Proceedings of the 5th IEEE International Symposium on Requirements Engineering (RE '01)*, pages 174–181. IEEE Computer Society, 2001.

[Fow03]   Martin Fowler. *UML Distilled: A Brief Guide to the Standard Object Modeling Language*. Addison-Wesley Longman Publishing Co., Inc., Boston, MA, USA, 2003.

[FP97]   Norman Fenton and Shari Lawrence Pfleeger. *Software Metrics (2nd ed.): a Rigorous and Practical Approach*. PWS Publishing Co., Boston, MA, USA, 1997.

[GC87]   Robert B. Grady and Deborah L. Caswell. *Software Metrics: Establishing a Company-wide Program.* Prentice-Hall, Inc., Upper Saddle River, NJ, USA, 1987.

[Gen07]   Nicolas Genon. Modelling Security during Early Requirements: Contributions to and Usage of a Domain Model for Information System Security Risk Management. Master thesis, University of Namur, 2007.

[GL07]   Robin A. Gandhi and Seok-Won Lee. Discovering and Understanding Multidimensional Correlations among Certification Requirements with application to Risk Assessment. In *Proceedings of the 15th IEEE International Conference on Requirements Engineering (RE '07)*, pages 231–240. IEEE Computer Society, 2007.

[Gli07]   Martin Glinz. On Non-Functional Requirements. In *Proceedings of the 15th IEEE International Conference on Requirements Engineering (RE '07)*, pages 21–26. IEEE Computer Society, 2007.

[GMZ05]   Paolo Giorgini, Fabio Massacci, and Nicola Zannone. Security and Trust Requirements Engineering. In Alessandro Aldini, Roberto Gorrieri, and Fabio Martinelli, editors, *Foundations of Security Analysis and Design III*, volume 3655 of *Lecture Notes in Computer Science*, pages 237–272. Springer, 2005.

[GMZ07]   Paolo Giorgini, Haralambos Mouratidis, and Nicola Zannone. Modelling Security and Trust with Secure Tropos. In *Integrating Security and Software Engineering: Advances and Future Vision*. IDEA, 2007.

[GPW06]   Jaap Gordijn, Michael Petit, and Roel Wieringa. Understanding Business Strategies of Networked Value Constellations Using Goal- and Value Modeling. In *Proceedings of the 14th IEEE International Conference on Requirements Engineering (RE '06)*, pages 126–135. IEEE Computer Society, 2006.

[HD05]   Svetlana Hensman and John Dunnion. Constructing Conceptual Graphs using Linguistic Resources. In *Proceedings of the 4th WSEAS International Conference on Telecommunications and Informatics (TELE-INFO'05)*, pages 1–6. World Scientific and Engineering Academy and Society (WSEAS), 2005.

[HD08]   Andrea Herrmann and Maya Daneva. Requirements Prioritization Based on Benefit and Cost Prediction: An Agenda for Future Research. In *Proceedings of the 16th IEEE International Conference on Requirements Engineering (RE '08)*, pages 125–134. IEEE Computer Society, 2008.

[Her]   Hervé Schauer Consultants. ISO/IEC 27001 Lead Implementer training. 2008.

[HGF⁺05] Siv Hilde Houmb, Geri Georg, Robert France, James Bieman, and Jan Jürjens. Cost-Benefit Trade-Off Analysis Using BBN for Aspect-Oriented

Risk-Driven Development. In *Proceedings of the 10th IEEE International Conference on Engineering of Complex Computer Systems (ICECCS '05)*, pages 195–204. IEEE Computer Society, 2005.

[HIS05]   Peter Herrmann, Valérie Issarny, and Simon Shiu, editors. *Proceedings of the 3rd International Conference on Trust Management (iTrust '05)*, volume 3477 of *Lecture Notes in Computer Science*. Springer, 2005.

[HLMN04]   Charles B. Haley, Robin C. Laney, Jonathan D. Moffett, and Bashar Nuseibeh. The Effect of Trust Assumptions on the Elaboration of Security Requirements. In *Proceedings of the 12th IEEE International Conference on Requirements Engineering (RE '04)*, pages 102–111. IEEE Computer Society, 2004.

[HLMN06]   Charles B. Haley, Robin C. Laney, Jonathan D. Moffett, and Bashar Nuseibeh. Using Trust Assumptions with Security Requirements. *Requirements Engineering*, 11(2):138–151, 2006.

[HLMN08]   Charles B. Haley, Robin C. Laney, Jonathan D. Moffett, and Bashar Nuseibeh. Security Requirements Engineering: A Framework for Representation and Analysis. *IEEE Transactions on Software Engineering*, 34(1):133–153, 2008.

[HMLN05]   Charles B. Haley, Jonathan D. Moffett, Robin C. Laney, and Bashar Nuseibeh. Arguing Security: Validating Security Requirements Using Structured Argumentation. In *Proceedings of the 3rd Symposium on Requirements Engineering for Information Security (SREIS '05), in conjunction with the 13th IEEE International Conference on Requirements Engineering (RE '05)*, 2005.

[HMLN06a] Charles B. Haley, Jonathan D. Moffett, Robin C. Laney, and Bashar Nuseibeh. A Framework for Security Requirements Engineering. In *Proceedings of the 2nd International Workshop on Software engineering for Secure Systems (SESS '06), in conjunction with the 28th International Conference on Software Engineering (ICSE '06)*, pages 35–42. ACM Press, 2006.

[HMLN06b] Charles B. Haley, Jonathan D. Moffett, Robin C. Laney, and Bashar Nuseibeh. Arguing Satisfaction of Security Requirements. In Haralambos Mouratidis and Paolo Giorgini, editors, *Integrating Security and Software Engineering: Advances and Future Vision*. 2006.

[HR04]   David Harel and Bernhard Rumpe. Meaningful Modeling: What's the Semantics of "Semantics"? *Computer*, 37(10):64–72, 2004.

[HS05]   Ida Hogganvik and Ketil Stølen. On the Comprehension of Security Risk Scenarios. In *IWPC '05: Proceedings of the 13th International Workshop on Program Comprehension*, pages 115–124. IEEE Computer Society, 2005.

[HST+07]   Patrick Heymans, Pierre-Yves Schobbens, Jean-Christophe Trigaux, Raimundas Matulevičius, Andreas Classen, and Yves Bontemps. Towards the Comparative Evaluation of Feature Diagram Languages. In Tomi Mannisto, Eila Niemela, and Mikko Raatikainen, editors, *Proceedings of the Software and Services Variability Management Workshop - Concepts, Models and Tools (SVM-WS '07)*, pages 1–16. 2007.

[HV99]   John C. Henderson and N. Venkatraman. Strategic Alignment: Leveraging Information Technology for Transforming Organizations. *IBM Systems Journal*, 38(2/3):472–484, 1999.

[HWS⁺02]   Guy G. Helmer, Johnny S. Wong, Mark Slagell, Vasant Honavar, Les Miller, and Robyn R. Lutz. A Software Fault Tree Approach to Requirements Analysis of an Intrusion Detection System. *Requirements Engineering*, 7(4):207–220, 2002.

[IEE90]   IEEE. *Standard Glossary of Software Engineering Terminology*. IEEE Standard 610.12-1990, Geneva, 1990.

[IEE98]   IEEE. *IEEE Recommended Practice for Software Engineering Terminology*. IEEE Standard 830-1990, Geneva, 1998.

[Ins03]   Insight Consulting. *CRAMM (CCTA Risk Analysis and Management Method) User Guide version 5.0*. SIEMENS, 2003.

[ISA06]   ISACA. *CISA Review Manual 2006*. Information Systems Audit and Control Association, 2006.

[ISO98]   ISO/IEC 10746-1. *Information technology – Open Distributed Processing – Reference model: Overview*. International Organization for Standardization, Geneva, 1998.

[ISO00]   ISO 9001. *Quality management systems – Requirements*. International Organization for Standardization, Geneva, 2000.

[ISO02a]   ISO 19011. *Guidelines for quality and/or environmental management systems auditing*. International Organization for Standardization, Geneva, 2002.

[ISO02b]   ISO/IEC Guide 73. *Risk management – Vocabulary – Guidelines for use in standards*. International Organization for Standardization, Geneva, 2002.

[ISO04a]   ISO 14001. *Environmental management systems – Requirements with guidance for use*. International Organization for Standardization, Geneva, 2004.

[ISO04b]   ISO/IEC 13335-1. *Information technology – Security techniques – Management of information and communications technology security – Part 1: Concepts and models for information and communications technology security management*. International Organization for Standardization, Geneva, 2004.

[ISO05a]   ISO/IEC 24765. *Systems and software engineering – Vocabulary*. International Organization for Standardization, Geneva, 2005.

[ISO05b] ISO/IEC 27001. *Information technology – Security techniques – Information security management systems – Requirements.* International Organization for Standardization, Geneva, 2005.

[ISO05c] ISO/IEC 27002. *Information technology – Security techniques – Code of practice for information security management.* International Organization for Standardization, Geneva, 2005.

[ISO08] ISO/IEC 27005. *Information technology – Security techniques – Information security risk management.* International Organization for Standardization, Geneva, 2008.

[JÖ2] Jan Jürjens. UMLsec: Extending UML for Secure Systems Development. In *Proceedings of the 5th International Conference on The Unified Modeling Language (UML '02)*, pages 412–425. Springer-Verlag, 2002.

[JÖ4] Jan Jürjens. *Secure Systems Development with UML.* Springer, 2004.

[Jac95] Michael Jackson. *Software Requirements & Specifications: A Lexicon of Practice, Principles and Prejudices.* ACM Press/Addison-Wesley Publishing Co., New York, NY, USA, 1995.

[Jac97] Michael Jackson. The Meaning of Requirements. *Annals of Software Engineering*, 3:5–21, 1997.

[Jac01] Michael Jackson. *Problem Frames: Analyzing and Structuring Software Development Problems.* ACM Press Books. Addison-Wesley, 2001.

[JBR99] Ivar Jacobson, Grady Booch, and James Rumbaugh. *The Unified Software Development Process.* Addison-Wesley Longman Publishing Co., Inc., Boston, MA, USA, 1999.

[KCH+90] K. Kang, S. Cohen, J. Hess, W. Nowak, and S. Peterson. Feature-Oriented Domain Analysis (FODA) Feasibility Study. Technical Report CMU/SEI-90-TR-021, Carnegie Mellon University - Software Engineering Institute, Pittsburgh, Pennsylvania, 1990.

[KG00] Daryl Kulak and Eamonn Guiney. *Use Cases: Requirements in Context.* ACM Press, 2000.

[Kil01] Tapani Kilpi. Implementing a software metrics program at Nokia. *IEEE Software*, 18(6):72–77, 2001.

[KR97] Joachim Karlsson and Kevin Ryan. A Cost-Value Approach for Prioritizing Requirements. *IEEE Software*, 14(5):67–74, 1997.

[LBD02] Torsten Lodderstedt, David A. Basin, and Jürgen Doser. SecureUML: A UML-Based Modeling Language for Model-Driven Security. In *Proceedings of the 5th International Conference on The Unified Modeling Language (UML '02)*, pages 426–441. Springer-Verlag, 2002.

[LCJ05]   Samantha Lautieri, David Cooper, and David Jackson. SafSec: Commonali-
            ties Between Safety and Security Assurance. In F.Redmill and T. Anderson,
            editors, *Constituents of Modern System-Safety Thinking: Proceedings of the
            13th Safety-Critical Systems Symposium*, pages 65–78, 2005.

[Let01]   Emmanuel Letier. *Reasoning about Agents in Goal-Oriented Requirements
            Engineering*. PhD thesis, Université Catholique de Louvain, 2001.

[Lev95]   Nancy G. Leveson. *Safeware: System Safety and Computers*. ACM, New
            York, NY, USA, 1995.

[LGA05]   Seok-Won Lee, Robin A. Gandhi, and Gail-Joon Ahn. Security Require-
            ments Driven Risk Assessment for Critical Infrastructure Information Sys-
            tems. In *Proceedings of the 3rd Symposium on Requirements Engineering
            for Information Security (SREIS '05), in conjunction with the 13th IEEE
            International Requirements Engineering Conference (RE '05)*, 2005.

[LMFGL05]   Jurij Leskovec, Natasa Milic-Frayling, Marko Grobelnik, and Jurij
            Leskovec. Extracting Summary Sentences Based on the Document Semantic
            Graph. Technical Report MSR-TR-2005-07, Microsoft Research, 2005.

[LNI⁺03a]   Luncheng Lin, Bashar Nuseibeh, Darrel Ince, Michael Jackson, and
            Jonathan D. Moffett. Analysing Security Threats and Vulnerabilities Using
            Abuse Frames. Technical Report 2003/10, Open University, 2003.

[LNI⁺03b]   Luncheng Lin, Bashar Nuseibeh, Darrel Ince, Michael Jackson, and
            Jonathan D. Moffett. Introducing Abuse Frames for Analysing Security
            Requirements. In *Proceedings of the 11th IEEE International Conference
            on Requirements Engineering (RE '03)*, page 371. IEEE Computer Society,
            2003.

[LNIJ04]   Luncheng Lin, Bashar Nuseibeh, Darrel Ince, and Michael Jackson. Using
            Abuse Frames to Bound the Scope of Security Problems. In *Proceedings of
            the 12th IEEE International Conference on Requirements Engineering (RE
            '04)*, pages 354–355. IEEE Computer Society, 2004.

[LNN⁺96]   Gerald J. Langley, Kevin M. Nolan, Clifford L. Norman, Lloyd P. Provost,
            and Thomas W. Nolan. *The Improvement Guide: A Practical Approach to
            Enhancing Organizational Performance*, volume 96-05 of *The Jossey-Bass
            business & management series*. Jossey-Bass, 1996.

[LSS⁺08]   Marcia Lucena, Emanuel Santos, Carla Silva, Fernanda Alencar, Maria Jo-
            celia Silva, and Jaelson Castro. Towards a Unified Metamodel for i^*. In
            *Proceedings of the 2nd International Conference on Research Challenges
            in Information Science (RCIS '08)*, pages 237–246, Marrakech, Morocco,
            2008.

[LY01]   Lin Liu and Eric Yu. From Requirements to Architectural Design: Using
            Goals and Scenarios. In *Proceedings of the 1st International Workshop From
            Software Requirements to Architectures (STRAW '01)*, 2001.

[LYM02]   Lin Liu, Eric Yu, and John Mylopoulos. Analyzing Security Requirements As Relationships among Strategic Actors. In *Proceedings of the 2nd Symposium on Requirements Engineering for Information Security (SREIS '02)*. IEEE Computer Society, 2002.

[LYM03]   Lin Liu, Eric Yu, and John Mylopoulos. Security and Privacy Requirements Analysis within a Social Setting. In *Proceedings of the 11th IEEE International Conference on Requirements Engineering (RE '03)*, page 151. IEEE Computer Society, 2003.

[May05]   Nicolas Mayer. Managing Security IT Risk: a Goal-Based Requirements Engineering Approach. In *RE'05 Doctoral Consortium, in conjunction with the 13th IEEE International Conference on Requirements Engineering (RE '05)*, 2005.

[McD01]   J. McDermott. Abuse-Case-Based Assurance Arguments. In *Proceedings of the 17th Annual Computer Security Applications Conference (ACSAC '01)*, pages 366–376. IEEE Computer Society, 2001.

[MCY99]   John Mylopoulos, Lawrence Chung, and Eric Yu. From Object-Oriented to Goal-Oriented Requirements Analysis. *Communications of the ACM*, 42(1):31–37, 1999.

[MDHM08] Nicolas Mayer, Eric Dubois, Patrick Heymans, and Raimundas Matulevičius. Défis de la sécurité de l'information – Support à la gestion des risques de sécurité par les modèles. In Colette Rolland, Oscar Pastor, and Jean-Louis Cavarero, editors, *Nouveaux challenges dans les systèmes d'information*, volume 13, pages 37–74. Hermes, March 2008.

[MDMH08] Nicolas Mayer, Eric Dubois, Raimundas Matulevičius, and Patrick Heymans. Towards a Measurement Framework for Security Risk Management. In *Modeling Security Workshop (MODSEC '08), in conjunction with the 11th International Conference on Model Driven Engineering Languages and Systems (MODELS '08)*. Toulouse, France, 2008.

[MDR07]   Nicolas Mayer, Eric Dubois, and André Rifaut. Requirements Engineering for Improving Business/IT Alignment in Security Risk Management Methods. In *Enterprise Interoperability II: New Challenges and Approaches, Proceedings of the Third International Conference on Interoperability for Enterprise Software and Applications (I-ESA'07)*, pages 15–26. Springer-Verlag, 2007.

[MF99]   John McDermott and Chris Fox. Using Abuse Case Models for Security Requirements Analysis. In *Proceedings of the 15th Annual Computer Security Applications Conference (ACSAC '99)*, pages 55–65. IEEE Computer Society, 1999.

[MG04]   Haralambos Mouratidis and Paolo Giorgini. Enhancing Secure Tropos to Effectively Deal with Security Requirements in the Development of Multiagent Systems. In *Proceedings of the 1st International Workshop on Safety and Security Multiagent Systems (AAMAS '04)*. New York, USA, 2004.

[MG07a]   Haralambos Mouratidis and Paolo Giorgini. Secure Tropos: A Security-Oriented Extension of the Tropos Methodology. *International Journal of Software Engineering and Knowledge Engineering*, 17(2):285–309, 2007.

[MG07b]   Haralambos Mouratidis and Paolo Giorgini. Security Attack Testing (SAT) – Testing the Security of Information Systems at Design Time. *Information Systems*, 32(8):1166–1183, 2007.

[MG09]   Haralambos Mouratidis and Paolo Giorgini. *Social Modeling for Requirements Engineering*, chapter Extending *i** and Tropos to model security. Accepted for publication in MIT Press, 2009.

[MGM02]   Haralambos Mouratidis, Paolo Giorgini, and Gordon A. Manson. Using Tropos Methodology to Model an Integrated Health Assessment System. In *Proceedings of the 4th International Bi-Conference on Agent-Oriented Information Systems (AOIS '02)*, 2002.

[MGM03a]   Haralambos Mouratidis, Paolo Giorgini, and Gordon A. Manson. An Ontology for Modelling Security: The Tropos Approach. In Vasile Palade, Robert J. Howlett, and Lakhmi C. Jain, editors, *Proceedings of the 7th International Conference on Knowledge-Based Intelligent Information and Engineering Systems (KES '03)*, volume 2773 of *Lecture Notes in Computer Science*, pages 1387–1394. Springer, 2003.

[MGM03b]   Haralambos Mouratidis, Paolo Giorgini, and Gordon A. Manson. Integrating Security and Systems Engineering: Towards the Modelling of Secure Information Systems. In *Proceedings of the 15th International Conference on Advanced Information Systems Engineering (CAiSE '03)*, pages 63–78. Springer-Verlag, 2003.

[MGM04]   Haralambos Mouratidis, Paolo Giorgini, and Gordon A. Manson. Using Security Attacks Scenarios to Analyse Security during Information Systems Design. In *Proceedings of the 6th International Conference on Enterprise Information Systems 2004 (ICEIS '04)*, 2004.

[MGM05]   Haralambos Mouratidis, Paolo Giorgini, and Gordon A. Manson. When Security Meets Software Engineering: A Case of Modelling Secure Information Systems. *Information Systems*, 30(8):609–629, 2005.

[MGMP02]   Haralambos Mouratidis, Paolo Giorgini, Gordon A. Manson, and Ian Philp. A Natural Extension of Tropos Methodology for Modelling Security. In *Proceedings of the Agent Oriented Methodologies Workshop (OOPSLA '02)*. 2002.

[MHI05]   Nancy R. Mead, Eric D. Hough, and Theodore R. Stehney II. Security Quality Requirements Engineering (SQUARE) Methodology. Technical Report CMU/SEI-2005-TR-009, Carnegie Mellon University - Software Engineering Institute, Pittsburgh, Pennsylvania, 2005.

[MHM07]   Nicolas Mayer, Patrick Heymans, and Raimundas Matulevičius. Design of a Modelling Language for Information System Security Risk Management.

In *Proceedings of the 1st International Conference on Research Challenges in Information Science (RCIS '07)*, pages 121–132. Ouarzazate, Morocco, 2007.

[MHN04]   Jonathan D. Moffett, Charles Haley, and Bashar Nuseibeh. Core Security Requirements Artefacts. Technical Report 2004/23, The Open University, Milton Keynes, UK, 2004.

[MHO06]   Raimundas Matulevičius, Patrick Heymans, and Andreas Opdahl. Ontological Analysis of KAOS Using Separation of Reference. In *Proceedings of the Workshop on Exploring Modeling Methods for Systems Analysis and Design (EMMSAD '06), in conjunction with the 18th International Conference on Advanced Information Systems Engineering (CAiSE '06)*, pages 395–406. Printed by Namur University, 2006.

[MHO07]   Raimundas Matulevičius, Patrick Heymans, and Andreas Opdahl. Comparing GRL and KAOS Using the UEML Approach. In *Enterprise Interoperability II: New Challenges and Approaches, Proceedings of the Third International Conference on Interoperability for Enterprise Software and Applications (I-ESA'07)*, pages 77–88. Springer-Verlag, 2007.

[Mic04]   Microsoft. *The Security Risk Management Guide*. 2004.

[MJF06]   Haralambos Mouratidis, Jan Jürjens, and Jorge Fox. Towards a Comprehensive Framework for Secure Systems Development. In *Proceedings of the 18th International Conference on Advanced Information Systems Engineering (CAiSE '06)*, pages 48–62. Springer-Verlag, 2006.

[MMH08]   Raimundas Matulevičius, Nicolas Mayer, and Patrick Heymans. Alignment of Misuse Cases with Security Risk Management. In *Proceedings of the 4th Symposium on Requirements Engineering for Information Security (SREIS'08), in conjunction with the 3rd International Conference of Availability, Reliability and Security (ARES'08)*, pages 1397–1404. IEEE Computer Society, 2008.

[MMM⁺08]   Raimundas Matulevičius, Nicolas Mayer, Haralambos Mouratidis, Eric Dubois, Patrick Heymans, and Nicolas Genon. Adapting Secure Tropos for Security Risk Management during Early Phases of the Information Systems Development. In *Proceedings of the 20th International Conference on Advanced Information Systems Engineering (CAiSE '08)*, pages 541–555. Springer-Verlag, 2008.

[MN03]   Jonathan D. Moffett and Bashar Nuseibeh. A Framework for Security Requirements Engineering. Technical Report YCS 368, Department of Computer Science, University of York, UK, 2003.

[Moi77]   Jean-Louis Le Moigne. *La Théorie du système général: Théorie de la modélisation*. Presses Universitaires de France, Paris, 1977.

[Moo02]   Daniel L. Moody. Complexity Effects on End User Understanding of Data Models: an Experimental Comparison of Large Data Model Represetation

Mehods. In *Proceedings of the 10th European Conference on Information Systems (ECIS '2002)*, 2002.

[Moo06a]   Daniel L. Moody. Dealing with "Map Shock": A Systematic Approach for Managing Complexity in Requirements Modelling. In *Proceedings of the 12th International Workshop on Requirements Engineering: Foundation for Software Quality (REFSQ '06)*, pages 148–157. Washington, DC, USA, 2006.

[Moo06b]   Daniel L. Moody. What Makes a Good Diagram? Improving the Cognitive Effectiveness of Diagrams in IS Development. In *Proceedings of the 15th International Conference in Information Systems Development (ISD '06)*, pages 148–157. IEEE Computer Society, 2006.

[Moo08]   Daniel L. Moody. Evidence-based Notation Design: Towards a Scientific Basis for Constructing Visual Notations in Software Engineering. *Accepted at IEEE Transactions on Software Engineering*, 2008.

[Mou04]   Haralambos Mouratidis. *A Security Oriented Approach in the Development of Multiagent Systems: Applied to the Management of the Health and Social Care Needs of Older People In England*. PhD thesis, Department of Computer Science, University of Sheffield, UK, 2004.

[MPM03]   Haralambos Mouratidis, Ian Philp, and Gordon A. Manson. A Novel Agent-Based System to Support the Single Assessment Process of Older People. *Journal of Health Informatics*, 9(3):149–162, 2003.

[MR05]   Isabelle Mirbel and Jolita Ralyté. Situational Method Engineering: Combining Assembly-Based and Roadmap-Driven Approaches. *Requirements Engineering*, 11(1):58–78, 2005.

[MRD05]   Nicolas Mayer, André Rifaut, and Eric Dubois. Towards a Risk-Based Security Requirements Engineering Framework. In *Proceedings of the 11th International Workshop on Requirements Engineering: Foundation for Software Quality (REFSQ '05)*, pages 83–97, 2005.

[MS03]   Kevin D. Mitnick and William L. Simon. *The Art of Deception: Controlling the Human Element of Security*. John Wiley & Sons, Inc., New York, NY, USA, 2003.

[MS05]   Nancy R. Mead and Ted Stehney. Security Quality Requirements Engineering (SQUARE) Methodology. In *Proceedings of the 1st International Workshop on Software engineering for Secure Systems (SESS '05), in conjunction with the 27th International Conference on Software Engineering (ICSE '05)*, pages 1–7. ACM, 2005.

[NE00]   Bashar Nuseibeh and Steve Easterbrook. Requirements Engineering: a Roadmap. In *Proceedings of the 22nd International Conference on Software Engineering (ICSE'00), Future of Software Engineering Track*, pages 35–46. ACM, 2000.

[NF 01]   NF Z 42-013. *Archivage électronique - Spécifications relatives à la conception et à l'exploitation de systèmes informatiques en vue d'assurer la conservation et l'intégrité des documents stockés dans ces systèmes.* AFNOR, 2001.

[Nus01]   Bashar Nuseibeh. Weaving Together Requirements and Architectures. *Computer*, 34(3):115–117, 2001.

[Obj]   Object Management Group (OMG). UML Resource Page. http://www.uml.org/.

[Obj04]   Object Management Group (OMG). Unified Modeling Language: Superstructure, version 2.0, 2004.

[OHS05]   Andreas L. Opdahl and Brian Henderson-Sellers. A Unified Modelling Language without Referential Redundancy. *Data and Knowledge Engineering (DKE). Special Issue on Quality in Conceptual Modelling*, (277-300), 2005.

[OP04]   Alexander Osterwalder and Yves Pigneur. *Value Creation from E-Business Models*, chapter An Ontology For E-Business Models, pages 65–97. Butterworth-Heinemann, Newton, MA, USA, 2004.

[Pen03]   Tom Pender. *UML Bible.* John Wiley & Sons, Inc., New York, NY, USA, 2003.

[RB01]   Erhard Rahm and Philip A. Bernstein. A Survey of Approaches to Automatic Schema Matching. *The VLDB Journal*, 10(4):334–350, 2001.

[RBSS05]   Iris Reinhartz-Berger, Pnina Soffer, and Arnon Sturm. A Domain Engineering Approach to Specifying and Applying Reference Models. In *Proceedings of the Workshop on Enterprise Modeling Information Systems Architecture (EMISA '05)*, pages 50–63, 2005.

[RDGS02]   Dimitris Raptis, Theodosis Dimitrakos, Bjørn Axel Gran, and Ketil Stølen. The CORAS Approach for Model-Based Risk Management Applied to e-Commerce Domain. In Borka Jerman-Blazic and Tomaz Klobucar, editors, *Communications and Multimedia Security*, volume 228 of *IFIP Conference Proceedings*, pages 169–181. Kluwer, 2002.

[RFB88]   Colette Rolland, Odile Foucaut, and Guillaume Benci. *Conception des systèmes d'information: la méthode REMORA.* 1988.

[Rol07]   Colette Rolland. *Conceptual Modelling in Information Systems Engineering*, chapter Capturing System Intentionality with Maps, pages 141–158. Springer-Verlag, 2007.

[RR99]   Suzanne Robertson and James Robertson. *Mastering the Requirements Process.* ACM Press/Addison-Wesley Publishing Co., New York, NY, USA, 1999.

[SAS05]   Wes Sonnenreich, Jason Albanese, and Bruce Stout. Return On Security Investment (ROSI): A Practical Quantitative Model. In *Proceedings of the 3rd International Workshop on Security in Information Systems (WOSIS '05)*, pages 239–252, 2005.

[SB99]   R.van Solingen and E. Berghout. *The Goal/Question/Metric Method: A Practical Guide for Quality Improvement of Software Improvement.* McGraw-Hill, Cambridge, 1999.

[Sch04]   Bruce Schneier. *Secrets and Lies: Digital Security in a Networked World.* John Wiley & Sons, 2004.

[SFO03]   Guttorm Sindre, Donald G. Firesmith, and Andreas L. Opdahl. A Reuse-Based Approach to Determining Security Requirements. In *Proceedings of the 9th International Workshop on Requirements Engineering: Foundation for Software Quality (REFSQ '03)*, 2003.

[SGF02]   Gary Stoneburner, Alice Goguen, and Alexis Feringa. *NIST Special Publication 800-30: Risk Management Guide for Information Technology Systems.* National Institute of Standards and Technology, Gaithersburg, 2002.

[SHF04]   Gary Stoneburner, Clark Hayden, and Alexis Feringa. *NIST Special Publication 800-27 Rev. A: Engineering Principles for Information Technology Security (A Baseline for Achieving Security).* National Institute of Standards and Technology, Gaithersburg, 2004.

[SHTB06] Pierre-Yves Schobbens, Patrick Heymans, Jean-Christophe Trigaux, and Yves Bontemps. Feature Diagrams: A Survey and A Formal Semantics. In *Proceedings of the 14th IEEE International Conference on Requirements Engineering (RE '06)*, pages 139–148. IEEE Computer Society, 2006.

[SHTB07] Pierre-Yves Schobbens, Patrick Heymans, Jean-Christophe Trigaux, and Yves Bontemps. Generic Semantics of Feature Diagrams. *Computer Networks: The International Journal of Computer and Telecommunications Networking*, 51:456–479, 2007.

[Sin07]   Guttorm Sindre. Mal-Activity Diagrams for Capturing Attacks on Business Processes. In *Proceedings of the Working Conference on Requirements Engineering: Foundation for Software Quality (REFSQ '07)*, pages 355–366. Springer-Verlag, 2007.

[SO00]   Guttorm Sindre and Andreas L. Opdahl. Eliciting Security Requirements by Misuse Cases. In *Proceedings of TOOLS Pacific 2000*. IEEE Computer Society, 2000.

[SO01]   Guttorm Sindre and Andreas L. Opdahl. Templates for Misuse Case Description. In *Proceedings of the 7th International Workshop on Requirements Engineering, Foundation for Software Quality (REFSQ '01)*, 2001.

[SO05]   Guttorm Sindre and Andreas L. Opdahl. Eliciting Security Requirements with Misuse Cases. *Requirements Engineering*, 10(1):34–44, 2005.

[SOB02] Guttorm Sindre, Andreas L. Opdahl, and Gøran F. Brevik. Generalization/Specialization as a Structuring Mechanism for Misuse Cases. In *Proceedings of the Symposium on Requirements Engineering for Information Security (SREIS '02)*, 2002.

[Som95] Ian Sommerville. *Software engineering (5th ed.)*. Addison Wesley Longman Publishing Co., Inc., Redwood City, CA, USA, 1995.

[SoRiC02] United States Senate and House of Representatives in Congress (2002). Sarbanes-Oxley Act of 2002. Public Law 107-204 (116 Statute 745), 2002.

[Sow76] John F. Sowa. Conceptual Graphs for a Database Interface. *IBM Journal of Research and Development*, 20(4):336–357, 1976.

[SPM05] Angelo Susi, Anna Perini, and John Mylopoulos. The TROPOS Metamodel and its Use. *Informatica*, (29):401–408, 2005.

[SPW96] C. H. Pygott David J. Tombs Stephen P. Wilson, John A. McDermid. Assessing complex computer based systems using the goal structuring notation. pages 498–505, 1996.

[SSH^{+}03] Yannis Stamatiou, Eva Skipenes, Eva Henriksen, Nikos Stathiakis, Adamantios Sikianakis, Eliana Charalambous, Nikos Antonakis, Ketil Stølen, Folker den Braber, Mass Soldal Lund, Katerina Papadaki, and George Valvis. The CORAS Approach for Model-based Risk Management Applied to a Telemedicine Service. In *Proceedings of the Medical Informatics Europe (MIE '2003)*, pages 206–211. IOS Press, 2003.

[The01] The Project Management Institute. *Project Management Body of Knowledge*. 2001.

[UK 96] UK Ministry of Defence. Defence Standard 00-56, Safety Management Requirements for Defence Systems, Issue 2, 1996.

[VB93] Ludwig Von Bertalanffy. *General System Theory: Foundations, Development, Applications*. Georges Braziller, Inc., New York, USA, 1993.

[VdBLS05] Fredrik Vraalsen, Folker den Braber, Mass Soldal Lund, and Ketil Stølen. The CORAS Tool for Security Risk Analysis. In Herrmann et al. [HIS05], pages 402–405.

[vL01] Axel van Lamsweerde. Goal-Oriented Requirements Engineering: A Guided Tour. In *Proceedings of the 5th IEEE International Symposium on Requirements Engineering (RE '01)*, pages 249–262. IEEE Computer Society, 2001.

[vL03] Axel van Lamsweerde. The KAOS Meta-model: Ten Years After. Technical report, Université Catholique de Louvain, 2003.

[vL04] Axel van Lamsweerde. Elaborating Security Requirements by Construction of Intentional Anti-Models. In *Proceedings of the 26th International Conference on Software Engineering (ICSE '04)*, pages 148–157. IEEE Computer Society, 2004.

[vLBLJ03] Axel van Lamsweerde, Simon Brohez, Renaud De Landtsheer, and David
           Janssens. From System Goals to Intruder Anti-Goals: Attack Generation
           and Resolution for Security Requirements Engineering. In *Proceedings of
           Requirements for High Assurance Systems Workshop (RHAS '03)*, pages
           49–56, 2003.

[vLL00]   Axel van Lamsweerde and Emmanuel Letier. Handling Obstacles in Goal-
           Oriented Requirements Engineering. *IEEE Transactions on Software Engi-
           neering*, 26(10):978–1005, 2000.

[VLM⁺05]   Fredrik Vraalsen, Mass Soldal Lund, Tobias Mahler, Xavier Parent, and
           Ketil Stølen. Specifying Legal Risk Scenarios Using the CORAS Threat
           Modelling Language. In Herrmann et al. [HIS05], pages 45–60.

[VML⁺07]   Fredrik Vraalsen, Tobias Mahler, Mass Soldal Lund, Ida Hogganvik, Folker
           den Braber, and Ketil Stølen. Assessing Enterprise Risk Level: The CORAS
           Approach. In Djamel Khadraoui and Francine Herrmann, editors, *Advances
           in Enterprise Information Technology Security*, pages 311–333. Idea group,
           2007.

[Wie99]   Karl E. Wiegers. First Things First: Prioritizing Requirements. *Software
           Development*, 7(9), 1999.

[Wie03]   Karl Eugene Wiegers. *Software Requirements*. Microsoft Press, Redmond,
           WA, USA, 2003.

[Wik08a]   Wikipedia. Information System definition, 2008.

[Wik08b]   Wikipedia. Management System definition, 2008.

[Yu96]   Eric Yu. *Modelling Strategic Relationships for Process Reengineering*. PhD
           thesis, University of Toronto, Toronto, Ontario, Canada, 1996.

[Yu97]   Eric Yu. Towards Modeling and Reasoning Support for Early-phase Re-
           quirements Engineering. In *Proceedings of the 3rd IEEE International
           Symposium on Requirements Engineering (RE'97)*, pages 226–235. IEEE
           Computer Society, 1997.

Appendices

Appendix A

Definitions extracted from the different sources

A.1 ISO/IEC Guide 73

The definitions related to ISSRM for the ISO/IEC Guide 73 are extracted from the *"Terms and definitions"* section of the standard [ISO02b].

Risk: combination of the probability of an event and its consequence

Consequence: Outcome of an event
NOTE 1: There can be more than one consequence from one event.
NOTE 2: Consequences can range from positive to negative. However, consequences are always negative for safety aspects.

Event: Occurrence of a particular set of circumstances.
NOTE 1: The event can be certain or uncertain.
NOTE 2: The event can be a single occurrence or a series of occurrence.

Source: Item or activity having a potential for a consequence
NOTE: In the context of safety, source is a hazard.

Risk criteria: terms of reference by which the significance of risk is assessed

Risk treatment: process of selection and implementation of measures to modify risk
NOTE 2: **Risk treatment measures** can include avoiding, optimizing, transferring or retaining risk.

Risk control: actions implementing **risk management decision**.

A.2 AS/NZS 4360

The definitions related to ISSRM for AS/NZS 4360 are extracted from the "*Definitions*" section of the standard [AS/04].

Consequence: outcome or impact of an event

Control: an existing process, policy, device, practice or other action that acts to minimize negative risk or enhance positive opportunities

Event: occurrence of a particular set of circumstances

Hazard: a source of potential harm

Loss: any negative consequence or adverse effect, financial or otherwise

Risk: the chance of something happening that will have an impact on objectives
NOTE 1: A risk is often specified in terms of an event or circumstance and the consequences that may flow from it.

Risk criteria: terms of reference by which the significance of risk is assessed

Risk treatment: process of selection and implementation of measures to modify risk
NOTE 1: The term 'risk treatment' is sometimes used for the measures themselves.
NOTE 2: **Risk treatment measures** can include avoiding, modifying, sharing or retaining risk.

A.3 ISO/IEC 13335

The definitions related to ISSRM for ISO/IEC 13335 are extracted from the document "*Information technology – Security techniques – Management of information and communications technology security – Part 1: Concepts and models for information and communications technology security management*" [ISO04b]. They are mainly extracted from the "Definitions" section, but also from the core of the standard, when specified.

Asset: anything that has value to the organization.
(Section 3.2) "These may include, without being limited to:
- physical assets (e.g., computer hardware, communications facilities, buildings),
- information / data (e.g., documents, databases), - software,
- the ability to provide a product or service,
- people, and
- intangibles (e.g., goodwill, image)."

Control: in the context of ICT security, the term "control" may be considered synonymous with "safeguard".

Impact: the result of an information security incident.
(Section 3.5) "**Impact** is the result of an information security incident, caused by a threat, which affects assets. The impact could be the destruction of certain assets, damage to the ICT system, and compromise of confidentiality, integrity, availability, non-repudiation, accountability, authenticity or reliability. Possible indirect impact includes financial losses, and the loss of market share or company image."

Risk: the potential that a given threat will exploit vulnerabilities of an asset or group of assets and thereby cause harm to the organization. It is measured in terms of a combination of the probability of an **event** and its consequence.
(Section 3.6) "**Risk** is the potential that a given threat will exploit vulnerabilities of an asset or group of assets and thereby cause harm to the organization."
(Section 3.6) "The **risk** is characterized by a combination of two factors, the probability of the incident occurring and its impact. Any change to assets, threats, vulnerabilities and safeguards may have significant effects on risks."

Safeguard: a practice, procedure or mechanism that treats risk. Note that the term "safeguard" may be considered synonymous with the term "control".
(Section 3.7) "**Safeguards** are practices, procedures or mechanisms that may protect against a threat, reduce a vulnerability, limit the impact of an information security incident, detect incidents and facilitate recovery."
(Section 3.7) "Examples of specific **safeguards** are: policies and procedures, access control mechanisms, anti-virus software, encryption, digital signatures, monitoring and analysis tools, redundant power supplies, and back-up copies of information."

Threat: a potential cause of an incident that may result in harm to a system or organization.
(Section 3.3) "A **threat** has the potential to cause an incident that may result in harm to an asset and therefore an organization."
(Section 3.3) "**Threats** may be of environmental or human origin and, in the latter case, may be either accidental or deliberate.
Examples of threats are: Eavesdropping, Information modification, System hacking, Malicious code, Theft, Errors and omissions, File deletion, Incorrect routing, Physical accidents, Earthquake, Lightning, Floods, Fire"

Vulnerability: a weakness of an asset or group of assets that can be exploited by one or more threats.
(Section 3.4) "**Vulnerabilities** associated with assets include weaknesses in physical layout, organization, procedures, personnel, management, administration, hardware, software or information."
(Section 3.4) "[...] a **vulnerability** is merely a condition or set of conditions that may allow a threat to affect an asset."
(Section 3.4) "An example of a **vulnerability** is lack of access control, which could

allow the threat of an intrusion to occur and assets to be lost."

(Section 4.1) "**ICT security requirements**, e.g., in terms of confidentiality, integrity, availability, nonrepudiation, accountability, authenticity and reliability, particularly with regard to the views of the asset owners, [. . .]"

A.4 Common Criteria

The definitions related to ISSRM for CC are extracted from the document *"Common Criteria for Information Technology Security Evaluation - Part 1: Introduction and general model"* [Com06a].

(12) **assets**: entities that the owner of the TOE presumably places value upon.

(74) **security objective**: a statement of intent to counter identified threats and/or satisfy identified organisation security policies and/or assumptions.

(153) **vulnerability**: a weakness in the TOE that can be used to violate the SFRs in some environment.

(192) **Assets** are entities that someone places value upon. Examples of assets include:
- contents of a file or a server;
- the authenticity of votes cast in an election;
- the availability of an electronic commerce process;
- the ability to use an expensive printer;
- access to a classified facility.
but given that value is highly subjective, almost anything can be an asset.

(195) Examples of **threat agents** include hackers, malicious users, non-malicious users (who sometimes make errors), computer processes and accidents.

(196) The owners of the assets will perceive such **threats** as potential for impairment of the assets such that the value of the assets to the owners would be reduced. Security-specific impairment commonly includes, but is not limited to: loss of asset confidentiality, loss of asset integrity and loss of asset availability.

(197) These **threats** therefore give rise to **risks** to the **assets**, based on the likelihood of a **threat** being realised and the **impact** on the assets when that threat is realised. Subsequently **countermeasures** are imposed to reduce the risks to assets. These countermeasures may consist of IT countermeasures (such as firewalls and smart cards) and non-IT countermeasures (such as guards and procedures).

(202) The Security Target then describes the **countermeasures** (in the form of **Security Objectives**) and demonstrates that these countermeasures are sufficient to counter these threats: if the countermeasures do what they claim to do, the threats

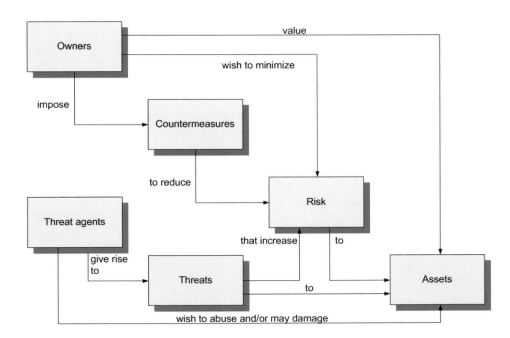

Figure A.1: 'Security concepts and relationships' for CC (as appears in [Com06a] *(194)*)

are countered.

(292) A **threat** consists of a **threat agent**, an **asset** and an **adverse action** of that threat agent on that asset.

(293) **Threat agents** are entities that can adversely act on assets. Examples of threat agents are hackers, users, computer processes, TOE development personnel, and accidents. Threat agents may be further described by aspects such as expertise, resources, opportunity and motivation.

(296) **Adverse actions** are actions performed by a **threat agent** on an asset. These actions influence one or more properties of an asset from which that asset derives its value.

(304) The **security objectives** are a concise and abstract statement of the intended solution to the problem defined by the security problem definition. The role of the security objectives is threefold:
- provide a high-level, natural language solution of the problem;
- divide this solution into two part wise solutions, that reflect that different entities each have to address a part of the problem;
- demonstrate that these part wise solutions form a complete solution to the problem.

(327) The **SFRs**[1] are a translation of the security objectives for the TOE. They are usually at a more detailed level of abstraction, but they have to be a complete translation (the security objectives must be completely addressed).

---

[1]Security Functional Requirements

A.5   ISO/IEC 27001

The definitions related to ISSRM for ISO/IEC 27001 are extracted from the document "*Information technology – Security techniques – Information security management systems – Requirements*" [ISO05b].

(p.2) **asset**
anything that has value to the organization

(p.2) information security
preservation of confidentiality, integrity and availability of information; in addition, other **properties** such as authenticity, accountability, non-repudiation and reliability can also be involved

(p.3) **risk treatment**: process of selection and implementation of measures to modify risk [ISO/IEC Guide 73:2002]
NOTE: In this International Standard the term '**control**' is used as a synonym for '**measure**'.

(p.4) "Identify the **risks**.
1) Identify the **assets** within the scope of the ISMS, and the owners of these assets.
2) Identify the **threats** to those assets.
3) Identify the **vulnerabilities** that might be exploited by the threats.
4) Identify the **impacts** that losses of confidentiality, integrity and availability may have on the assets."

(p.5) "Identify and evaluate options for the **treatment of risks**.
Possible actions include:
1) applying appropriate **controls**;
2) knowingly and objectively accepting risks, providing they clearly satisfy the organization's policies and the criteria for risk acceptance;
3) avoiding risks; and
4) transferring the associated business risks to other parties, e.g. insurers, suppliers."

(p.13 to 32) Examples of **controls**

A.6   ISO/IEC 27005

The definitions related to ISSRM for ISO/IEC 27005 are extracted from the document "*Information technology – Security techniques – Information security risk management*" [ISO08].

(p.1) **impact**
adverse change to the level of business objectives achieved

(p.1) information security **risk**
potential that a given **threat** will exploit **vulnerabilities** of an **asset** or group of assets and thereby cause harm to the organization.
NOTE: It is measured in terms of a combination of the likelihood of an **event** and its consequence

(p.8) "Risk evaluation **criteria** [...]
- Operational and business importance of availability, confidentiality and integrity"

(p.8) "Impact **criteria** [...]
- Breaches of information security (e.g. loss of confidentiality, integrity and availability)"

(p.10) "A **risk** is a combination of the **consequences** that would follow from the occurrence of an unwanted **event** and the likelihood of the occurrence of the event"

(p.10) "An **asset** is anything that has value to the organization and which therefore requires protection."

(p.11) "A **threat** has the potential to harm **assets** such as information, processes and systems and therefore organizations. Threats may be of natural or human origin, and could be accidental or deliberate. Both accidental and deliberate threat sources should be identified. A threat may arise from within or from outside the organization."

(p.12) "**Vulnerabilities** that can be exploited by **threats** to cause harm to assets or to the organization should be identified (relates to ISO/IEC 27001, Clause 4.2.1 d) 3))."

(p.13) "The **consequences** that losses of confidentiality, integrity and availability may have on the assets should be identified (see ISO/IEC 27001 4.2.1 d) 4))."

(p.15) "**Consequences** or business **impact** may be determined by modelling the outcomes of an event or set of events, or by extrapolation from experimental studies or past data."

(p.17) "Information security **properties**: if one **criterion** is not relevant for the organization (e.g. loss of confidentiality), then all risks impacting this criterion may not be relevant"

(p.17) "There are four options available for **risk treatment**: risk reduction (see 9.2), risk retention (see 9.3), risk avoidance (see 9.4) and risk transfer (see 9.5)."

(p.19) "ISO/IEC 27002 provides detailed information on **controls**."

(p.30) "The **primary assets**:
- Business processes & activities
- Information
The **supporting assets** (on which the primary elements of the scope rely) of all types:
- Hardware
- Software
- Network
- Personnel
- Site
- Organization's structure"

(p.35) "**Criteria** [...]
Another basis for the valuation of assets is the costs incurred due to the loss of confidentiality, integrity and availability as the result of an incident. Non-repudiation, accountability, authenticity and reliability should also be considered, as appropriate."

(p.40, Left column of the table) **Threat source / Origin of threat**: "Hacker, cracker, computer criminal, terrorist [...]"

A.7   NIST Special Publication 800-27 Rev A and 800-30

The definitions related to ISSRM from the NIST '800' serie of standards are extracted first from the glossary of the NIST SP 800-27 Rev A *"Engineering Principles for Information Technology Security"* [SHF04] and second from the NIST SP 800-30 *"Risk Management Guide for Information Technology Systems"* [SGF02].

*"**NIST SP 800-27 Rev A - Engineering Principles for Information Technology Security**"*

IT-related risk / Risk: The net mission/business impact considering (1) the likelihood that a particular **threat source** will exploit, or trigger, a particular information system **vulnerability** and (2) the resulting **impact** if this should occur. IT-related risks arise from legal liability or mission/business loss due to, but not limited to:
1. Unauthorized (malicious, non-malicious, or accidental) disclosure, modification, or destruction of information.
2. Non-malicious errors and omissions.
3. IT disruptions due to natural or man-made disasters.
4. Failure to exercise due care and diligence in the implementation and operation of the IT.

Security goals: The five security goals are confidentiality, availability, integrity, accountability, and assurance.

Threat: Any circumstance or event with the potential to harm an information system through unauthorized access, destruction, disclosure, modification of data, and/or denial of service. Threats arise from human actions and natural events.

Threat source: Either (1) intent and method targeted at the intentional exploitation of a vulnerability or (2) the situation and method that may accidentally trigger a vulnerability.

Vulnerability: A weakness in system security requirements, design, implementation, or operation, that could be accidentally triggered or intentionally exploited and result in a violation of the system's security policy.

"*NIST SP 800-30 - Risk Management Guide for Information Technology Systems*"

(p.12) **Threat**: "The potential for a threat source to exercise (accidentally trigger or intentionally exploit) a specific vulnerability."

(p.14 Table 3.1) "Human **Threats**: **Threat-Source**, Motivation, and **Threat Actions**"

(p.14 Table 3.1) **Threat action**: "Hacking, Social engineering, System intrusion, Break-ins, Unauthorized system access, Blackmail [...]"

(p.14 Table 3.1) **Threat source**: "Floods, earthquakes, tornadoes, landslides, avalanches, hacker, cracker, terrorist [...]"

(p.19) "The goal of this step is to analyze the **controls** that have been implemented, or are planned for implementation, by the organization to minimize or eliminate the likelihood (or probability) of a **threat**'s exercising a system **vulnerability**."

(p.22) "The following list provides a brief description of each security goal and the **consequence** (or **impact**) of its not being met:
- Loss of Integrity. [...]
- Loss of Availability. [...]
- Loss of Confidentiality. [...]"

(p.27) Risk mitigation can be achieved through any of the following **risk mitigation options**:
- Risk Assumption. To accept the potential risk and continue operating the IT system or to implement controls to lower the risk to an acceptable level
- Risk Avoidance. To avoid the risk by eliminating the risk cause and/or consequence (e.g., forgo certain functions of the system or shut down the system when risks are identified)
- Risk Limitation. To limit the risk by implementing controls that minimize the adverse impact of a threat's exercising a vulnerability (e.g., use of supporting, preventive, detective controls)
- Risk Planning. To manage risk by developing a risk mitigation plan that prioritizes,

implements, and maintains controls

- Research and Acknowledgment. To lower the risk of loss by acknowledging the vulnerability or flaw and researching controls to correct the vulnerability
- Risk Transference. To transfer the risk by using other options to compensate for the loss, such as purchasing insurance.

(p.33-34) **Controls**: "Identification, Cryptographic Key Management, Security Administration, Authentication, Protected communication, Audit [...]"

A.8   The IT-Grundshutz

The definitions related to ISSRM from the IT-Grundshutz are extracted first from the glossary of the Catalogues *"The IT-Grundschutz Catalogues 2005"* [Bun05d] and second from the Risk analysis standard *"BSI Standard 100-3 Risk analysis based on IT-Grundschutz"* [Bun05c].

"The IT-Grundschutz Catalogues 2005"

Applied threat
An applied threat is a **basic threat** which has a direct effect on an object as the result of a **vulnerability**. A basic threat therefore only becomes an applied threat for an object when combined with a vulnerability.
For example, are computer viruses a basic or applied threat to the user who is surfing the Internet? According to the above definition it can be ascertained that all users are principally exposed to a basic threat by computer viruses on the Internet. The user who downloads an infected file is exposed to an applied threat by the computer virus if his computer is vulnerable to this type of computer virus. Users with an effective anti-virus programme, a configuration which prevents the function of the virus, or an operating system which cannot execute the virus code is, however, not exposed to an applied threat as a result of downloaded malicious program.

Asset
Everything which is important for an organisation (financial assets, knowledge, objects, health).

Basic IT security parameters
The IT-Grundschutz defines three fundamental IT security values: confidentiality, availability and integrity.
Each user is naturally free to include additional fundamental values when assessing protection requirements if this is helpful in individual cases. Other generic terms concerning IT security are, for example:
- Authenticity
- Liability
- Reliability

Basic threat

A basic threat in general terms is an event or condition which involves the risk of damage. The **damage** is related to a concrete value such as financial assets, knowledge, objects or health. In IT terms a basic threat is a condition or an event which can negatively affect the availability, integrity or the confidentiality of information, which in turn results in **damage** to the owner of the information. Basic threats can result from the effects of force majeure, organisational shortcomings, human errors, technical failure or deliberate acts.

IT assets

IT assets refers to all the infrastructural, organisational, personnel and technical components which serve to perform tasks in a particular field of information processing. IT assets can refer to all the information technology of an organisation or to individual areas defined in terms of organisational structures (e.g. departmental network) or shared IT applications (e.g. personnel information system).

Risk

A risk is the prediction of possible damage, often based on calculation, in a negative case (danger), or in a positive case a possible advantage (chance). The definition of damage or advantage depends on the benchmark values.

Risk is also often defined as the combination of the probability of the occurrence of damage and the extent of this damage.

Security safeguard

The term security safeguard refers to all actions which serve to control and counter security risks. This includes organisational, personnel, technical or infrastructural security safeguards. The terms security precaution and protective measure are often used synonymously. "Safeguard" is used as a general term. In addition to "**safeguard**" the term "**control**" is often used.

Vulnerability

A vulnerability can result in the manifestation of a **basic threat** and **damage** to an organisation or a system. As a result of a vulnerability an object (an organisation or a system) is susceptible to threats.

"BSI Standards 100-3 Risk Analysis based on IT-Grundschutz"

(Section 1.2) "The methodology outlined below demonstrates how the **threats** listed in the IT-Grundschutz Catalogues can be used to carry out a simplified analysis of **IT risks**."

(Section 1.2) "Have a high or very high security requirement in at least one of the three **basic parameters** of confidentiality, integrity or availability"

(Section 2) "An IT structure analysis must have been performed for the **IT assets**, as specified in Section 4.1 of the IT-Grundschutz Methodology."

(Section 2) "The standard **security measures** stated in the individual modules form the basis for the IT-Grundschutz security concept for the **IT assets** under review."

(Section 3) "In contrast to the "IT-Sicher-heitshandbuch", **threats**, **vulnerabilities** and **risks** are not examined separately here."

(Section 6) "Therefore, a **decision** on how to deal with the remaining **threats** has to be taken."

A.9 EBIOS

The definitions related to ISSRM for the EBIOS method are extracted from the document *"EBIOS - Expression of Needs and Identification of Security Objectives, Section 1 - Introduction"* [DCS04c].

Asset: Any resource of value to the organisation and necessary for achieving its objectives. There is an important distinction between essential elements and entities needing to be protected.
Examples: - list of names; - certification request; - invoice management; - encryption algorithm; - laptop computer; - Ethernet; - operating system; - etc.

Attack: Exploiting one or more vulnerabilities using an attack method with a given opportunity.
Examples: - strong opportunity of using counterfeit or copied software resulting from total absence of awareness or information concerning copyright legislation; - software damaged by a virus through easy loading of malicious programmes onto the organisation's office network; - etc.

Attack method: Standard means (action or event) by which a threat agent carries out an attack.
Examples: - theft of media or documents; - software entrapment; - attack on availability of personnel; - passive wiretapping; - flood; - etc.

Entity: An asset such as an organisation, site, personnel, equipment, network, software, system.
Examples: - facilities management company; - the organisation's premises; - system administrator; - laptop computer; - Ethernet; - operating system; - teleprocedure gateway; - etc.

Essential element: Information or function with at least one non-nil sensitivity.
Examples: - list of names; - certification request; - invoice management; - encryption algorithm; - etc.

Impact: Consequences for an organisation when a threat is accomplished.

Examples: - loss of customers' confidence in a trade mark; - financial loss of 10% of turnover; - infringement of laws and regulations leading to legal proceedings against the Director; - etc.

Risk: Combination of a threat and the losses it can cause, i.e.: of the opportunity, for a threat agent using an attack method, to exploit one or more vulnerabilities of one or more entities and the impact on the essential elements and on the organisation.
Examples: - a former member of the personnel with little technical ability but possibly strong motivation, deliberately damages the system software by introducing a virus, taking advantage of the ease of installing harmful programmes on the organisation's office network; this could affect, for example, the functions generating estimates or signature certificates, which could result in the inability to provide a service, impossibility of fulfilling contractual obligations and serious consequences in terms of confidence in a trade mark; - a cracker with a good level of expertise, standard equipment and paid for his actions, steals confidential files by remotely accessing the company's network, causing a transaction with a partner to fail and loss of customers' confidence; - etc.

Security criterion: Characteristic of an essential element allowing the various sensitivities to be assessed.

Security functional requirements: to contribute to covering one or more security objectives for the target system.
Examples: - the system must generate the encryption keys in compliance with a specified encryption key generation algorithm and with the specified sizes of encryption keys in compliance with specified standards; - the system must unambiguously detect a physical intrusion that could compromise it; - a lightning conductor must be installed at the organisation's premises; - etc.

Security measure: A measure designed to improve security, specified by a security requirement and implemented to comply with it. The effect of the measures may be to anticipate, prepare, dissuade, protect, detect, confine, combat, recover, restore, compensate, etc.

Security objectives: Expression of the intention to counter identified threats or risks (depending on the context) and/or comply with the organisational security policies and assumptions; an objective can concern the target system, its development environment or its operational environment.
Examples: a) "open" objectives (security objective can be covered by a wide range of means): - the configuration of internal network stations must be upgradable; - the rooms must be protected against lightning; - etc. b) "closed" objectives (security objective can only be covered by a narrow range of means): - the system must allow unique identification and authentication of users before any interaction between the system and the user; - two different and compatible antivirus programmes must be installed and the signature bases updated every two weeks; - etc.

Threat: Possible attack of a threat agent on assets.

Examples: - a former member of the personnel with little technical ability but possibly a strong motivation to carry out an attack deliberately damages the system software by introducing a virus, taking advantage of the ease of installing harmful programmes on the organisation's office network; this could affect, for example, the functions generating estimates or signature certificates; - a cracker with a good level of expertise, standard equipment and paid for his actions, steals confidential files by remote access to the company's network; - a developer or member of the personnel with a very good level of expertise in source codes but little ISS knowledge deliberately modifies the source code; - a visitor steals equipment containing confidential information; - etc.

Threat agent: Human action, natural or environmental element that has potentially negative consequences on the system. It can be characterised by its type (natural, human or environmental) and by its cause (accidental or deliberate). In the case of an accidental cause, it is also characterised by exposure and available resources. In the case of a deliberate cause, it is also characterised by expertise, available resources and motivation.
Examples: - former member of the personnel with little technical ability and time but possibly a strong motivation to carry out an attack; - cracker with considerable technical ability, well equipped and strongly motivated by the money he could make; - very wet climate for three months of the year; - virus; - users; - developers; - etc.

Vulnerability: Characteristic of an entity that can constitute a weakness or flaw in terms of information systems security.
Examples: - no fire safety arrangements for an Organisation type entity; - little attention drawn to security problems for a Personnel type entity; - ease of intrusion into site for a Site type entity; - possibility of creating or modifying system commands for a Network type entity; - etc.

A.10 MEHARI

The definitions related to ISSRM for the MEHARI method are extracted from the document "*MEHARI 2007: Concepts and Mechanisms*" [CLU07a]

(p.3) "Critical **assets** + High **vulnerability** = Unacceptable **risk**"

(p.6) "Classification of **assets** using the three basic **criteria** (Availability, Integrity, Confidentiality)."

(p.6) "It is usual to distinguish **primary assets** (business activities and related information) and **supporting assets**."

(p.7) "The **vulnerability** of an information system is the addition of its weak points whereby an accident, error or deliberate act could damage the organization."

(p.7) "A **security service** is a response to a security need, expressed in generic and

functional terms that describe what the service should do, and generally referring to certain types of threat. A **security service** describes a **security function**. This function is independent of the real **mechanisms** or **solutions** that ensure the effective implementation of the service. For example: the access control service is designed (as its name implies) to control user access, or to only allow access to authorized users."

(p.8) "**Security services** provide functions that can, themselves, require complementary services, or **sub-services**, as they will be called."

(p.8) "A "**Mechanism**" is a specific way of ensuring the function of a service or subservice (whether totally or partially). This may take the form, for example, of a procedure, an algorithm, or some specific technology."

(p.8) "A **security solution** is the real implementation of a mechanism and includes the hardware and/or software components required for its deployment, the installation procedures, and operational support, as well as organizational structures needed for its correct use."

(p.8) "Some services can be considered to be general measures, where others are technical.
- General measures are **security measures** that are considered to be generally useful, or even necessary, to the security of the information system. However, their effect may be felt at the level of the organization, security operation or awareness, but with no direct influence on specific risk situations.
- Technical measures have a specific role, a direct objective and have an immediate effect in certain risk situations that can be defined."

(p.11) "**Security services**, as defined in MEHARI, are **security functions** and these functions are implemented through **security solutions** that are, or will be, installed in the organization."

(p.13) "A **risk scenario** is the description of a malfunction and the way in which the malfunction can happen. The malfunction states the potential damage, or the direct deterioration caused by the malfunction, and any indirect consequences. It is usual to speak of a risk situation, where it is understood that the organization is potentially exposed to such a scenario.
A **risk situation** is often identified as a result of a stakes analysis. However, it could also be identified at the level of a project, or detected through systematic search."

(p.14) "Each scenario will therefore be described as follows:
- The type of **consequence** (sometimes in relation with predefined value scale)
- The type of **assets** implicated by the scenario (sometimes in relation with the predefined critical resources)
- The types of **causes** that can lead to the risk situation
A risk scenario that could be envisaged is described below:

Scenario description		
Description of the event and its consequence(s)	*Description of its cause and origin*	
Destruction of basic data used for paying salaries (calculations & parameters)	...due to an operational error: a disk crash preventing data from being read	,,
Destruction of basic data used for paying salaries (calculations & parameters)	...due to intentional deletion of the files by a member of the operations staff	

A.11   OCTAVE

The definitions related to ISSRM for the OCTAVE method are extracted from the document *"OCTAVE criteria, Version 2.0"* [AD01a] which has a common glossary with the OCTAVE method [AD01b].

Actor: a property of threat that defines who or what may violate the security requirements (confidentiality, integrity, availability) of an asset.

Area of Concern: a situation or scenario where someone is concerned about a threat to important assets. Typically, areas of concern have a source and an outcome - a causal action that has an effect on the organization.

Asset: something of value to the organization. Information technology assets are the combination of logical and physical assets and are grouped into specific classes (information, systems, software, hardware, people).

Impact: the effect of a threat on an organization's mission and business objectives.

Key classes of components: types of devices that are important in processing, storing, or transmitting critical information. They represent related assets to critical assets.

Outcome: a property of threat that defines the immediate outcome (disclosure, modification, destruction, loss, interruption) of violating the security requirements of an asset.

Protection Strategy Practice: actions that help initiate, implement, and maintain security within an organization. A protection strategy practice is also called a security practice.

Risk: the possibility of suffering harm or loss. It is the potential for realizing unwanted negative consequences of an event. Risk refers to a situation where a person could do something undesirable or a natural occurrence could cause an undesirable outcome, resulting in a negative impact or consequence.
(p.5) "It breaks down into three basic components: asset, threat, and vulnerability" [AD01a]

Security requirements: requirements outlining the qualities of information assets that are important to an organization. Typical security requirements are confidentiality, integrity, and availability.

Threat: an indication of a potential undesirable event. A threat refers to a situation in which a person could do something undesirable (an attacker initiating a denial-of-service attack against an organization's email server) or a natural occurrence could cause an undesirable outcome (a fire damaging an organization's information technology hardware). Threats have defined properties (asset, actor, motive, access, outcome).

Vulnerability: a weakness in an information system, system security practices and procedures, administrative controls, internal controls, implementation, or physical layout that could be exploited by a threat to gain unauthorized access to information or disrupt processing. There are two basic types of vulnerabilities (organizational and technology).

Risk mitigation plans: a plan that is intended to reduce the risks to a critical asset. Risk mitigation plans tend to incorporate actions, or **countermeasures**, designed to counter the threats to the assets.

A.12   CRAMM

The definitions related to ISSRM for the CRAMM method are extracted from the document "*CRAMM User Guide*" [Ins03].

(p.3-1) "**Assets** within an information system or network can be considered under three categories:
- information or data assets
- software assets
- physical assets, such as file servers, workstations, bridges, routers."

(p.3-2) "Typical **threats** include:
- deliberate attacks such as hacking, spoofing, insertion of false messages, introduction of damaging or disruptive software, theft, wilful damage
- disasters such as fire, flood, lightning strike
- errors by individuals
- technical failures."

(p.3-2) "The level of **risk** is identified from the value of the **assets**, the level of **threat** and the extent of the **vulnerability**."

(p.7-33) "For each data asset, you need to discuss with the interviewee the effect of the following **impacts**.
Unavailability
The consequences resulting from data being unavailable may vary depending on the length of the loss of service. CRAMM allows you to investigate these consequences

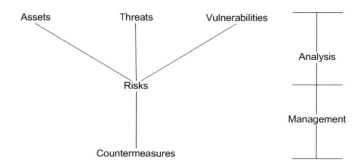

Figure A.2: 'The IT risk analysis and management process' for CRAMM (as appears in [Ins03] *(p.3-3))*

against the following timeframes: [...]
Destruction
This impact investigates the consequences that could result from:
- loss of data since the last successful back-up
- total loss of data including back-ups.
You need to find out how often back-ups are taken and where they are stored when looking at this impact.
Disclosure
This impact is investigated in terms of:
- disclosure to insiders (those people working for the organisation, but who are not authorised to see the data)
- disclosure to contracted service providers (staff of third party organisations who may have legitimate access to the system or network, but not necessarily to the data - examples include those organizations running outsourced IT services or virtual private networks)
- disclosure to outsiders (all other individuals).
Modification
The issues to explore when examining this impact vary according to the end-user service that the data is using, as follows. [...]"

(p.8-4) "**Countermeasures** in each sub-group are arranged in a hierarchical structure, with all countermeasures being assigned to one of three possible categories:
- category 1: **security objectives** - a high-level statement
- category 2: a detailed description of the **security functions** that help to achieve the security objectives
- category 3: **examples** of how the functions can be implemented."

(p.B-2) Accountability: The **property** that ensures that the actions of an entity may be traced uniquely to the entity. (ISO 7498-2/3.3.3)

(p. B-3) **Asset**: A component or part of the total system. Assets may be of four types:
- physical
- application software

- data
- end user services.

(p.B-4) Availability: The **property** of being accessible and usable upon demand by an authorised entity. (ISO 7498-2/3.3.11)

(p.B-8) Confidentiality: The **property** that information is not made available or disclosed to unauthorised individuals, entities or processes. (ISO 7498-2/3.3.16)

(p.B-9) **Countermeasure**: A check or restraint on a system, designed to enhance security in one of the following ways:
- reducing the threat of an attack occurring
- reducing the vulnerability to an attack
- reducing the impact of an attack
- detecting an attack
- recovering from an attack.

(p.B-9) **Countermeasure** category: CRAMM's countermeasure library is hierarchical in structure. Countermeasures can be in one of the following three categories:
- **Security Objectives**
- **Functions**
- **Examples** or **implementation options**.

(p.B-16) **Impact**: The effect on the organisation of a breach in security.

(p.B-29) **Security risk**: The likelihood of a system's inherent vulnerability being exploited by the threats to the system, leading to the system being penetrated.

(p. B-34) **Threat**: A potential violation of security.
(ISO 7498-2/3.3.55)
NOTES
1 For example, disclosure, modification, destruction, or denial of service.
A threat is defined by its source, motivation, path, target, and result.
See also - accidental threat, intentional threat, active threat, passive threat and physical threat.

(p. B-38) **Vulnerability**: A weakness or lack of controls that would allow or facilitate a threat actuation against a specific asset or target.
NOTES
1 A vulnerability may be an omission or it may relate to a deficiency in a control's strength, completeness or consistency.
A vulnerability may be technical, procedural or operational.

A.13   CORAS

The definitions related to ISSRM for the CORAS method are extracted from the paper *"Assessing Enterprise Risk Level: The CORAS Approach"* [VML$^+$07].

(p.313) "**Assets** are the parts or features of the target which have value to the client of the analysis, such as physical objects, know-how, services, software and hardware, and so on."

(p.313) "A **vulnerability** is a weakness of the system or organization."

(p.313) "A **threat** may exploit a vulnerability and cause an unwanted incident."

(p.313) "[...] **an unwanted incident**, an event which reduces the value of one or more of the assets."

(p.313-314) "A **risk** is an unwanted incident along with its estimated likelihood and consequence values."

(p.314) "**Treatments** represent various options for reducing risk."

(p.317) "Part of defining the scope is selecting which **security properties** are to be considered in the analysis, such as confidentiality, integrity and availability, as well as other aspects of interest."

(p.321) "**Assets** are the parts or features of the target of analysis that have value to the client and that the client wants to protect, such as physical objects, key personnel, services, software and hardware, or more intangible things such as know-how, trust, market share and public image."

(p.325) "**Vulnerabilities** can also be system characteristics that are impossible to treat; an internet connection that is crucial to the system, for example."

(p.325) "**Vulnerabilities** can be thought of as control mechanisms that ideally should be in place, but for some reason are missing or not sufficiently robust."

(p.325) "[...] a **threat** (e.g., a disloyal employee or a computer virus) [...]"

(p.325) "An **unwanted incident** is an event resulting in a reduction in the value of the target asset. Furthermore, an unwanted incident may initiate or lead to other unwanted incidents, forming chains of events."

(p.325) "[...] **threat scenario**, which is a sequence of events or activities leading to an unwanted incident."

A.14   Firesmith

The definitions related to ISSRM from the Firesmith research work are extracted first from the technical report *"Common Concepts Underlying Safety, Security, and Survivability Engineering"* [Fir03] and second from the paper *"A Taxonomy of Security-Related Requirements"* [Fir05].

"Common Concepts Underlying Safety, Security, and Survivability Engineering"

(p.3) "Safety is largely about protecting **valuable assets** (especially people) from harm due to accidents. Security is largely about protecting **valuable assets** (especially sensitive data) from harm due to attacks. [...] In all three cases, a primary focus is in **dangers** (**hazards** and **threats**) and their associated **risks** and the system's **vulnerabilities** to them."

(p.15) "In fact, security has historically been defined more often in terms of its most popular **subfactors** (typically availability, integrity, and privacy) than in terms of its subclasses."

(p.29) "**Asset** (with regard to safety engineering) is anything of value that should be protected from accidental harm."

(p.30) "**Harm** (when dealing with safety requirements) is significant damage to or a negative impact (i.e., negative outcome) associated with an asset due to an accident. Harm must be sufficiently significant to warrant relatively prompt remedial action to prevent such harm in the future."

(p.30) "**Hazard** is a situation that increases the likelihood of one or more related accidents.
A hazard thus consists of hazardous states (i.e., a set of one or more incompatible system conditions or states, possibly including one or more conditions in the system's environment) together with the accident (type) they may cause. Potential hazards should be identified early during requirements engineering or architecting, while actual hazards may be identified in existing systems. The following are two examples of such potential and actual hazards with their various components identified:
- Potential hazard: The subway doors are opening, open, or closing while the subway is moving (hazardous conditions), which may result in passengers and/or their property (assets) falling out (accident) and being injured, killed, or damaged (harm).
- Actual hazard: Riders and/or their property within the doorway when the subway doors are closing (hazardous conditions) may result in the passengers and their property (assets) being crushed (accident) and thus injured, killed, or damaged (harm).
Examples of primarily internal hazardous conditions include dangerous conditions involving hazardous chemicals, high voltages, and robotic-controlled moving machinery. A more specific example would be a moving elevator with open doors, two incompatible states of an elevator. Examples of primarily external hazardous conditions include fires and such natural disasters as earthquakes, floods, hurricanes, and tornadoes."

(p.31) "**Safety mechanism** (also known as a **safeguard** or **safety tactic**) is an architectural mechanism (i.e., strategic decision) that helps fulfill one or more safety requirements and/or reduces one or more safety vulnerabilities."

(p.31) "**Safety requirement** is a quality requirement that specifies a required amount of safety (typically a subfactor of safety) in terms of a system-specific criterion and a minimum mandatory level of an associated quality metric that is necessary to meet one or more safety policies."

(p.31) "**Safety risk** is the potential risk of harm to an asset due to accidents.
Safety risk is defined as the sum (over all relevant hazards) of the products of the following two terms: (1) the largest negative impact of the harm to the asset (i.e., its criticality, severity, or damage) times (2) the likelihood that the hazard will result in an accident.
Using the basic theory of conditional probability, the likelihood that a hazard results in an accident causing harm can be calculated/estimated as the product of the following terms: (1) the likelihood that the hazard exists, (2) the likelihood that other necessary conditions also exist (also known as latency), and (3) the likelihood that the hazard will lead to an accident if it and the other necessary conditions exist (also known as danger)."

(p.31) "**Safety vulnerability** is a weakness in the system that increases the likelihood that an accident will occur and cause harm.
This weakness may be in the architecture, design, implementation, integration, deployment, and configuration of the system. Examples of safety vulnerabilities include the lack of safety features, the lack of warning mechanisms, or defects that could cause failures."

(p.34) "**Asset** (with regard to security engineering) is anything of value that should be protected from malicious harm."

(p.34) "**Attacker** (also known as adversary) is an agent (e.g., person or program) that causes an attack due to the desire to cause harm to an asset."

(p.34) "**Harm** (when dealing with security requirements) is a negative impact associated with an asset due to an attack. Harm is due to an accident when dealing with safety requirements, is due to an attack when dealing with security requirements, and may be due to both accidents and attacks when dealing with survivability requirements."

(p.34) "**Threat** is a situation that increases the likelihood of one or more related attacks.
The threat consists of the existence of one or more potential attackers together with a set of one or more system conditions or states that provide motivation to the attackers. Thus, the threat of theft may result in an actual theft (attack), and threats

correspond to attacks that are typically classified by attacker motivation (e.g., theft) as opposed to technique (e.g., spoofing). In some books and articles, the different but highly related terms "attack" and "threat" are sometimes confounded by being used as synonyms."

(p.35) "**Security mechanism** (also known as **countermeasure** or **security tactic**) is an architecture mechanism (i.e., strategic decision) that helps fulfill one or more security requirements and/or reduces one or more security vulnerabilities.
Security mechanisms can be implemented as some combination of hardware or software components, manual procedures, training, etc. It should also be noted that the same architectural mechanism (e.g., redundancy) can often be used as a safety, security, and survivability mechanism."

(p.35) "**Security requirement** is a quality requirement that specifies a required amount of security (actually a quality subfactor of security) in terms of a system-specific criterion and a minimum level of an associated quality metric that is necessary to meet one or more security policies."

(p.35) "**Security risk** is the potential risk of harm to an asset due to attacks.
Security risk is the sum (over all relevant threats) of the negative impact of the harm to the asset (i.e., its criticality) multiplied by the likelihood of the harm occurring. Using the basic theory of conditional probability, the likelihood that harm results from an attack can be calculated/estimated as the product of the following terms: (1) the likelihood that the threat of attack exists, (2) the likelihood that other necessary conditions (e.g., vulnerabilities) also exist, and (3) the likelihood that the threat will lead to a successful attack if it and the other necessary conditions exist. The term "likelihood" is used rather than probability because the probability is typically not accurately or precisely known but rather only grossly estimated ("guesstimated")."

(p.36) "**Security vulnerability** is any weakness in the system that increases the likelihood that a successful attack (i.e., one causing harm) will occur.
Security vulnerability is not restricted to only those vulnerabilities due to programming problems. It also includes vulnerabilities in the system's architecture and design, how the system is installed and configured, how its users are trained, etc. The vulnerabilities of a system may involve its data components, hardware components, software components, human-role components (i.e., wetware or personnel), and document components (i.e., paperware)."

(p.46) "**Asset** is anything of value that should be protected from harm."

(p.46) "**Harm** is significant damage to or negative impact (i.e., negative outcome) associated with a valuable asset that is due to an incident. Harm can be decomposed according to the type of asset harmed (e.g., harm to people includes such things as injury, illness, death, or victimization by a cybercrime) or the type of incident (e.g., harm due to attack may include exposure of sensitive information). Harm must be sufficiently significant to warrant relatively prompt remedial action to prevent such

harm in the future."

(p.48) "**Danger** (also known as obstacle) is a situation (i.e., a set of one or more incompatible conditions or states of the system, possibly including one or more conditions in the system's environment) that increases the likelihood of one or more related incidents. As such, dangers are ways of organizing related categories of incidents.
- **Hazard** is a danger that may result in one or more related accidents.
- **Threat** is a danger that may result in one or more related attacks."

"A Taxonomy of Security-Related Requirements"

(p.2) "Safety and security are subtypes of defensibility quality factor because they are both primarily concerned with the protection of **valuable assets** from **harm**, which is a significant negative consequence to the asset."

(p.3) "Specifically, a **danger** is one or more conditions, situations, or states of a system that in conjunction with conditions in the environment of the system can cause or contribute to the occurrence of one or more related incidents."

(p.3) "[...] **dangers** are classified into **hazards** and **threats**, whereby hazards can cause safety incidents and threats can cause security incidents."

(p.3) "Risk is usually defined as the probable magnitude of the potential harm to one or more assets that can occur due to a danger and is conservatively estimated as the maximum credible harm multiplied by the estimated probability that the associated accident or successful attack occurs. And as before, risks can be classified as either **safety risks** due to hazards or **security risks** due to threats."

A.15   Haley *et al.* and Moffett and Nuseibeh

The definitions related to ISSRM from the Haley *et al.* research work are extracted from the research paper *"Security Requirements Engineering: A Framework for Representation and Analysis"* [HLMN08] and for Moffett and Nuseibeh from the technical report *"A Framework for Security Requirements Engineering"* [MN03].

"Security Requirements Engineering: A Framework for Representation and Analysis"

(Section 2.1) "Security needs arise when stakeholders establish that some resource involved in a system, be it tangible (e.g., cash) or intangible (e.g., information or reputation), is of value to the organization. Such resources are called **assets**, and the stakeholders naturally wish to protect themselves from any **harm** involving these assets."

(Section 3.1) "The security community has enumerated some general **security concerns**: confidentiality, integrity, and availability (labeling them CIA, and more re-

cently adding another A for accountability).”

(Section 3.1) “By enumerating the assets in a system, then postulating actions that would violate these security concerns for the assets, one can construct descriptions of possible **threats** on assets. For example, one can erase (the **action**) customer records (the **asset**) of a company to cause loss of revenue (the **harm**).”

(Section 3.1) “Knowing the goals of **attackers** could be useful when determining security goals for the system, for example when enumerating assets or quantifying harm.”

(Section 3.2) “We define **security requirements** as constraints on the functions of the system, where these constraints operationalize one or more security goals. Security requirements operationalize the security goals as follows:
- They are constraints on the system’s functional requirements, rather than themselves being functional requirements.
- They express the system’s security goals in operational terms, precise enough to be given to a designer/architect. Security requirements, like functional requirements, are prescriptive, providing a specification (behavior in terms of phenomena) to achieve the desired effect.”

(Section 3.5.2.3) “In general, **harm** is caused by the negation of the **security concerns** described in Section 3.1: confidentiality, integrity, availability, and accountability.”

“A Framework for Security Requirements Engineering”

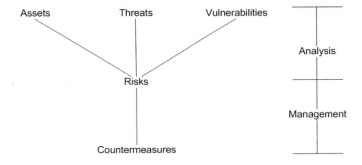

Figure A.3: ’Security Risk Analysis & Management Framework’ for Moffett and Nuseibeh (as appears in [MN03] *(Section 2.2)*)

(Section 2.2) “The meanings of terms in this area are not universally agreed. We will use the following
- **Threat**: Harm that can happen to an asset
- **Impact**: A measure of the seriousness of a threat
- **Attack**: A threatening event
- **Attacker**: The agent causing an attack (not necessarily human)
- **Vulnerability**: a weakness in the system that makes an attack more likely to succeed”

(Section 2.2.1) "There are many types of **asset** controlled by a system, including:
- Information
- Money
- Intangibles, such as an organisation's confidence and public reputation."

(Section 2.2.2) "For each asset type, it is necessary to identify the **threats** that apply. Thus for stored information there are the following possibilities:
- Unauthorised exposure
- Unauthorised alteration
- Loss of availability.
How much **impact** (**harm**) will the business suffer if each of these threats come to pass?"

(Section 2.2.3) "For each threat, the baseline is analysed in order to identify the **vulnerabilities**, i.e. the means of exploiting a threat successfully."

(Section 2.2.3) "Risk assessment combines the results of **vulnerability** analysis with the **impact** valuation of **threats to assets**, and reaches an overall conclusion about the level of **risk** to an asset."

(Section 2.4) "We define **security requirements** to be the constraints, on functional requirements, that are derived from security goals. A simple example is: The system shall not display salary information except to members of Human Resources Dept."

A.16 The DITSCAP automation framework

The definitions related to ISSRM for the DITSCAP automation are extracted from the research paper "*Discovering and Understanding Multi-dimensional Correlations among Certification Requirements with application to Risk Assessment*" [GL07].

(Section 2.2.1) "To support an overall risk-based strategy, C&A requirements should explicitly identify relevant risk components. These are the **threats** to and **vulnerabilities** of the **assets** to be protected, and **countermeasures** that can mitigate or reduce the **vulnerabilities** to acceptable levels."

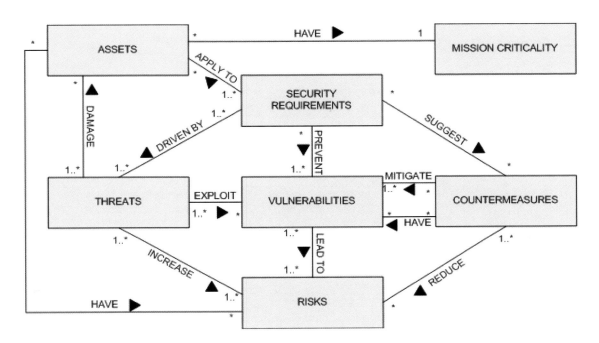

Figure A.4: 'Requirements and Risk Model' for the DITSCAP automation framework (as appears in [GL07] *(Section 2.2.1)*)

Appendix B

Alignment table for ISSRM concepts

Type	Concept	RISK MANAGEMENT STANDARDS		SECURITY-RELATED STANDARDS		SECURITY RISK MANAGEMENT STANDARDS		
		ISO/IEC Guide 73:2002	AS/NZS 4360:2004	ISO/IEC 13335-1:2004	Common Criteria v3.1	ISO/IEC 27001:2005 / ISO/IEC 27006:2008	NIST 800-27 REV A / NIST 800-30	The IT-Grundschutz
Concepts related to assets	Asset	/	/	Asset	Asset	Asset	/	Asset
	Business asset	/	/			Primary asset	/	
	IS asset	/	/			Supporting asset		IT asset
	Security criterion	Risk criterion	Risk criterion	ICT security requirement	/	Property / Criterion	Security goal	Basic parameter / Basic IT security parameter
Concepts related to risk	Risk	Risk	Risk	Risk	Risk	Risk	(IT-related) Risk	Risk
	Event	Event	Event	Event	/	Event	Threat	Applied threat
	Impact	Consequence	Consequence / Loss / Harm	Impact	Impact	Impact / Consequence	Impact / Consequence	Damage
	Threat	Source	Hazard		Threat	Threat	Threat	Basic threat
	Vulnerability	/	/	Vulnerability	Vulnerability	Vulnerability	Vulnerability	Vulnerability
	Threat agent		/		Threat agent	Threat source / Origin of threat	Threat source	/
	Attack method		/	Threat	Adverse action	Threat action	Threat action	
Concepts related to risk treatment	Risk treatment	Risk treatment measure / Risk management decision	Risk treatment measure	/	/	Risk treatment	Risk mitigation option	Decision
	Security requirement		/		Countermeasure / Security objective / Security (functional) requirement	Control	/	/
	Control	Risk control	Control	Safeguard / Control	/	Control	Control	Safeguard / Security measure / Control

Type	Concept	SECURITY RISK MANAGEMENT METHODS					SECURITY RE FRAMEWORKS		
		EBIOS v2	MEHARI 2007	OCTAVE 2.0	CRAMM v6.0	CORAS	Moffett and Nuseibeh / Haley et al.	Firesmith	The DITSCAP automation
Concepts related to assets	Asset	Asset	Asset	Asset	Asset	Asset	Asset	Asset / Valuable asset	Asset
	Business asset	Essential element	Primary asset	/	/	/	/	/	/
	IS asset	Entity	Supporting asset	Key component	Asset	/	Asset	/	/
	Security criterion	Security criterion	Criterion / Classification criterion	Security requirement	Property	Security property	Security concern	Quality subfactor	/
Concepts related to risk	Risk	Risk	Risk / Risk scenario	Risk	Risk	Risk	Risk	Risk / Safety risk / Security risk	Risk
	Event	Threat	Cause	Area of concern / Outcome	/	/	/	/	/
	Impact	Impact	Consequence	Impact	Impact	Unwanted incident	Impact / Harm	Harm	/
	Threat			Threat	Threat	Threat scenario	Threat	Danger / Hazard / Threat	Threat
	Vulnerability	Vulnerability	Vulnerability	Vulnerability	Vulnerability	Vulnerability	Vulnerability	Safety vulnerability / Security vulnerability	Vulnerability
	Threat agent	Threat agent	/	Actor	/	Threat	Attacker	Attacker	/
	Attack method	Attack method	/		/	/	Action	/	/
Concepts related to risk treatment	Risk treatment	/	/	Risk mitigation plan	/	/	/	/	/
	Security requirement	Security objective / Security (functional) requirement	Security service / Security function / Security sub-service / Security measure		Countermeasure / Security objective / Security function	Treatment	Security requirement	Safety requirement / Security requirement	Security requirement
	Control	Security measure	Mechanism / Security solution	Protection strategic practice / Countermeasure	Countermeasure / Implementation options (or examples)	/	/	Safety mechanism / Safety tactic / Safeguard / Security mechanism / Countermeasure	Countermeasure

Figure B.1: Alignment table for ISSRM concepts

Appendix C

Extraction of relationships between the concepts of ISO/IEC Guide 73

Legend
Concepts involved are *in italic*. Information about relationships are **in bold**.

Risk: **combination** of the probability of an *event* and its *consequence*

Consequence: **Outcome of** an *event*
NOTE 1: There can be more than one consequence from one event.
NOTE 2: Consequences can range from positive to negative. However, consequences are always negative for safety aspects.

Source: Item or activity **having a potential for** a *consequence*

Risk criteria: terms of reference by which the **significance** of *risk* **is assessed**

Risk treatment: process of selection and implementation of measures to **modify** *risk*
NOTE 2: **Risk treatment measures** can include avoiding, optimizing, transferring or retaining risk.

Risk control: actions **implementing** *risk management decision*.

Appendix D

Summary of ISSRM approaches performing concept estimation

Legend
Concepts measured are **in bold**.
Metrics are *in italic*.

D.1 NIST 800-30

These different steps are extracted from the document NIST SP 800-30 *"Risk Management Guide for Information Technology Systems"* [SGF02].

- The *likelihood* that a potential **vulnerability** could be exercised by a given **threat-source** that can be described as high, medium, or low. (p.21)

- Determine the adverse **impact** and its *magnitude* resulting from a successful threat exercise of a vulnerability. (p.22)

- The determination of **risk** (*risk level*) for a particular threat/vulnerability pair can be expressed as a function of: (p.25)

  - The likelihood of a given threat-source's attempting to exercise a given vulnerability

  - The magnitude of the impact should a threat-source successfully exercise the vulnerability

  - The adequacy of planned or existing security controls for reducing or eliminating risk

Figure D.1 summarises the metrics proposition of NIST 800-30 regarding the ISSRM domain model.

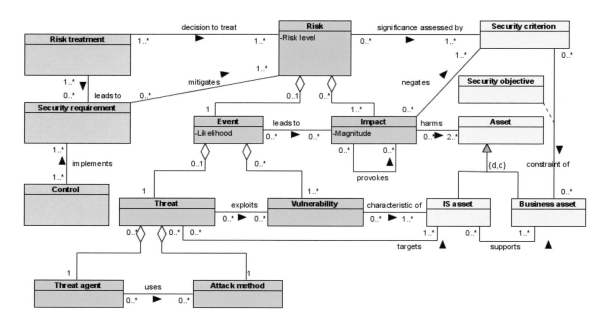

Figure D.1: ISSRM domain model enriched with the metrics proposed by NIST 800-30

D.2 MEHARI

These different steps are extracted from the document "*MEHARI 2007: Concepts and Mechanisms*" [CLU07a]

- For each **asset**, check if a loss of confidentiality, integrity or availability (**classification criteria**) can lead to a relevant malfunction and so what is its value. This level is so the asset *classification value* for the considered criterion. (p.6)

- For each **security service**, assess its *quality* with the help of a questionnaire or a guideline, based on the following characteristics: service efficiency, robustness, permanency. (p.8-10)

- Define: *Natural exposure to risk, Effectiveness of dissuasive measures, Effectiveness of preventive measures*, directly or based on quality of security services. (p.16-19)

- Estimate *potentiality* of **cause** of risk leading to risk, based on natural exposure to risk, effectiveness of dissuasive measures, effectiveness of preventive measures, with tables or directly. (p.19)

- Define : *Intrinsic impact, Effectiveness of protective or confinement measures, Effectiveness of palliative measures, Effectiveness of recuperative measures*, directly or based on quality of security services. (p.20-25)

- Estimate *impact* of **consequence** based on intrinsic impact, effectiveness of protective or confinement measures, effectiveness of palliative measures, effectiveness of recuperative measures, with tables or directly. (p.25)

- Estimate *seriousness* of **risk**, defined by potentiality and impact, based on tables. (p.26)

Figure D.2 summarises the metrics proposition of MEHARI regarding the ISSRM domain model.

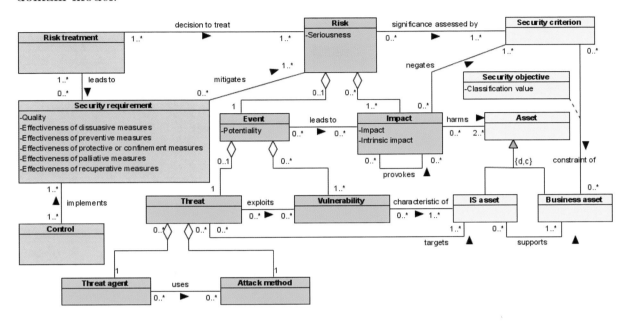

Figure D.2: ISSRM domain model enriched with the metrics proposed by MEHARI

D.3 OCTAVE

These different steps are extracted from the document "*OCTAVE Method Implementation Guide*" [AD01b]. Page numbers are extracted from the "Complete example results" that shows the complete path of the method.

- Define for each asset the *impact level* of the **impact** based on the scale High, Medium, Low. (p.57-59)

Figure D.3 summarises the metrics proposition of OCTAVE regarding the ISSRM domain model.

D.4 CRAMM

These different steps are extracted from the document "*CRAMM User Guide*" [Ins03].

- Define **impact** *severity* (level of the impact) and *cost*, used only for Unavailability and Physical Destruction impacts, with the help of interviews. (p.7-35 to 7-38 ; Appendix E)

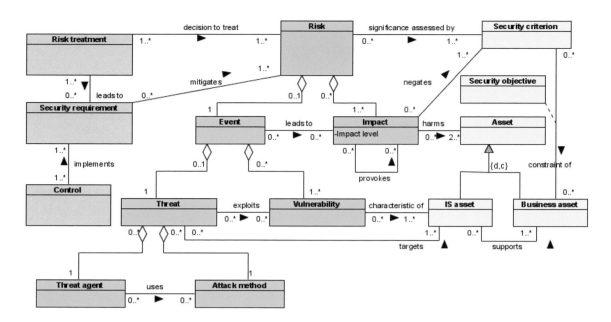

Figure D.3: ISSRM domain model enriched with the metrics proposed by OCTAVE

- Define **asset** *value* by gathering every impact applicable on the asset or by replacing the asset value of physical assets (to be determined) by the one (if higher) of data or application assets supported by this physical asset. (p.7-35 to 7-38 ; Appendix E)

- Define *threat level* of identified **threats**. This is done with the help of questionnaires or manually for rapid risk assessment. (p.8-12 ; p. 8-20)

- Define *vulnerability level* for **vulnerabilities** associated to the identified threat. This is done with the help of questionnaires or manually for rapid risk assessment. (p.8-12 ; p. 8-20)

- Define for each **risk** the *measure of risk*, identified from the value of the assets, the level of threat and the extent of the vulnerability. This is done based on the risk matrix. (p.9-1 ; Appendix G)

- Select **countermeasures** with appropriate *security level*, where the measure of risk falls within the range of security levels provided by the countermeasure. (p.8-7)

- *Prioritization* of **countermeasures**, depending on many factors: (p.8-19 to 8-20)

    - it protects against several threats
    - it is required to protect a high risk system
    - there are no alternative countermeasures already installed
    - *cost*
    - *effectiveness*

– the type of protection provided by the countermeasure

Figure D.4 summarises the metrics proposition of CRAMM regarding the ISSRM domain model.

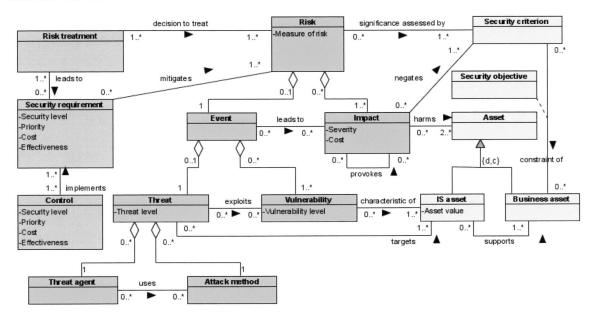

Figure D.4: ISSRM domain model enriched with the metrics proposed by CRAMM

D.5   CORAS

These different steps are extracted from the document *"Assessing Enterprise Risk Level: The CORAS Approach"* [VML⁺07].

- Define *value* of **assets** by interviews. (p.13)

- Define *likelihood* and *consequence* of **risk** by interviews. (p.14)

- Define *level* of **risk** based on likelihood and consequence of risk. (p.14)

- Define *risk reduction* and *cost* of **treatment** by interviews and analysis. (p.21)

Figure D.5 summarises the metrics proposition of CORAS regarding the ISSRM domain model.

D.6   The IT-Grundschutz

These different steps are extracted from the document *"Risk analysis based on IT-Grundschutz"* [Bun05c]

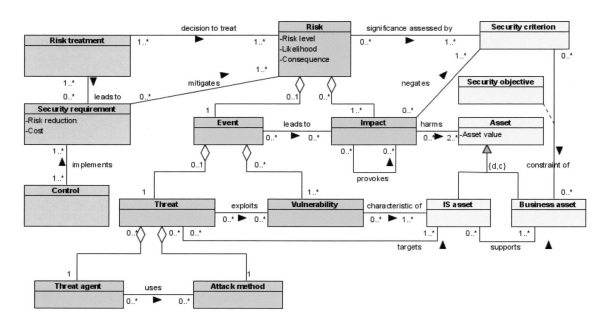

Figure D.5: ISSRM domain model enriched with the metrics proposed by CORAS

- Define the *level* of **security requirements** referring to the basic parameters of confidentiality, integrity and availability based on three levels, namely normal, high, very high. (p.5)

Figure D.6 summarises the metrics proposition of the IT-Grundschutz regarding the ISSRM domain model.

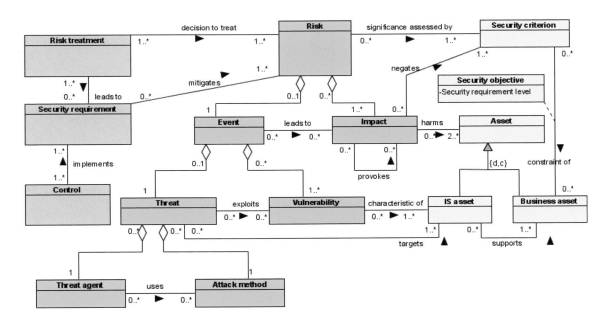

Figure D.6: ISSRM domain model enriched with the metrics proposed by the IT-Grundshutz

ABSTRACT

During the last twenty years, the impact of security concerns on the development and exploitation of information systems never ceased to grow. Security risk management methods are methodological tools, helping organisations to take rational decisions, regarding the security of their IS. Feedbacks on the use of such approaches show that they considerably reduce losses originating from security problems. Today, these methods are generally built around a well structured process. However, the product coming from the different risk management steps is still largely informal, and often not analytical enough. This lack of formality hinders the automation of the management of risk-related information. Another drawback of current methods is that they are generally designed for being used a posteriori, that is, to assess the way existing systems handle risks, and are with difficulty usable a priori, during information system development. Finally, with method using its own terminology, it is difficult to combine several methods, in the aim of taking advantage of each of them. For tackling the preceding problems, this thesis proposes a model-based approach for risk management, applicable from the early phases of information system development. This approach relies on a study of the domain's own concepts.

This scientific approach is composed of three successive steps. The *first step* aims at defining a reference conceptual model for security risk management. The research method followed proposes to base the model on an extensive study of the literature. The different risk management and/or security standards, a set of methods representative of the current state of the practice, and the scientific works related to the domain, are analysed. The result is a semantic alignment table of the security risk management concepts, highlighting the key concepts taking place in such an approach. Based on this set of concepts, the security risk management domain model is built. This model is challenged by domain experts in standardisation, risk management practitioners and scientists.

The *second step* of this research work enriches the domain model with the different metrics used in a risk management method. The proposed approach combines two methods to define this set of metrics. The first one is the Goal-Question-Metric (GQM) method applied on the domain model. This method allows to focus on reaching the best return on security investment. The second one enriches the metrics identified with the first approach, through a study of the literature based on standards and methods addressed during the first step. An experimentation on a real case of these metrics is performed, in the frame of supporting a SME towards the ISO/IEC 27001 certification.

Finally, in a *third step*, a set of conceptual modelling languages dedicated to information security is noticed in the literature. These languages are mainly coming from the requirements engineering domain. They allow to tackle security during the early phases of information system development. The conceptual support proposed by each of them is evaluated, and thus the gap to bridge for being able to completely model the different steps of risk management too. This work ends in an extension proposal of the Secure Tropos language, and a process to follow for using this extension in the frame of risk management, illustrated by an example.

Made in the USA
Charleston, SC
16 July 2013